THE MATTAWA SONG CYCLE

from Pageant Song, composed by Carolyn Brown Senier in 1954

© 1954, © 2005 by Carolyn Brown Senier

The Mattawa Song Cycle

music by
CAROLYN BROWN SENIER

with a biographical profile by
MARY-ANN DEVITA PALMIERI

Haley's
Athol, Massachusetts

© 2005 by Carolyn Brown Senier. Copyright includes words and music by Carolyn Brown Senier.

Biographical profile © 2005 by Mary-Ann DeVita Palmieri.

Foreword © 2005 by Kathleen Deignan, CND.

Publisher's note © 2005 by Marcia Gagliardi.

Essay about Carolyn's music © 2005 by Geoffrey Hudson.

Sidebars © 2005 by Barbara Arnesen, Gladys Barron, Richard Brown, Donald Brown, Kathleen Brown-Carrano, Margaret Mary Chiara, Florence Clark, Robert Grady, Aine Graham, Lee Howe, Claire Lamontagne, Dorothy Johnson, Anne C. Leonard, Katherine Brown Mark, Lola McGrail, Joan McGrath, Ann Burns Macqueen, Cara Morris, Patricia Morris, Joseph Moylan, Fergus O'Farrell, Joan Page, Richard Senier, Diane Sweet, Samuel A. Turner, William Williams.

All rights reserved. With the exception of short excerpts in a review or critical article, no part of this book may be reproduced by any means, including information storage and retrieval or photocopying equipment, without written permission of the publisher, Haley's. The proprietary trade dress, including the format, is the property of Haley's and may not be reproduced without the expressed permission of Haley's.

Book and cover designed by Marcia Gagliardi in collaboration with Carolyn Brown Senier.

Photographs from the collection of Carolyn Brown Senier unless otherwise acknowledged with the list of illustrations beginning on Page xv.

Music edited by Geoffrey Hudson.

Copy edited by Miryam Ehrlich Williamson. Index compiled by Rand Haven with Edna Haven.

Music transcribed by Ted Horman, Jeremy van Buskirk, and Susan Aery.

Printed by Charles River Publishers, Boston. Cover printed by Highland Press, Athol, Massachusetts.

This work was supported with a generous grant from the International Music and Art Foundation of Vaduz, Liechtenstein. Additional support was received from the Composer Assistance Program of the American Music Center, New York, New York, and The Valley Charitable Fund administered by Fleet National Bank through the Community Foundation of Western Massachusetts. The 1794 Meetinghouse, New Salem, Massachusetts, was a helpful resource, especially through the consideration of Patience Bundschuh and Philip Rabinowitz. Additional support was provided by businesses and individuals listed on Page 405. Diane Lincoln provided crucial assistance. Haley's is grateful for Doris Abramson, Dorothy Johnson, and Richard Senier and their dependable understanding, for Mary-Ann DeVita Palmieri and her steady insight, and for Carolyn Brown Senier and her beautiful music, heartfelt laughter, and remarkable capacity to collaborate.

With special thanks to Nicholas Thaw.

Grateful acknowledgment is made to Warner Bros. Publications U.S. Inc. for the reassignments of rights and release for "O, Praise Ye the Lord," "Three Christmas Carols" (formerly called "For He Comes"), and "Thou Makest the Winds Thy Messengers" from McLaughlin & Reilly Co. to Carolyn Brown Senier.

Library of Congress Catalogue-in-Publishing data:
    Palmieri, Mary-Ann DeVita.
  The Mattawa song cycle : music by Carolyn Brown Senier / with a biographical profile by Mary-Ann DeVita Palmieri.
    p. cm.
Includes bibliographical references and index.
ISBN 1-884540-73-2
1. Brown Senier, Carolyn. 2. Composers--Massachusetts--Biography. I. Brown Senier, Carolyn. II. Title.
ML410.S4522P35 2005
782.4'7'092--dc22
          2004021024

Haley's
488 South Main Street
Post Office Box 248
Athol, Massachusetts 01331
haley.antique@verizon.net
800.215.8805

for my husband Richard
. . . and for the rest of things

Carolyn Brown Senier, c. 1986

I have had my invitation to this world's festival,
and thus my life has been blessed.
My eyes have seen and my ears have heard.
It was my part at this feast to play upon my instrument,
and I have done all I could.

from *Gitanjali*
Rabindranath Tagore, 1913

Carolyn Brown Senier, c. 1975

contents

illustrations xv
One Ordained to Praise, a foreword by Kathleen Deignan, CND xix
Carolyn's Excellent Offering, a note by Marcia Gagliardi xxiii
Mingling with the Music of the World, an introduction by Carolyn Brown Senier xxv
Luminous Spirit, a biographical profile by Mary-Ann DeVita Palmieri 1
   raised under a lucky star in Waterbury, Connecticut 5
      playing the descending scale as fast as she can by Don Brown 7
      a tomboy who played football by Dick Brown 9
      a butterfly floating over snow-covered fields by Bob Grady 25
   honoring a religious life illuminated by music 31
      sensitivity, compassion, interest in others by Anne C. Leonard, CND 40
      delighting in little things, sensitive to others by Barbara Arnesen 47
      sharing sorrows, celebrating successes by Margaret Mary Chiara 56
      Mother prayed her child would be a girl by Kaye Brown Mark 60
      providing an excellent music education program by Samuel A. Turner 63
      responding with a personal touch for each friend by Ann Burns Macqueen 64
   keeping shop in Boston's Faneuil Hall Marketplace 69
      a belief that good outcomes are always possible by Joan Page 72
      interfaith celebrations and rousing musicales by Gladys Barron 80
      beautiful clothing in soft shades of heather and green by Aine Graham 84
      positive attitude, delighting in beauty—lucky streak and all by Joan McGrath .. 87
      hospitality, music, great conversations, good food by Pat Morris 90
      hurtling across Rome at midnight by Fergus O'Farrell 97
      despite disparity, adding a new dimension to life by Lola McGrail 98
      gifted eye for design, impeccable taste in the finest products by Cara Morris . 100
      talent for product selection and display by Diane Sweet 101
      catching a herring red-handed by Joseph Moylan 103
      singing, guitar playing, an inspiration to many by Claire Lamontagne 110
      a cosmetic makeover at Bloomingdale's by Kathleen Brown-Carrano 111
   creating beautiful music in a secluded Lake Mattawa cove 115
      fast friends through devotion to music by Florence Clark 119
      "Why couldn't she write a duet for Richard and herself?" by Dorothy Johnson . 121
      she listens to you when you speak by Lee Howe 122
      a friendship leading to special evenings by Buck Williams 124
Ancient Song, Modern Harmony, music by Carolyn Brown Senier 129
   sing it bold and strong, an essay from the music editor by Geoffrey Hudson 131
   The Mattawa Song Cycle, with annotations by Carolyn Brown Senier 135
   songs for concert 137
      De Profundis 140
      In Praise of Names 163
      Song of Abraham 218
      Thou Makest the Winds Thy Messengers (in three versions) 244
      You Know Me 258

(continued)

xi

songs for concert, continued

- Four Songs for a Woman of Galilee 273
  - Pageant Song 276
  - Respice Stellam 281
  - Hail, Mary (Supplication in Time of War or Sorrow) 291
  - Assumpta Est, Maria 294
- Love Songs 298
  - I'd Give You the Moon 300
  - Listen to Your Heart 304
  - Summer Days 312
  - When I Knew 317

songs for congregational singing and for choir 331
- Adoremus 332
- Lamb of God 334
- Celtic Prayer 338
- Creator, Spirit 341
- O, Praise the Lord, All Ye Nations 348
- O, Praise Ye the Lord 351
- The Ram 355
- Sing Joy to the Lord 358
- Three Christmas Carols 361
  - Let the Heav'ns Be Glad 362
  - Lowly Shepherds 363
  - Come, Sing Alleluia 364
- Mass in Honor of Marguerite Bourgeoys 366
  - Lord, Have Mercy 368
  - Glory to God 369
  - Creed 374
  - Holy, Holy, Holy 386
  - Blessed 387
  - Lamb of God 388
- Meditation Doxology 390

good fortune has been my traveling companion, acknowledgments by Carolyn Brown Senier .. 401

supporters of The Mattawa Song Cycle 405

music in progress: Carolyn at work on manuscripts 407

a Brown family primer 413

music as an integral part of conemporary liturgical celebrations: master's thesis 416

index 430

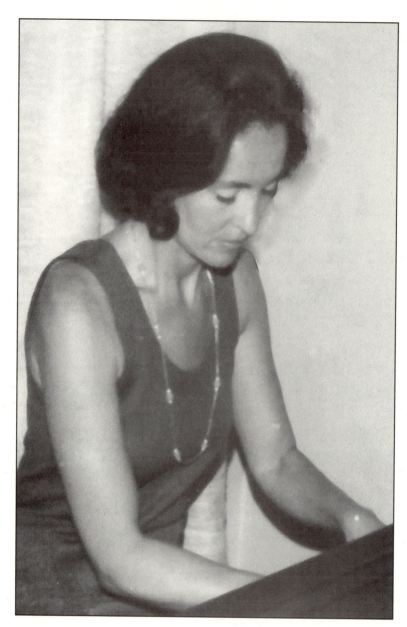
Carolyn Brown Senier, c. 1974

Illustrations

from "Pageant Song"	ii
Carolyn Brown Senier, 1986	viii
Carolyn Brown Senier, 1975	x
Carolyn Brown Senier, 1982	xiii
Carolyn Brown Senier, 1974	xiv
Carolyn Brown	xviii
"O, Praise Ye, the Lord" (published by McLaughlin & Reilly in 1966)	xx
"In Praise of Names" (2005)	xxi
Carolyn Brown, c. 1939; Sister Carolyn Brown . . .	1
Carolyn Brown, c. 1936; Carolyn on a pony . . .	3
Carolyn, c. 1940, with her brothers Robert, Richard, and Donald	4
The Brown family summer home . . .	6
In their canoe that eventually became half a canoe . . .	8
Carolyn's father Edward Godfrey Brown . . .	10
Carolyn's parents Rosalene and Eddie Brown . . .	11
Carolyn's family home at 226 Sylvan Avenue, Waterbury, Connecticut . . .	12
Joan Brown, Rosalene Carolan Brown, Kaye Brown Mark, Edward Godfrey Brown	13
Carolyn, Joan, Roselyn, Kaye . . .	14
Lieutenant Joseph D. Shea with a photo of his wife Roselyn . . .	15
Carolyn, c. 1948	15
Rosalene and Eddie at Cape Cod, c. 1955	16
Among frequent visitors to the Brown household were the Moriartys . . .	18
Carolyn's eighth grade graduating class from Saint Francis Xavier School in Waterbury	19
Carolyn's friend Georgia Breithaupt and Carolyn . . .	20
Carolyn and her classmates occasionally played hookie . . .	21
Father Peter Cuny of Waterbury's Saint Cecilia's Church hired Carolyn as organist . . .	22
Eddie Brown at the piano, c.1946, with Emil Mark, Sr. . . .	23
Carolyn in the male lead singing the "Gypsy Love Song" in her high school senior play	24
When she was in high school, Carolyn sometimes visited her sister Roselyn . . .	26
"The beautiful shades of Brown, Carolyn's three sisters . . .	27
Sister Carolyn Brown, c. 1968 . . .	29
Sister Carolyn Brown, c. 1968 . . .	30
Carolyn and friends pulled a successful prank on their former teachers . . .	32
Marguerite Bourgeoys, founder of the Congregation de Notre Dame	33
The crucial scriptural moment for the CND is the visit made by Mary . . .	34
Sister Frances McManus (Sister Saint John Joseph) . . .	36
Carolyn corresponded by letter and telephone with her family. Her father typed . . .	38
Eddie and Rosalene, c. 1954	42

Eleanor Roosevelt, c. 1958 42
Sister Carolyn directs a Stamford Catholic High School choir, c. 1966................................. 43
Carolyn's dad at the piano at the family home in Waterbury 44
Carolyn visiting Roselyn's grave at Chipping Campden, England 45
Sister Carolyn's boys choir at Stamford Catholic High School, c. 1959 46
During a series of early 1960s summers on the campus of Manhattanville College 48
The Manhattanville recital hall where Piux X students performed and heard ancient music .. 48
Sister Carolyn's massed choir at Stamford Catholic, c.1959 50
The liturgical commission of the Roman Catholic Diocese of Bridgeport, c. 1966 51
The "Glory to God" section from Carolyn's mid 1960s English language Mass 51
Carolyn saved clippings (but unfortunately not their dates) 52
Rehearsing for Confraternity of Christian Doctrine religious education conference 53
Carolyn, family members including her mother. Carolyn's brother Dick behind Rosalene . . . 55
Carolyn learning to waterski in Florida, c. 1968 58
The SS Bahama Star captain with singer John Raitt 59
Sister Carolyn, c. 1968, making music 60
. . . . in 1969, Carolyn continued a masters of music program 61
During her first summer as "just plain" Carolyn Brown, she took full advantage 62
As a member of the Massachusetts Teachers Association 65
Carolyn, c. 1969 67
Carolyn and her husband Richard Senier in Tenerife, c. 1978 68
The Senier family was still growing in 1935 70
Dick and Carolyn honeymooned in New Orleans 71
Richard Senier, c. 1973, snapped by Carolyn 71
Carolyn, right, with her friend Joan Page at a fountain in Rome, c. 1974 73
On a business trip to Italy with Dick 74
A schematic map of Boston's Faneuil Hall Marketplace 75
In the nineteenth century, Quincy Market was a vibrant place 76
Thomas Senier, Dick's father, with bolts of his Celtic Weavers cloth 77
Carolyn had a fashionable palazzo pants outfit sewn from Thomas Senier's cloth 78
Carolyn selling hats from the Faneuil Hall Marketplace pushcart, c. 1977 79
Carolyn and Dick in their first South Market shop 82
Carolyn modeling a Celtic Weavers outfit in a Quincy Market fashion show, c. 1978............ 83
A page from Rosalene's recipe book and Rosalene stirring up a batch of tomato catsup 85
Carolyn and her dog Farley, c. 1979... 86
Possibly as an outcome of stress, Carolyn developed rheumatoid arthritis 88
Carolyn and Dick mailed a catalogue to thirty thousand recipients, c. 1980 89
A Celtic Weavers window display, c. 1982.. 92
A busy springtime day in Quincy Market at Faneuil Hall Marketplace 92
Carolyn and Dick—Herself and Himself—keeping shop at Celtic Weavers 93

Rosalene cruising Long Island Sound on her son Don's boat, c. 1980 94
Celtic Weavers, a stone's throw from Faneuil Hall 95
Carolyn plays the organ in the home church of Dick's mother 96
The Seniers often travel with family or friends 99
Cara Morris in Carolyn's shoes, c. 1978 100
Dick, c. 1997, president of the Faneuil Hall Merchants Association 102
The Seniers' Mendum Street house 104
Carolyn with Farley, c. 1988 105
Carolyn enjoys cooking 106
Peace activist and writer Gary Maceoin 107
At holidays, Carolyn made the most of the Brown party tradition 108
Carolyn's nieces and their families at Lake Mattawa with Dick and Carolyn 109
Family and friends tune up at one of the Seniers' Mendum Street musical evenings 110
Carolyn, c. 1996; the composer Carolyn Brown Senier, 2004 113
Carolyn at Lake Mattawa, c. 2004 114
Carolyn and Dick in Lake Como, Italy, c. 1992 116
"In general," says Dick of his marriage with Carolyn, "life has always been the same 117
There can be more or fewer depending on who's traveling 120
Dick and Carolyn and their friends Tony and Mary-Ann Palmieri 125
Directed by Geoffrey Hudson, The Lake Mattawa Singers and musicians 127
Carolyn Brown Senier, 2004 128
a manuscript page from Carolyn's "De Profundis," 2003 129
Geoffrey Hudson, composer, conductor, and editor of music 130
Geoffrey Hudson, above, with pianist Gretchen Saathoff 132
The Lake Mattawa Singers and Richard Chase 133
Abraham Barron 219
Carolyn works on the evolving manuscript for "In Praise of Names" 407
manuscript page from Carolyn's "De Profundis," 2003 408
a manuscript page from Carolyn's "Pageant Song," 1953 409
a manuscript page from Carolyn's "Song of Abraham," 2003 410
a manuscript page from Carolyn's "I'd Give You the Moon," 1999 411
Carolyn's brother Ed offers a song 413
Katherine, Patricia, Roselyn, Joan, Edward, Donald, Richard, Robert, Carolyn 414
Carolyn with Mary-Ann Palmieri; Kathleen Deignan 438

Photographs are from the collection of Carolyn Brown Senier and the Brown and Senier family archives except the following: by Marcia Gagliardi on the front cover and pp. v, 48, 95, 104, 113, 114, 127, 128, 132, 133 (both), 135, and 407 from public domain Internet sources: pp. 33, 34, 42 (Eleanor Roosevelt), 75, and 92; by Michael Phillips: back cover and 1; by Susan Wilson, www.susanwilsonphoto.com: 113, 129, 130, 136, 140, 163, 218, 244, 258, 274, 298, 299, 329, 330, 332, 333, 334, 341, 348, 351, 352, 355, 358, 361, 367, and 390

Special thanks to Carolyn's nieces Kathleen Brown-Carrano and Claire Lamontagne for redigitizing early Brown family pictures and to Richard Senier for his assistance with archival searches and correspondence.

Carolyn Brown, c. 1966

a foreword from the composer's friend
One Ordained to Praise

by Kathleen Deignan, CND

Praising, that's it! One ordained to praise . . .
— Rainer Maria Rilke

Carolyn Brown Senier's musical corpus resounds with the spirit of *praise.* For Carolyn, praise is an acknowledgement and celebration of a great mystery in which we live and move and have our being. It partakes of wonder, of awe, and it is at once the deepest and highest note resounding through all her music. Praising is a vocation. It is a gift and a calling, like healing, teaching, marrying, or parenting. In some profound sense it is the vocation of every living thing, but few human beings ever embody its invitation so completely that it can be said they are "ordained to praise." Carolyn Brown Senier is one ordained to praise.

When I first met Carolyn in 1965, she was in the act of praising—of leading, inspiring, engendering praise. It was Lent, and I had come to visit the novitiate of the Congregation of Notre Dame, a Catholic sisterhood dedicated to a life of service and contemplation. In that brief encounter, I saw and heard a beautiful young nun preparing the CND novices for the Holy Week Triduum, the richest liturgical week of the Christian year. I do not know if I doubted more my ears or my eyes, because in Sister Saint Roselyn I beheld a beauty that opened an inner and outer door through which I too would pass into the mystery of sung praise. That fleeting experience changed the course of my life, and Carolyn has been the muse, mentor, and inspiration of my own musical creativity ever since.

> **The Poet Speaks of Praising**
>
> O speak, poet, what do you do?
> —I praise.
> But the monstrosities and the murderous days,
> How do you endure them, how do you take them?
> —I praise.
> But the anonymous, the nameless grays,
> How poet, do you still invoke them?
> —I praise.
> What right have you in all displays,
> In very mask, to be genuine?
> —I praise.
> And that the stillness and the turbulent sprays
> Know you like star and storm?
> —since I praise.
>
> —Rainer Maria Rilke,
> translated by John J. L. Mood

The next year I was one of those novices learning at her side the art of praise and exploring the mysticism of song. She was the mistress of that domain for the religious community of sisters who came together in a vow to make a "Magnificat" of their whole lives. And it was Carolyn who composed the music that would become the soul of our shared lives in community. It was a season of grace for all of us who were awakened and formed by her musical ministry, a season of grace we revisit each time we hear or sing one of her exquisite compositions.

Music was the gift of Carolyn Brown's lineage, flowing through the Celtic soul of her family for whom it was an environment, a habit, and a joyous expectation. Her father was a piano teacher, and her home was ever alive with the sounds of song and instruments of every kind. By fifteen, she was the organist at Saint Cecilia's Church in Waterbury, Connecticut. But in her soul there was another music sounding, drawing her toward mystery, and she pursued that calling when she was eighteen years old with the Sisters of the Congregation of Notre Dame. Whether she knew it then or not, the community she joined was itself committed to sacred song: Mary's "Magnificat" of praise was the inspiring canticle sung with one voice in the varied harmonious ministries of the CND, which celebrated its own treasured musical heritage. The nuns recognized her gift immediately and because they needed to sing their prayer, the young novice began to compose music that arose out of their shared spiritual life. Soon she was sent on for musical studies, and it became clear that she would do more than teach music as a member of this educating order, she would create it. In the 1960s during the *aggiornamento* of Catholic life inspired by the Second Vatican Council, Carolyn would be distinguished among the new musicians composing new songs of praise for a new time.

Spiritual life in the Catholic form is rooted in liturgy, where the rich symbolism of the Christian faith is dramatized in word and song throughout various seasons of the year: Advent, Christmastide, Epiphany, Lent, Eastertide, Pentecost. These festivals and sacred cycles gave Carolyn the scaffolding for her compositions, providing her the necessity, occasions, form, and inspiration for her early works. Rooted in the Jewish and Christian scriptures, the office of daily sung prayer supplied rich poetry for her imagination in the psalmody of lauds, vespers, and compline, and its variety and dynamism became the studio where her creativity flourished. Within the musical framework of "the Mass" she composed Credos and Glorias, Introits and Alleluias, entrance songs and communion hymns for many feasts and

O, Praise Ye the Lord, *Carolyn Brown Senier's hymn published in 1966 by McLaughlin & Reilly Co. of Boston, when Carolyn was known as Sister Saint Roselyn, CND.*

O Praise Ye the Lord © 1961 and © 1966 by Carolyn Brown and © 2002 and © 2005 by Carolyn Brown Senier.

festivals with her signature sound—an ecstatic utterance of glory. Indeed Carolyn was herself a "Magnificat," magnifying the life of everything by her praise. But her liturgical expressiveness was fed by a deeper, silent life of contemplation, and Carolyn's early repertoire oscillates between the celebratory music of the worshiping faithful, and the quieter, intimate movements of the soul who lives with God.

During her advanced musical studies Carolyn returned to the novitiate in Ridgefield to conduct the musical training of the young nuns and be the medium of transmission for the musical gift that was part of the charism of the Congregation. During this time she composed some of her most exquisite pieces and those of us who lived with her were privileged to be the choir augmenting her song. At night sometimes, after "grand silence," novices would find their way to the chapel simply to listen in rapt attention to Carolyn in the act of composing. Music was her prayer and we found ourselves blessed to overhear her prayer laboring in the night to be born after her long hours before the Presence, searching for the notes that would give expression to her spirit. By morning we knew we would have a new song to sing, and such songs became the form of our own prayer in concert with hers. Always her dominant theme was praise, even when such lifting of the heart was nearly impossible, as at the death of her sister, when she composed perhaps the most profound, wordless expression of a soul drawn into the dark depths, and finally, gloriously surfacing into a doxology to the Trinity—at once an expression of grief, acceptance, and hope. And yes, of praise.

It is rare for a composer to be a perfect medium of her own song, but Carolyn has been just that. And this is challenging given the complexity of her music. Her unique "voice" discloses a range that plays between worlds, revealing a rich soprano soul that can in an interval descend to the depths and then suddenly scale the heights, as her voice skillfully sweeps the vault of heaven. Lush, elegant, and powerful, her songs can also be tender, humble, and innocent. Influenced by the breathfulness and ethereal flow of Gregorian

In Praise of Names, *Carolyn's anthem in honor of all. Composed in 2004, it sometimes combines as many as eleven separate voices in opposing choirs offering English affirmations and Latin words of sung praise: Te Deum, Gaudeamus, Magnificat, Laudamus.*

In Praise of Names © 2005 by Carolyn Brown Senier

chant, her music also evokes the intensity of romantic and modern composers, vocally painting with rich colors a strength and solidity into her often free-form, lyrical style. Her music arises out of a "deep grounding," rooted in awe, replete with joy that, however capable of reaching the sky, manages always to return to earth. In fact her music, for all its unearthly sublimity, is richly earthy, as if composed by a gypsy queen—it is at once regal and real. Though luscious, there is nothing excessive or superficial about her music; rather it bears an elegance born of authenticity that, while lifting the soul to heaven, gathers the world in its wake.

As Carolyn minded those deep promptings that led her to the convent, she likewise attended the inner movements of soul that invited her beyond it into a new season of living. With her spouse and fellow music lover, Dick Senier, she has created a life redolent with friends all over the world who share their passion for music of every kind. Busy for more than twenty years with her work at Celtic Weavers in Faneuil Hall Marketplace, Boston, Carolyn did not have the creative leisure to compose as before, but with retirement the muse has returned and her original creativity is in full flow. Still a composer of the spirit, Carolyn creates her newer music from more fluid expressions of spirituality, more elemental movements of soul, more inclusive and global forms of prayer. Now the "scriptures" that speak to her broaden—Hindu *Vedas*, Zen koans, Native American incantations become the wisdom that moves her to compose universal invocations of peace, intercession, and protest. With *The Mattawa Song Cycle,* we celebrate the mature harvest of her tremendous gift as she brings forth distinctive pieces of her expansive repertoire, now more fully realized beyond the simplicity of piano, guitar, or even of organ to rich orchestration and complex choral forms. In this collection she continues to touch the world with her music as she gathers up those she loves in her prayer and lifts them to God in song. In it she lets us hear what she has so deeply attended: the duet of the human spirit and divine Spirit singing toward each other.

As one ordained to praise Carolyn Brown Senier has been faithful to her calling and we, her many audiences, are ever blessed by her fidelity. What she has bountifully received as gift she has generously given with magnanimity of heart that has only one name. Though all her songs are manifestations of her own luminous spirit, she once made music of a poem by Gerard Manley Hopkins that is particularly revelatory of her true nature and sings like a manifesto of her musical vocation—its grace, its source, its profound intention :

I have found my music in a common word . . .
I have found the dominant of my range and state:
Love.

a note from the publisher
Carolyn's Excellent Offering

by Marcia Gagliardi

When Carolyn Brown Senier accepted the invitation in autumn 2001 to allow us to present her life and music in this book, I knew we had received quite a gift. I imagined it would mean countless pleasant and challenging hours collaborating with Carolyn and a fine team of professionals on a vibrant project, and so it has.

But this enterprise has surpassed all expectations. The marvelous gift keeps giving in untold ways because—joyfully, constructively, gently, patiently, certainly, conscientiously—Carolyn and her music defy easy definition. As I write the adverbs, I am reminded of the formal gifts of the Holy Spirit listed in the *Baltimore Catechism*. The mental jog seems appropriate. Carolyn's music invokes the spirit, feels religious, sounds modern, sings in Latin, and washes you through familiar emotions.

Whether or not you were raised Roman Catholic as she was, Carolyn's music does these things. She grew up when Catholic service music was in Latin. There were candles and incense. Sometimes an organ played. Sometimes, the priest sang, but usually the worshipers didn't. In those days, people in the congregation (who were also supposed to be praying) watched or read along in a missal that had Latin on one side and English on the other. The priest conducted a ritual invested in tradition and majesty.

> *Carolyn's music opens the heart. One might venture to say it opens the soul.*

Carolyn professed her religious vows in the same institution. Then the Second Vatican Council, the Catholic Church reform initiative of the 1960s, changed the American church as much as flower power changed American life. Carolyn was a direct instrument of the change.

Nurtured in the intellectual climate leading to and proceeding from Vatican II statements about sacred music and worship, the spirit of Carolyn's songs embraces the church's exhortations toward transcendence. Her music reveals familiarity with Catholic chant, polyphony, and twentieth century Catholic liturgical concerns. At the same time, her carefully crafted music is accessible, lyrical, singable, and inviting to the instrumentalist.

Carolyn (then known as Sister Saint Roselyn, CND) served as music director for the liturgical commission of the Diocese of Bridgeport, Connecticut. The commission addressed worship provisions of Vatican II, and so Carolyn was at the heart of American Roman Catholic bureaucratic efforts to implement the council's changes. She was thirty-two and the only woman at the Bridgeport table.

Photographs from the time show her working hard to encourage the joyful noise that should have been the legacy of Vatican II's edict for liturgical music. *Sacrosanctum Concilium*, the main Vatican

II document about worship music, declares that vernacular language will be allowed. The document "does not offer a formal definition of Roman Catholic worship music, but affirms its preeminence among the arts associated with worship," according to Jan Michael Joncas in his study of twentieth century Roman Catholic worship music, *From Sacred Song to Ritual Music.* Carolyn succeeded in giving life to those remarkable ecclesiastical dictates, and her music today embodies all of the heart, soul, and spirit from those days and more besides.

Carolyn's music opens the heart. One might venture to say it opens the soul. She takes a weighty vocabulary, the traditional Latin Roman Catholic lexicon, and redefines it. The bishop and members of the Bridgeport Liturgical Commission no doubt counted on her to convey the worship intentions of Vatican II. Together, they worked to elevate the level of active participation in the liturgical experience.

One of the things I've learned while working with her is that Carolyn has been touched by genius. She is plugged in to eternity, and she can make you feel that, too. She has made herself familiar with the sounds, pulses, horizons, and journeys of the world beyond our usual experience.

It is thrilling to be present when this genius is at work. Nonchalantly, she may lean across the piano during an interview and say, almost shyly, "I've been working on something new. Do you want to hear it?" You just know she wants to split herself into five so she can play the accompaniment and sing all of the parts at once, and somehow, she manages to become at least three. Heavenly, transcendent, and elegant, sound fills her music room for minutes on end, but time really does stand still.

Then you catch a glimpse at the sheets of music paper, apparently willy-nilly on her piano's music rack, and you realize that Carolyn has made sketches of a few measures here, a few bars there, leaving plenty of white space to fill in notations later. Those pages are really not for her. The music, after all, is in her very being. They are for the rest of us, so that we may sing and play and listen to what she has created.

Here—following our introductory words and presentation of a biographical profile to help you know her better—is Carolyn's excellent offering.

a preface to *The Mattawa Song Cycle*
Mingling with the Music of the World

by Carolyn Brown Senier

In Psalm 138 / 139, the poet speaks about our journeys and our rest being scrutinized. This notion causes me to look back at how and where all the music began in my life, why it flourished in a certain manner, when it rested and waited for expression.

I was born into a rich Irish family—rich not in the way one ordinarily thinks of riches, such as having lots of money or jewels. But rich in laughter, in warmth, rich in its cast of characters, and rich in a tradition of music making. I cannot think of those early years without connecting them to certain sounds and harmonies, to all the songs my father taught me, and to the music rising from the living room and flowing through the rest of the house, to sounds of school and church and choirs, to friends harmonizing on the front stoop or in the car.

I did not know then that I would be writing music and that there would be a *Mattawa Song Cycle* and that its foundation was already in the ground of my being. It was only after I entered the convent that I began composing. The first song was a simple "Ave Maria."

After I wrote it, it was sung at my sister Joan's wedding. I had been named organist for my novitiate and became totally involved in a liturgical musical life. It touched some creative mode in me, and the music began flowing. I would jot this

> *Life was a balancing act on a high wire, and the stabilizer was music.*

melody and that one down as the inspiration or liturgical need arose.

Certain compositions in *The Mattawa Song Cycle* were still only jots in a closet until the fall of 2001. Some songs were more or less written out for my choirs to learn. A few had been published earlier by McLaughlin and Reilly of Boston.

I'm not sure what most people think about nuns other than that they are off somewhere living a mysterious way of life. True, there is a certain mystery to it all involving inward motives, prayer, and the spiritual draw, as it were. But let me tell you, nuns are really busy and as hard-working as any member of society. I received my higher education in such a busy environment. It was a different era fifty years ago, and at that time, even as undergraduates, we taught full-time and studied at the same time. We were writing our own term papers and taking exams in colleges and universities even while we were assigning papers and correcting exams of our students.

Summers were wonderful because they gave me music in full force. Those weeks at Pius X School of Liturgical Music in Purchase, New York, were like a balm. I would reach for those classes and choruses long before they began, knowing how full of music's knowledge I would become. A student's experience at Pius X was like gaining weight in sound, a little note here, a little chord there, a symphony of sorts developing in each of us on that campus.

All in all, those sixteen years of sisterhood were rich with teaching, with being taught, with recitals, concerts, liturgical conferences. Life was a balancing act on a high wire, and the stabilizer was music.

After I left the convent, I continued teaching music in Newton, Massachusetts, for about eight years. Then my husband Richard and I began a business called Celtic Weavers. Musically, it was a period of creative rest. Color and cloth texture supported a different form of creativity and provided financial stability. The twenty-three-year endeavor meant extensive travel opportunities and an interesting life, although not without hard work. It was a long time of gestation for music composition.

I felt I had nothing else to say musically, although occasionally I would long for those earlier tonal sparks. Basically, I was too darned busy to compose. Even the word "compose" implies not only arranging things in proper form or state but also to be calm, to be quiet.

It is only now, in the quiet of a life on Lake Mattawa, that I have found my voice again. I am now privileged to have my songs mingling with the music of the world.

Luminous Spirit

a biographical profile of the composer Carolyn Brown Senier

by Mary-Ann DeVita Palmieri

Carolyn Brown, c. 1939; Sister Carolyn Brown after a Stamford, Connecticut, concert, c. 1968, when most of the CNDs adopted simpler habits and returned to their own given names; Carolyn Brown Senier at Lake Mattawa, 2004; Carolyn Brown Senier and her husband Richard, c.1995; clockwise from upper left

On the seashore of endless worlds children meet.
The infinite sky is motionless overhead
and the restless water is boisterous.
On the seashore of endless worlds the children meet
with shouts and dances.

from *Gitanjali*
Rabindranath Tagore, 1913

Carolyn Brown, c. 1936; Carolyn on a pony, c. 1939; Carolyn's school pictures c. 1949, c. 1947; c. 1947; c. 1945, clockwise from top left

Carolyn, c. 1940, with her brothers, from left, Robert, Richard, and Donald

growing up in a household with a musical legacy
raised under a lucky star in Waterbury, Connecticut

Whenever I visit my friend, the composer Carolyn Brown Senier, at her home on Lake Mattawa, I am struck by the serenity and dramatic beauty of the place. To get there I have to bump down a steep, pot-holed road past converted camps and abandoned vehicles that are characteristic of small lakes in mill towns like Orange, Massachusetts. But as soon as I walk through her gardens filled with icicle pansies and tall yellow tulips or covered with holly, boxwood, and varieties of hosta and open her door, I find a different world. The walls of the large kitchen / dining room are painted bright coral, banana yellow, and aqua with touches of hot pink, Mediterranean colors that play with the blue of the cove outside the picture window. Shelves sag under the weight of Irish pottery, earth-colored with decorations of pansies and antique roses. A bowl of shallots, soil still clinging to their roots, or a platter of apples from a local orchard sits on the round table at the door. Pots and pans hang ready for dinner preparations or entertaining the unexpected friend.

It's no surprise that Carolyn has chosen to spend her retirement at Lake Mattawa. She grew up in Waterbury, Connecticut, but during the summer, as soon as school was out, the family packed up for nearby Wolcott and moved to the Hitchcock Lake cottage Carolyn's father inherited from his father.

> *I considered summers at the lake gifted space in our lives.*

As Carolyn describes it, the cottage on Hitchcock Lake looked like many on Lake Mattawa. It had a big living room and dining room overlooking the water. To the side was an old rowboat spilling over with petunias. Out back and up the hill was the outhouse, a small room with a "throne." Citing James Whitcomb Riley's "The Passing of the Backhouse," Carolyn says, "The torture of that icy seat would make a Spartan sob." The cottage had two bedrooms. Carolyn and some of her sisters were in one and Carolyn's parents in the other. Her brothers slept near the house in a small cabin often pressed into service as a first home when one of the siblings married. Carolyn says,

I considered summers at the lake gifted space in our lives. It was here I learned to catch night crawlers with a flashlight after a rain. My brothers finally got me to bait my own fishing hooks with worms. At first I felt queasy, but I got over it. After a catch, I learned how to scale and clean the fish. I wanted to be with my brothers, so all these childhood activities, so natural to them, became mine as well.

Hitchcock Lake was only five miles from Waterbury, but it seemed like the depths of the country to Carolyn. By the time Carolyn, the youngest of nine, was six or so, her three older sisters were married or working, and her oldest brother was off to World War II. Carolyn spent her days romping with her three brothers still at home. Carolyn's mother was content to have the children playing together, and they were careful not to let her know about the times they rolled Carolyn into the water in a tire or paddled the lake in half a canoe. The four of them rowed on the lake, swam, caught fish, played with frogs, or picked blueberries.

Blueberry picking was serious business! We devised great timesaving methods. Each of us took wire, bored holes into the top of a huge tomato juice can, and created handles. We tied the cans around our waists so we could pick with both hands. Quart by quart, we added them to a large bucket. Eventually, we sold them to a local restaurant or a neighborhood store called Löfblad's. My brothers and I usually spent the money from the sale on ice cream, parties, or some such thing.

I remember Don, Dick, Bob, and my mother's Aunt Nell (with a large straw hat) picking the berries on early mornings before the sun and mosquitoes joined forces to thwart us. I especially remember my wise mother and a remarkable life's lesson. During one summer, the blueberry crop was unusually abundant. One day, my brothers and I picked nearly forty quarts. We felt quite proud and candy-store-rich as we set off to sell our berries. Mother, who made gorgeous pies, had asked us for a few quarts. We greedy children thought it over and decided to sell her enough blueberries for the evening dessert. She quietly paid us and made the pies.

That evening, my mother cut a piece of pie for Dad, for Joan, for Aunt Nell, for Maryann Carolan who lived with us, and for herself. She did not, however, offer any pie to the four young blueberry pickers. If we wanted a piece, she said, we had to pay for it. She charged us each for a piece of pie and even made a profit. We ate humble pie that night. My brother Don admitted many years after, with a mighty laugh, to being the sales instigator.

Like Carolyn's house on Lake Mattawa, the cottage fronted a cove looking across to a point, the one at Hitchcock Lake called Figgy's Point. The water was clear and cold, and five-year-old Carolyn learned to swim there. Her oldest sister Kaye's husband Emil taught her, and he accompanied her on her

The Brown family summer home on Hitchcock Lake near Waterbury, Connecticut. The setting is remarkably similar to the place at Lake Mattawa where Carolyn and her husband Richard Senier make their home in Orange, Massachusetts.

Little Miss Sunbeam "out de yake"
playing the descending scale as fast as she can

by Don Brown

Carolyn always was the vibrant one of the four youngest children. Our mother's call of "Bobby-Donny-Dicky-Carolyn" was a separate identity that distinguished us from the elders who were Kaye, Roselyn, Joan, and Ed.

When Mom and Dad were doing our annual move to our summer cottage on Hitchcock Lake, we kids all piled into the rear seat of the family car. Just as we came over the crest of the hill on Fairview Avenue and the lake came into view, Carolyn started singing: "We're out de yake, we're out de yake." Then the rest of us—we who could speak clearly, including Mom and Dad—would join in: "We're out de yake, we're out de yake."

Carolyn had a brief stint at our local radio station in Waterbury, Connecticut. She sang and played on the "Uncle Louis" program. The sponsor was the Sunbeam Bread Company which had as its trademark the image of Little Miss Sunbeam eating a slice of Sunbeam Bread. Carolyn came to be known as Little Miss Sunbeam to some of her family and friends.

The radio station was playing its men's baseball team against a competing team at the local ball field. Carolyn attended as a spectator to watch and applaud. It was an informal game, more like an outing. Because her team was losing, in desperation, they asked her to bat. She hit a homer and drove in two runs.

We Brown kids had a genius of a father who solved a very muddy problem for us at the lake. We were the only known people on earth who swam in a lake using an underwater boardwalk. This was his invention to solve the problem of a muddy bottom. The underwater boardwalk was quite large, but when we played underwater tag we sometimes ventured away from it to escape being tagged. It became a diversionary tactic to muddy up the water with our hands so that the tagger could not see his prey. We engaged in the tactic quite often, and I was better at it than anyone else. But Carolyn started it. She may deny this, but you should not believe someone who still thinks she can play a descending scale with the right hand faster than I can.

Don Brown is Carolyn's late older brother. Death claimed him as this book went to press.

first long distance swim. She remembers the cheers of her family when she completed the trip across the cove and back, Emil swimming nearby for safety.

As she got older, Carolyn became serious about swimming, spending long hours in the water in front of her house, practicing the crawl and the butterfly she later used in competition at the Waterbury YWCA. She enjoyed the sport's solitude and discipline. Often Carolyn practiced swimming to music. She loved to listen to a Tchaikovsky piano concerto at full volume on the record player as she swam in long easy strokes.

The house on the lake was often filled with family and visitors. Sometimes fifteen or twenty people sat at the grown-ups' dinner table and as many or more children would be at the kids'.

In the evening, some of the family and guests gathered around the piano to sing while others played whist.

Carolyn loves to talk about her large Irish-American family. Her mother, Rosalene Carolan, was one of eleven children. Her forebears came to the United States during the Irish immigration of the mid-nineteenth century. Family was very important to her, and during the years when she was raising her own children, she always made room for relatives and friends around her large dining room table. While Carolyn was growing up, her aging aunt Nell Finley Daly Downey lived with the Browns until her death when Carolyn was fifteen. Aunt Nell had buried two husbands whom she fondly remembered as "dear Jimmy and poor Bill." The Brown children loved Aunt Nell but couldn't resist chuckling every time they heard the refrain.

During summers, Rosalene invited her elderly cousin Maryann to the lake so she could enjoy a vacation. Maryann helped by watching the younger children and baking bread, sixteen loaves

In their canoe that eventually became half a canoe, left above, from front to back, Don, Dick, Carolyn, and Bobby. When Carolyn's mother called the children, it was "Bobby-Donny-Dicky-Carolyn." Maryann Carolan, a distant cousin at left in the other photo, who lived with the Browns at the lake every summer. The oldest of a large family, Maryann assisted Carolyn's mother by watching the children, who often attempted to get the better of her. Ellen Finley Daly Downey (Aunt Nell, at right) was Aunt Nellie to the children. She owned a saloon in Waterbury. She was good to people in need in the family. As she got older and throughout Carolyn's growing up, she lived with the Browns. Maryann died in the late 1950s. Aunt Nellie died between Carolyn's freshman and sophomore years of high school, about 1951. Carolyn looked after Aunt Nellie after school when her mother was at work in a factory. Once Carolyn was detained at school for misbehavior. When she arrived at home, there was Aunt Nellie in the road directing traffic. Carolyn encouraged the confused elderly woman into the house by offering her a cup of tea.

at a time. Carolyn smiles at the thought of warm bread and butter waiting for them in the afternoons.

When I think of dinner table hours at the lake, Maryann is always in the picture. She was a major presence in our family and aided my mother in birthing my older siblings at home in the days before women had their babies in hospitals. She was there for my mother throughout a lifetime. When I knew Maryann, she was always old, had no teeth, and resembled the comic strip character Andy Gump. Her laugh was a cackle. She loved us and watched over us, even when we played tricks on her.

They enjoyed teasing her by diving under the raft so she couldn't find them. Or they climbed a tree next to the house where they dug out acorns to make pipes, smoking dry corn silk. When Maryann asked why there was smoke in the tree, they told her the birdhouse was on fire.

The tree was a secret hideout for us. We had other secret places, hideouts we considered our wonders of the world.

One place is the Gorge. This waterfall lay hidden deep in the forest, which is how we referred to the top of Southington Mountain. Although we knew the landmarks in the woods, we always felt relief when we had the certainty of the waterfall's crashing sound within our hearing. There we sat on the ledges with falling water pounding our bodies, absolutely free. Occasionally we reached the deep smooth pool at the bottom of the Gorge, where we would swim. If, during your visits, we ever brought you to the Gorge, consider it a great honor.

Another place was "the lookout," a big flat promontory overlooking Meriden and the wide valley. Now and then, we found blueberries there, but mostly, we picnicked or —and this is in a hushed tone so the family ghosts won't hear—smoked a cigarette or acorn pipe.

Bobby-Donny-Dicky-Carolyn
a tomboy who played football

by Dick Brown

Carolyn was a tomboy and played football and baseball. She swam and ice-skated as well as any boy and often, better.

During our summer expeditions at Hitchcock Lake, the four of us—Bobby-Donny-Dicky-Carolyn—would pass a neighborhood cornfield and "help" the farmer harvest his crop. We stuffed the corn into Carolyn's pants hoping no one would notice. She looked as if she weighed 250 pounds and wobbled all the way home. We told our parents we traded blueberries for the corn.

We had an old canoe we paddled all over the lake. One day we hit a large rock and put a hole in the center of the canoe. We decided to salvage the canoe by sawing it in half. We needed that boat to sell our blueberries to houses around the lake. The only problem was we had to sit way in the back of the canoe with the cut end sticking up in the air so we wouldn't sink—dangerous but fun, and we were all strong swimmers.

We used some of our spending money on cigarettes (a no-no), but before that, we tried smoking dried out tree leaves we called Indian cigars. We sat high on a rock smoking and watched our parents below to make sure they didn't spot us.

Our many walks would sometimes include rolling old tires in front of us. Sometimes we put Carolyn inside the tire and rolled her down the driveway and into the lake. Our mother and father did not see this as funny.

When we became teenagers, Carolyn really developed her musical skills both vocal and at the piano, and we all knew music would always be a great part of her life.

Dick Brown is Carolyn's older brother.

The large willow tree that spread its branches over the shoreline close to the end of our cove created another secret place. In our canoe, we glided under those branches, giving ourselves a push off its sturdy bark while ducking under its bough. I remember it as a shady, peaceful, mysterious spot.

We thought we owned other parts of the world, also, like certain dirt roads for rolling our hoops, Perch Rock where we anchored our boats and went swimming, and the "point" where we caught bullheads—catfish—my mother's favorite. They were difficult to clean, and there was a little fear in the task because their fins could sting, but Dad would sometimes help us.

Carolyn's father, Edward Godfrey Brown, was an only child. His mother died not long after emigrating with her husband from the Wexford area of Ireland at the turn of the twentieth century. Carolyn remembers her sister Roselyn had a switch of her grandmother's hair, a family treasure. As an only child, Eddie Brown spent days by himself during the summer at the lake while his father worked. Carolyn's grandfather died when she was two, but her father told her wonderful stories of how his father took him everywhere with him, to boxing matches and the pool parlor, but also to the opera and concerts. One of Eddie's favorite experiences was attending a New York City performance by Josef Hoffman, a legendary pianist, with his father. Carolyn's grandfather loved music and passed that love to his son, who learned to play piano as a child and was giving lessons by the time he was sixteen. Even Rosalene took lessons from Eddie before they were married.

Years later, dressed up to go out for an evening and waiting for Dad to get ready, my mother played piano; he always took longer to get dressed than she did. My father sometimes liked to remind old friends that he gave my mother piano lessons—and she gave him lessons on the couch. After a pause, he would remark, "And she was the better teacher."

Growing up in a household with a musical legacy, a fine piano, and a father who had infectious enthusiasm for the instrument and talent for teaching about it, Carolyn began playing piano at an early age just as many of her sisters and brothers had. She sometimes found herself performing at the lake. On occasion, a neighbor, Rocco D'Orio, called her out of the water. D'Orio owned a prestigious restaurant, the Waverly Inn, and had an imposing house on the lake. He hosted grand parties and sometimes persuaded Carolyn to stop swimming and come to his living room and play for his guests. The twelve-year-old would arrive in her wet bathing suit, long light-colored hair plastered to her back, and sit on a big beach towel folded for her on the piano bench. She played pieces her father had taught her, melodies she still plays today.

When Carolyn talks about her family, it's easy to see where she gets her sense of humor.

Carolyn's father Edward Godfrey Brown, left, with his father, Patrick Brown.

Her mother and father must have had a busy life with a house full of children, but they thoroughly enjoyed teasing each other. I can picture Carolyn's mother smiling mischievously the same way that Carolyn does.

Carolyn tells about the time the family returned home after a particularly trying trip to the lake cottage. It was spring, and one of the children's assignments had been to clean up the remains of the winter's mouse droppings and cobwebs. The boys and Carolyn hadn't exactly done their best, and her mother was a bit annoyed on the ride home. When Carolyn's brother Bob asked, "What do you want for Mother's Day?" her mother remarked, "Oh, give me a load of horse manure." And that's just what their dad did. The day before Mother's Day, he had a load of horse manure dropped on the front lawn. But Rosalene had the last laugh. She marshaled her family and got them to cart every last bit to the back yard where she had them spread it on the small garden, enlarging it to about three times its original size. They had terrific tomatoes that year—and some terrific rotten-tomato fights.

Rosalene and Eddie habitually put their heads together about raising their children and managing the household.

> My parents were a real team. My mother told me that on many evenings, in order to make ends meet during the early days of their marriage, Dad hurried home from work and took off his shirt so my mother could wash it, iron it, and get it back to him in time to give a piano lesson to someone in the neighborhood or in the next parish. He only had the one shirt.

Carolyn was six when the United States entered World War II, but she remembers the day Pearl Harbor was bombed in December, 1941. Riding her bicycle in the Browns' Ridge Street

Carolyn's parents Rosalene and Eddie Brown, left, on a trip to the shore, c. 1922, and at Race Point Beach in Provincetown, c. 1947

neighborhood of Saint Francis Xavier parish, she heard the neighbors talking about something important and ominous. She wasn't sure what was going on and put things together years later. Her brother Ed would eventually go off to the war in the merchant marines. Like other American families in the 1940s, the Browns supported the war effort not only by sending their children to participate but also by growing Victory gardens and saving salvage, including tin foil.

In 1943, when Carolyn was eight, her family moved to Sylvan Avenue, a neat middle class neighborhood.

> Our house on Sylvan Avenue was directly across the street from Washington Park. It provided tennis courts, a ball field, a small swimming pool, climbing bars we called monkey bars, and, in winter, an ice skating pond created by flooding the baseball field.

Carolyn's family home at 226 Sylvan Avenue, Waterbury, Connecticut. Carolyn's father died in 1959, while the family was still living in the house, which was sold several years later.

> We spent hours skating in winter. Skating was free and not fancy. We sped across the ice having races and snapping the whip, a game where a leader skates backwards followed by a long row of skaters holding on to each other. Of course, in those days, no one wore protective helmets. When the speed and timing are just right, the leader turns abruptly and stops, causing those in line to lose control and land every which way—particularly the last skater, who may fly off into the woods.

We put on our skates in the warm community house, but then we would take our shoes and find a place for them in the stone wall surrounding the field. One time right before dark, I went to get my shoes, and they were gone. I was late for supper and realized I had to walk home in my skates. It was very difficult. There was a hill to climb, and the snow was full of icy ridges. I was eleven years old, and it was slow going, getting dark. I became afraid. While the distance may not have been great, in my young eyes, it was enormous. I looked up and saw John Kiley, a friend of the family, walking toward me. John was a tall man. Sizing up my problem, he reached down like a gentle giant, picked me up, and carried me home.

The new house, still in Saint Francis Xavier parish, was also big like the one on Ridge Street. The Browns needed a good-sized house. There were a lot of them, with frequent live-in relatives—and of course, the piano. Any house they lived in had to have a piano. When they moved to Sylvan Avenue, they replaced an upright with a grand, the one that now stands in Carolyn's music room at Lake Mattawa.

Joan Brown, Rosalene Carolan Brown, Kaye Brown Mark, Edward Godfrey Brown, Roselyn Brown, from left, and Carolyn as flower girl for Kaye's wedding at Hitchcock Lake in 1942

Carolyn, Joan, Roselyn, Kaye, front left to right; Carolyn's parents, Rosalene and Eddie, second row; Dick, Don, Bob, and Ed, back row, on the day Carolyn and her brother Dick didn't clean up diligently enough at the lake. As a result, horse manure made the tomato patch especially bountiful that year.

    The family divides naturally into two groups. What could be called the "first" family consisted of three girls, Katherine, Roselyn, and Joan, and a boy, Edward. There was also Patricia, but she died young, long before Carolyn was born. Kaye is fifteen years older than Carolyn, who was flower girl at her wedding. Carolyn's brother Edward married Barbara O'Brien. Roselyn married handsome Lieutenant Joseph Shea, a Boston College track athlete. He was a navy pilot, and Eleanor Roosevelt often requested that he be assigned to fly her to the Solomon Islands and Philippines on visits to the troops. Joe was killed in World War II. Roselyn herself died of cancer when she was thirty-eight during a trip to England. Joan, the youngest girl of the older family, married Ed McElligott.

    Nearer Carolyn's age were her brothers Robert, who joined the religious order of the Holy Cross; Donald, married to Jeannette Lamontagne, and Richard, married to Lorraine Swanson. The "second" family, whom Rosalene often addressed as Bobby-Donny-Dicky-Carolyn, played together as a unit. Carolyn's brother Don died in 2004.

    Despite having three beautiful sisters as role models, Carolyn grew up a tomboy. She loved playing baseball and football and insists that she could throw a baseball or climb a tree as well as any of her brothers.

Lieutenant Joseph D. Shea with a photo of his wife Roselyn behind him on the night of a squadron party when the pilots all received leis. On the back, the picture says, "Guess who the letter is from. My sweet, precious wife." Carolyn shared a room with Roselyn when Joe, to whom she had been married for two years, went missing in action. He was missing for a long time. Eventually, the navy identified a missal (a Catholic prayer book) as Joe's. Eleanor Roosevelt attended a memorial service for him in Waterbury.

One evening at dusk, a few members of our seventh grade were stealing cherries in the tree behind the rectory. When the priests saw the movement in the high old branches, they sat on the stoop waiting for us to descend to see exactly who we were. They didn't really care about the cherries as much as the idea that kids would be so brazen—and in their very yard. Suddenly my branch broke. Don Maloney, one of my classmates, was on the same branch. Down went Don, then the branch, and then me on top of everything. I heard Father Sullivan cry, "Oh, my god! It's a girl!" Luckily I didn't get hurt. Explaining that prank at home was not an easy matter.

Flagpole swinging did hurt. The flagpole was near the cannon. My pals and I made notches in the rope for our feet, and someone would begin pushing the rider until momentum took over. I was in mid air flying around the pole about ten feet off the ground when the rope broke. My friends had to apply artificial respiration on me to get my breath back.

At the lake, the unmistakable sound of clanking horseshoes could be heard from yard to yard. Carolyn had quite a reputation for pitching horseshoes. Her father loved to brag about her, and one day the neighbor, Rocco D'Orio, overheard him. He set up a friendly match between Carolyn and an old friend known for horseshoe pitching. She narrowly lost, so they scheduled a rematch for the next weekend. She got up at five every morning that week to practice, and she won.

Carolyn had an audience while she practiced for the match.

> I saw my mom and dad watching and laughing at me from their bedroom window as I practiced.

Carolyn, c. 1948

Some people hold the horseshoes on the end where the letters or numbers are embossed. I hold mine where the raised metal in the center creates a place for my thumb. It makes it easier to throw ringers. I like it best when the only sound is a thud in the dirt as the shoe lands around the peg—one flip of the horseshoe, a clean ringer: worth practicing for the rematch.

My mother loved to play horseshoes. She was very competitive and played the game with Dad, my uncles, my brother Ed, and my sisters' boyfriends—the adult players. If it became dark during the games, she would call for candles to be lit and placed directly in the horseshoe pegs. I watched from the tree above them, rooting for her.

As children, the Brown siblings were on vacation all summer. Eddie worked at Scovill Manufacturing Company in Waterbury to support them. When he had his two-week vacation, everyone headed for Cape Cod, sometimes to Eastham, but mostly to Provincetown. There used to be a large ice house in Provincetown, and nearby there was a bed and breakfast called Sandra Lodge where the family often stayed.

Our days consisted of early morning walks on the fishing pier, dune rides in those vehicles with large balloon tires, picnicking at Race Point, and riding the waves. Aunt Nell was with us, too, on some of those Cape Cod getaways. We had to push her up the sandy hill separating the beach from the road. It was too steep for her legs and her age.

Later, I went with my husband Richard to these places, and we found Sandra Lodge under a different name and ownership. The owner showed me the early registers, and there in the book in my mother's handwriting are names of our family and friends who spent many happy vacations there.

Rosalene and Eddie at Cape Cod, c. 1955

All of Carolyn's brothers and sisters had musical interests. Some of them played one or more instruments, several sang, and all enjoyed listening. Sheet music was plentiful around the piano, where the family sometimes gathered to sing. Carolyn was tiny when her father began to teach her to play the piano—so young she can hardly remember when she didn't play. Lessons weren't formal. He or one of her brothers or sisters might help her with a piece she wanted to learn. When she was older, her father devised a method he called "the piano class," when several students met in someone's living room. There were refreshments, and Carolyn's dad presided. He called on each student to play a prepared piece and also offered quick-thinking exercises: "Find middle C. Play a tonic D chord. Show me an arpeggio."

Her father was really proud of her. He liked to play four-hand music with her, and he knew early that she had talent. Once, in a childish tantrum, she announced that she wasn't going to play the piano any more and that running about outdoors with her friends was more important. Her father never lectured or scolded her, but she eventually started playing again when he was away at work. Carolyn says he knew her so well, he knew she'd find her way back to the piano.

When he heard from her mother that she had returned to playing, he sat down with Carolyn and told her the parable of the talents from the gospel of Saint Matthew. Jesus tells the story of a servant who doubles money given him by his master and is rewarded, unlike the servant who hides his money in the ground. Carolyn's father told the story to emphasize the duty one has to one's gifts. In large measure because of her father's devotion to the idea, she believes you should do the best you can with the gifts you have been given. Her dad was a kind man with a dry sense of humor and the ability to make every one of his children feel special. Even today, Carolyn and her surviving brothers and sister banter about whom he liked best. Each of them thinks he or she was that one.

Her dad read avidly and had many books, among them a leather-bound set of the complete works of Sinclair Lewis. Carolyn says he liked to discuss his reading and also to show his books. He read *Life*, *Saturday Evening Post,* and *Esquire* magazines, too, and daily newspapers. Sometimes of a summer evening, while Rosalene worked in the kitchen or garden, he and Carolyn sat on the porch— "I remember leaning back in the porch chair with my feet on the rail"—and had a leisurely talk about his childhood, current events, or his family.

One year, Eddie's old friend Bill Lawlor, a concert bass baritone, moved back to the neighborhood after a career in New York where he had made his living as a singer of classical music. Widowed, he moved in with his sister. When the Browns heard he was back, they immediately invited him over. Their father told the children there would be singing. But Carolyn and her brothers really wanted to hear their favorite radio program *Inner Sanctum*, a thirty-minute weekly thriller that opened with the sound of a squeaking door. They managed some excuse and hid out in their rooms. When Bill Lawlor arrived, Carolyn's dad offered to accompany him. The accomplished singer stood by the piano, his hallmark matchbook in hand like Pavarotti's handkerchief. His rich baritone floated through the house. The sounds of "No rose in all the world . . ." from the song "Until," one of her mother's favorites, found the cracks in Carolyn's door. Drawn to the music, she and her brothers huddled on the top step and listened. Bill Lawlor's singing became a regular feature of Sunday nights. The next time he came, Carolyn was right there listening and joining in.

The Browns loved to have parties, especially at the holidays. There was always music and good food and sometimes costumes. Generations mingled, conversed, played cards, and sang. One Halloween, Carolyn's Aunt Helen entered with a beach blanket, plunked it down on the floor, set up a beach umbrella, and spent the evening there in her antique bathing suit. Eddie Brown carried on his dad's tradition of cooking quantities of steak and sausage for famished attendees when they returned from midnight Mass on Christmas Eve. Musical evenings enlivened many a week.

On Saturday afternoons, Carolyn's mother and dad listened to opera radio broadcasts.

> Good old-fashioned radio carried the music from the Metropolitan Opera to us, letting us hear the world's greatest voices. My parents revered those moments, and we knew enough to tiptoe around the house and listen. If we didn't want to listen, at least we had to let listening happen by being very quiet. I remember a stunning performance of *Mignon* by Tomas, rarely performed now. To this day, I love and enjoy the pleasure of Saturday

Among frequent visitors to the Brown household were, clockwise from upper left, the Moriartys; a singing neighbor, Helen McGrath; Jeanette Cody (with Rosalene, seated) on a Christmastime visit to the McElligott family; Emil Mark's mother dancing with Rosalene. At the table, Carolyn's sister Joan Brown McElligott tends her baby.

afternoon opera on the radio. As I write, *Nabucco* is being performed at the Met and being sent to my living room.

Co-ed grade school at Saint Francis Xavier's was great fun for Carolyn. There were games of dodge ball and kickball at recess. She was a valuable pitcher on the eighth grade baseball team as well. But her dad was protective. He was worried that she might injure her hands.

Playing baseball with the boys as a youngster was as natural for me as scaling flat stones on a lake. I played softball, too, but preferred baseball. I loved the strong sound of that ball and bat. My brothers taught me how to play, and we often had local games in the park across from our house. I remember my brother Bob hitting a line drive right into the barrel of a civil war cannon situated at the end of the playing field. For a few moments, we couldn't figure out where the ball had disappeared—causing the most unusual home run ever.

The grammar school coach watched me one day fielding without a glove. He also watched me pitch and asked me to join the team, which was made up of boys from the parish I usually played with. I had the best time until my father found out. Dad really wanted me to stop playing baseball. You have to remember how hard a baseball is and how important it is for a pianist to have agile fingers and dexterity. I guess he must have put up with it all for a while, but when Dad found out I got hit in the head with a pitch, he put his foot down and made me stop playing.

Carolyn also sang in the school chorus and harmonized with friends. Often she was called out of class to provide piano accompaniment for the kindergarten or teach the children songs.

Carolyn's eighth grade graduating class from Saint Francis Xavier School in Waterbury. She is third from left in the front row, wearing spectator pumps.

She loved working with the little children. Many years later, when Carolyn was in her shop at Boston's Faneuil Hall Marketplace, a woman stopped by and asked Carolyn if she remembered her. Carolyn searched back through the years. Finally it dawned on her that the woman before her was one of the kindergarten students from Saint Francis Xavier.

> She always stood right next to me and watched every move I made. Those eyes looking across the counter in my shop were the eyes of that little girl in kindergarten waiting for the piano music to begin.

In eighth grade, Carolyn was chosen to represent her school in a citywide talent contest sponsored on the radio by the Sunbeam Bread Company. The school basketball team had a game that day. The coach and team, however, found a way to satisfy all spectra of school pride. They stopped the game, turned up the radio, and listened to Carolyn play "The Last Smile" by Wallenhaupt. After she finished, the game resumed. When it came over the gym loudspeaker that she had placed first in the contest, kids, parents, and teachers cheered. Carolyn won five dollars. She can still play the flamboyant piece from memory.

When Carolyn was fourteen, she left behind the comfort of the small familiar parish school at Saint Francis Xavier. She entered Waterbury Catholic High, a girls' school staffed by sisters of the Congregation of Notre Dame, a group that would play a significant role in her life. Waterbury Catholic was a large brick edifice like so many built in the early part of the twentieth century. There were long dark halls and open airy classrooms with tall windows that students opened and closed using six-foot, hooked poles. Catholic High wasn't Carolyn's first choice. She had wanted to go to Crosby, Waterbury's public school. Crosby had a gym, school sports, and boys. One of her brothers had gone there, but she took her parents' advice and followed her sisters to Waterbury Catholic. When her sister Joan asked her how she liked high school, Carolyn said vehemently, "I hate it!"

Carolyn had a hard time finding things she liked to do. She missed the rough and tumble coed sports of elementary school, and she missed singing with the kindergarten students and taking part in the many musicals the school put on. Then, to make matters worse, during Christmas vacation of her first year, she

Carolyn's friend Georgia Breithaupt, left, and Carolyn on the bottom; Marie Capella on top, c. 1949

Carolyn and her classmates occasionally played hookie by heading for a friend's home when the parents were at work. Carolyn is in the front row, right. All are wearing the uniforms of Waterbury Catholic High School.

had a serious accident. She and her cousin Dede Carolan went skiing. They used old wooden skis with straps they buckled around their overshoes. Her equipment tripped her up while she took a jump, and she fell hard in a sitting position on the frozen ground. Painfully, she made her way home, but thinking she had a simple bruise, she didn't tell her mother or father what had happened. She remembered the time she had fallen out of a tree and received little sympathy. In her family, you were expected to take your knocks. If something was truly wrong, you got the support you needed, but you were expected to deal on your own with everyday scrapes.

The pain grew increasingly worse, and by the second half of the school year, one of the nuns noticed Carolyn was not working up to par. She asked her what was wrong and then convinced Carolyn to tell her mother. As soon as Rosalene realized that Carolyn had had a serious accident, she took her to the doctor. He discovered that Carolyn had broken her coccyx bone and, after extensive treatment, scheduled an operation for the following summer. In the meantime she had to give up her only sports activity, swimming competitively at the Y.

Because she was often in pain, her grades plummeted and she even failed Latin. Aware that Carolyn needed help, her father decided, in the good Brown tradition, that music was the cure.

Father Peter Cuny of Waterbury's Saint Cecilia's Church hired Carolyn as organist and choir director when she was fifteen. He is shown here in the 1940s.

He suggested that Carolyn take organ lessons with Sister Reine LaFontaine (Sister Saint Reine Marie), music director at the high school. Although Carolyn initially had no interest in the organ, the challenge, discipline, and tonal discoveries were intriguing. She grew to enjoy the lessons for the next three years.

Those lessons ushered Carolyn into a wider world of music. Father Peter Cuny, pastor of Saint Cecilia's Church, needed an organist. The first person he consulted was Father John Sullivan, Catholic Youth Organization adviser for Saint Francis Xavier Church. He told Father Cuny he knew of only one person who might be available, and that was a high school student in his parish, Carolyn Brown. Father Cuny was not ready to entrust the job to a sophomore, so he consulted Father Philip Hussey, Waterbury Catholic Youth Organization director. Father Hussey thought carefully and told him the only person he knew who played the organ and was not engaged at some other church was a high school student named Carolyn Brown. Father Cuny was beginning to see a pattern, but he continued his search. Finally, he went to Waterbury Catholic High and asked Sister Reine. Again the answer came back, Carolyn Brown. Father Cuny made his decision and, although he must have had some doubts, took a chance with Carolyn.

When Carolyn heard the choir at Saint Cecilia's, she was horrified at how bad it sounded. Her first thought was, "How can I get it to sound good?" All the members were at least twice her age and had been in the choir for years. In desperation she convinced her friend Terri Pugliese, who had a fine alto voice, to join. Terri was a great addition and served as a model for other members. Carolyn had misgivings about taking on an adult group, but after the first rehearsal, Father Cuny came to her with a fifty-dollar check. "But I haven't done anything yet," she said. He told her that he always gave a bonus at Thanksgiving, and since she was the choir director / organist, the bonus was hers. Carolyn took the check —and the challenge.

Then she had to make sure she could play the organ well enough. After all, she was new at it, and although she could play the piano well, an organ has stops, pedals, and more than one keyboard. Furthermore, sight-reading was not one of her strengths. She tracked down Father Cuny whenever she could, got the key to the church, and practiced. When she returned the key,

Father Cuny and she sat and talked in his study among piles of books and newspapers. Father Cuny invariably smoked a cigar as they chatted. As time passed, he became one of her idols as well as her staunch supporter.

The choir needed extra practice, so she invited them to her house one Sunday evening. Her mother filled the living room with sandwiches, cake, and coffee, and the ten people who showed up became the core of the choir. By Christmas, the singers made Carolyn proud. The high point came when Terri and Carolyn sang "Stille Nacht" to a congregation crowded with ethnic German parishioners, some of them with tears in their eyes.

Father Cuny saw that Carolyn had the pluck and savvy to do whatever she set out to do. Teasing her one evening, he invited her to have a cigar, assuming the beautiful young woman would refuse. Except for the acorn pipes and occasional experiment with a cigarette, Carolyn did not smoke. Characteristically, however, she took him up on it and joined Father Cuny as they each lit up. She smoked the whole thing. Father Cuny remembered the joke years later when Carolyn was on the brink of a new life, and he gave her a present, beautifully wrapped—a huge cigar with an inscription on the box, "Holy Smoke."

Failing Latin turned out to provide an opportunity for Carolyn. Since she had to repeat first-year Latin, her schedule was rearranged. She then had a study period where the juniors and seniors had choral club. Sister Ann Kiley (Sister Saint Ann of Jesus), her homeroom teacher, discovered Carolyn had a good voice. "You've got to get this girl into our singing group," she urged Sister Reine. Carolyn passed an audition and that was that. The only sophomore in the group, she got in an extra year of singing. She loved it and was soon asked to join the Ambrosians, a select smaller group. Music had rescued her.

Carolyn had more musical opportunities. Her friend Georgia Breithaupt told her about a radio show on Waterbury's WBRY. On Saturday mornings, Louis "Uncle Louis" Boisvert hosted a show called *Young Stars on Parade* where he presented local high school talent. Georgia asked Carolyn if she wanted to try to get on the show. When she entered the downtown studio on the second floor of a brick business block, Uncle Louis was sitting at a piano. He saw Carolyn in the doorway, struck a note, and asked her to sing it. She did, and it must have been the right one, because Uncle Louis said, "Okay, you're on the show." When Uncle Louis found out she could play the piano, he asked her to play something. She drew on her old favorite, Debussy's "Clair de Lune." The next day she performed it live on the radio.

Eddie Brown at the piano, c.1946, with Emil Mark, Sr., father-in-law of Carolyn's sister Kaye

Every week the show aired something different. Once the teenagers sang the entire score from *The King and I* by Rodgers and Hammerstein. Sometimes they sang solos or played instruments. Rehearsals were on Fridays. Saturdays were live. Carolyn sang and played on the program for three years.

Carolyn in the male lead singing the "Gypsy Love Song" in her high school senior play, c.1953; crowning the new queen with her good friend, Barbara Brodeur, c. 1952; the Mellotones, singing group, including, from left, Beverly Larrivee, Georgia Breithaupt, Faith Garrity, Marie Capella, and Carolyn, c. 1952; in a school fashion show, c. 1950, clockwise from top left

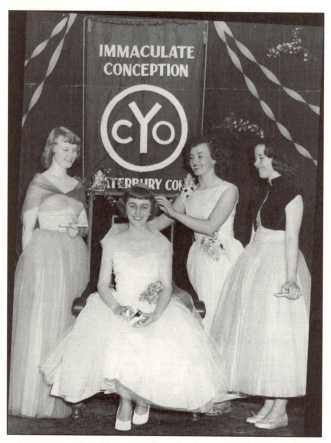

Young Stars on Parade was quite an experience. Uncle Louis taught them to baby a microphone by "modulating your tone, turning away a bit when the volume is too strong, huddling close to it during pianissimo sections." He also started a group, the MelloTones, five girls including Carolyn singing in close harmony. Sometimes he arranged their music, and sometimes Carolyn did. They wore matching dresses and sang for women's clubs and the Knights of Columbus.

Carolyn learned that in show business you have to take on any part and not everyone gets a solo. In her last appearance on the show, she did sound effects for "How Much Is That Doggie in the Window?" Her father joked, "You began with a classic and you ended with a bark."

At Uncle Louis's, Carolyn met Rosemary and John Monagan, two local singers. John was a politician and Rosemary, a music teacher. They invited Carolyn to join the Chansonneures, a group they coached that specialized in French songs. Carolyn, the only teenager, had to work to keep up with the others. Everyone was expected to sight-read a challenging repertoire. Carolyn later took singing lessons from Rosemary in exchange for babysitting. Rosemary, whom Carolyn remembers as "breathtakingly beautiful," taught her "When I Marry Mr. Snow" from *Carousel*. Carolyn still sings it at Lake Mattawa parties.

Her teenage years were happy. Although she started

---

in my dreams, at least
a butterfly floating over snow-covered fields
by Bob Grady

I have been in love (well, in my dreams, at least) with Carolyn since we first met at—where else but a piano! She and the girl next door were classmates playing and singing together when I came to the house to listen to them. It was the beginning of a friendship that has survived fifty-five years.

Our teenage dates included New Haven Pops concerts at the Yale Bowl as well as the usual movies. What else impressed me was how much the family was into music. There was hardly a time when I came to pick her up that there was not someone, or many someones, around the piano or playing different instruments, especially around the holidays. It seemed to be a loving, close-knit family.

But life moved on. I joined the navy and Carolyn, the convent—though the two facts were not connected. I heard about her accomplishments from her cousin, my best friend, over the years. As fate would have it, we met again some seventeen years later as both affiliations had changed. She was living in Newton, Massachusetts and teaching music. I had left the navy. I visited her from my home in Waterbury, and we attended the *Fiddler on the Roof* film because she was thinking of making that production the spring musical at the school where she was teaching. She did and, as usual, it was a smash hit. She has since gone on to more and greater things with a great partner at her side who has also become a friend of mine since first we met some twenty years ago. To me knowing Carolyn is like coming upon a butterfly floating over snow-covered fields—an inspiration you will always remember!

Bob Grady lives in retirement in Waterbury, Connecticut.

When she was in high school, Carolyn sometimes visited her sister Roselyn in New York City. Emil Mark, Carolyn's brother-in-law, ran an advertising company, and Roselyn was Emil's assistant. Carolyn; the Brown family friend, Paul Haight; and Georgia Breithaupt are from left, above, walking in Midtown. Carolyn's sister Roselyn works at top right with Emil.

out hating high school, she came to accept the flow of life. She enjoyed walking back and forth to school with friends. Evenings she did her homework, read a book, or played four-handed piano with her father. Like many middle class families in the early 1950s, the Browns didn't have television. When there were special services in the church, some of them went, and Carolyn liked to meet her friends there. Sometimes, Carolyn and a friend traveled to New York City to visit her sister Roselyn.

Georgia Breithaupt and I were fourteen and staying with my sister on the Upper East Side. We decided to stroll around New York City, going in and out of stores as teenagers do. We actually walked into the Steinway Piano Company and pretended our parents were planning to buy us a piano. We then "tested" each instrument for action and tone. After that, we continued on to Carnegie Hall, bought tickets, and were directed to the balcony. We chose two seats: not our seats, just seats. Right in the front row. We were early. We thought we could sit any place at all until a beautifully fur-coated lady arrived and said, "Pardon, but I think you are in our seats." "Oh, no," we said. "We think you can just sit anywhere at all." She quietly insisted, "No. You are really in our seats." We finally realized how naïve we were and found our own seats—in the next to the last row. The lesson is not the only thing I remember, however. I also remember the cellist's beautiful interpretation of Saint-Saëns's "The Swan."

In high school, Carolyn had lots of boyfriends. Pictures show a beautiful young woman with an easy smile and dark, honest eyes. By the time she was a senior, she was going to five or six proms a year at different schools. Once, she and her friend double-dated. The next night, the same foursome paired off for another double date: same gowns, same rented tuxedoes, but they had switched partners. Before one prom, Carolyn spent the afternoon playing three-outs on the wall with her next-door neighbor Marty Scully. In the game, you threw a tennis ball against the wall in such a way that your opponent couldn't catch it. Three successful catches by your opponent gave him or her the chance to be the thrower. It was a hot sweaty game with a touch of danger, since you had to run out into the street for most of the catches while keeping an eye on traffic as well as the ball. When Carolyn realized it was time to get ready for her date, she ran indoors, showered, changed, and went to the prom an hour later. Her next-door neighbor, Marty's uncle, couldn't believe the transition. "Look at her," he said. "And she was just playing ball on the street."

Carolyn never had to worry about what dress to wear. Her sister Joan not only shared a room but also her evening gowns. And her sister Kaye was known to go to New Jersey to shop for bargains. Carolyn remembers a prom dress that cost seven dollars. Although she wore school uniforms every day, she always had a variety of gowns. This was an advantage of being "little sister" to the older girls known throughout Waterbury as "the beautiful shades of Brown."

"The beautiful shades of Brown, Carolyn's three sisters, above left, from left, Roselyn, Joan, and Kaye, c. 1941; Carolyn's four brothers, at right: Dick and Bob, from left, front; Ed and Don at the lake, c. 1943;

*The same stream of life that runs through my veins night and day
runs through the world and dances in rhythmic measures . . . .
It is the same life that is rocked in the ocean-cradle
of birth and of death, in ebb and in flow . . . .*

*I put my tales of you into lasting songs.
The secret gushes from my heart . . . .
Let all my songs gather together their diverse strains
into a single current and flow to a sea of silence
in one salutation to thee.
Like a flock of homesick cranes flying night and day
back to their mountain nests
let all my life take its voyage to its eternal home
in one salutation to thee.*

from *Gitanjali*
Rabindranath Tagore, 1913

Sister Carolyn Brown, c. 1968, after the CNDs began wearing less complicated habits and sisters began using their own family names

Sister Carolyn Brown, c. 1968, practicing new music for the Roman Catholic Mass. At the request of her bishop, Carolyn organized twenty-one simultaneous liturgies on the campus of the University of Bridgeport, Connecticut, as a showcase for the potentials of congregational participation and vernacular language in Catholic worship, part of the mandate of the Second Vatican Council convened by Pope John XXIII in 1962. Students appreciate her accomplished technique, captured in motion, above.

celebration of Magnificat through faith and service

honoring a religious life illuminated by music

When I first heard that Carolyn had been a nun, I was surprised and curious. I was raised a Roman Catholic and had plenty of experience with nuns, the Sisters of Saint Joseph from whom I learned basic catechism and the Sisters of Notre Dame de Namur at Emmanuel College in Boston. These nuns wore long black habits, stiff white headgear, and rosary-bead belts. Carolyn did not fit this image. In 1994 when I met her she was an attractive business woman who talked about trips to Rome and Milan and wore fashionable clothes with panache. But there you have it. More than forty years earlier at the age of eighteen, Carolyn had joined the Congregation of Notre Dame (CND) and for the next sixteen years observed vows of poverty, chastity, and obedience.

Carolyn's choice did not come as a sudden revelation or with a clap of thunder. During her senior year, she struggled with the decision. She wanted to be of service and thought of nursing. She had helped her mother and sister Kaye take care of her bedridden Aunt Nell. She felt she was good at caring for the sick. She looked into nursing programs, but more and more she considered religious life.

> *I liked silence and I liked prayer. I wanted to be a Notre Dame sister. It was the right decision at the time.*

Carolyn's choice of the CNDs was logical. The sisters of the order had been her teachers at Waterbury Catholic. She admired many of them. Sister Reine had offered musical wisdom and kind support. Her senior homeroom teacher, Sister Margaret Young (Sister Saint Edward), was vibrant and intelligent. Her favorite teacher, Sister Ann, had a magic touch for reading the hearts and minds of students.

> She filled us with a respect for our own talents as well as those of each other.

The sisters of the CND at Waterbury Catholic were bright, dedicated women who loved their calling. Carolyn saw in their lives a combination of service and religious mysticism that attracted her.

She didn't talk much about her interest in religious life. Her decision was

> a gradual struggling with the notion. There were fewer options at the time, and I was drawn to a life of service and prayer.

She weighed pros and cons and, as with all of her major life decisions, allowed her heart to lead her.

When she told her family she planned to join the CNDs, her mother was delighted but surprised. "I thought you were head over heels for the young man down the street," was her comment. A child in the religious life was a blessing. Carolyn's brother Bob was already a member of the Brothers of the Holy Cross, and Carolyn's announcement, although a surprise, was greeted with support and encouragement. Her father was quite overcome when she told him, but he responded with a big hug. He didn't lose his humor, though. Hugging her as she left home that August, he lightened the moment by saying, "Remember, darling, keep your bowels open and your conscience clear."

The summer before she left was a busy one. Her sister Roselyn arrived in a Studebaker convertible to teach Carolyn to drive.

> She put me in the driver's seat, told me what to do, and after one long day on Connecticut back roads, she felt I knew how to drive. She had already made an appointment for the next day at the motor vehicle department.

Roselyn may have figured if the sisters needed a driver, Carolyn could volunteer. Or perhaps she wanted to be sure Carolyn could get away if she had to. Her brother Dick showed her how to start on a hill using a stick shift. He said she nearly stripped the gears. Roselyn tape-recorded the driving test booklet so Carolyn could memorize it. To everyone's surprise, including her own, she passed the test and got her license on the first try.

Her friends the Monagans from WBRY invited her to spend two weeks with them and their family in Bermuda. There she enjoyed the warm blue waters of the South Atlantic. One morning, she swam alone and dove deep into water so clear that she felt she could reach the bottom and then spring back up to the top. Taking strong long strokes, she headed down, realizing after a while that it was much farther to the bottom than she thought. Feeling her chest tighten, she turned and made her way to the surface, breaking through just in time to fill her lungs with air. That experience remains clear in Carolyn's memory.

> Should I keep going or turn back? Not knowing how deep the water really was, I turned. A bit disoriented, I wasn't sure if I were really heading up or down. Later, I discovered it was about fifty feet deep in that place. Its clarity had deceived me.

She remembers it as a wake-up call, an admonition that life is finite and she needed to take care and to know what she was diving into before she dropped over the edge.

When it came time for her to leave home, one of her brothers (no one remembers which one) drove her to Waterbury Catholic where a group of about a dozen girls, most from her high school, was gathering to fly to the novitiate in Illinois. There was neither celebration nor weeping. They just left. But Carolyn and a few others were not planning to go quietly. They arrived in

Carolyn and friends pulled a successful prank on their former teachers, the sisters at Waterbury Catholic High School, when they sent back two photos from a Chicago cabaret and some horrified nuns believed the soon-to-be CND postulants had overindulged. Carolyn, at right in both photos, labeled them "Before" and "After" to help the prank along.

Chicago, where arrangements had been made for them to stay in a downtown hotel before heading to the novitiate near Kankakee. Packed neatly in suitcases were their postulant habits, but they weren't quite ready to put them on. With some high school classmates, Carolyn took a cab to a performance by Les Paul and Mary Ford, the guitar-player / singer husband and wife. Then they went to the Loop area to hear jazz. They ordered soft drinks, the kind that came with umbrella stirrers and slices of lemon clinging to the edge of the glass, and had professional pictures taken of each other in front of their concoctions. Their teenage hijinks created quite a stir back home where some of the nuns at Waterbury Catholic thought they had gotten drunk. Carolyn grins mischievously at the thought.

The Congregation of Notre Dame is a Canadian order with its motherhouse in Montreal. French-born Marguerite Bourgeoys founded it in 1653. Like other women who began orders in seventeenth century Canada, she went to Montreal to educate the women and children of the colony, both French and native. The CND was among the first uncloistered Roman Catholic orders for nuns. Mother Bourgeoys established her school in a stone Montreal stable in the 1650s and supervised construction of the beautiful Our Lady of Bon Secours Chapel from 1655 to 1675. Canonized in 1982 by the Roman Catholic

Marguerite Bourgeoys, founder of the Congregation de Notre Dame

Church, she had been revered in Canada for centuries. In 1988, a statue by sculptor Jules La Salle, depicting her as a sturdy strong woman with arms outstretched and gown flowing, was placed by the Canadian government on Place Marguerite Bourgeoys in Montreal.

The order's mission:

To follow Jesus in a preferential option for the poor and to live our mission of liberating education in fidelity to the prophetic charism of Marguerite Bourgeoys in today's world, we commit ourselves to live close to the reality of the impoverished, excluded, and the oppressed. In solidarity with them, we commit ourselves to participate actively in the transformation of society for a more just world.

For the community, the crucial event in the story of Jesus is his mother Mary's visit to her cousin Elizabeth when both are pregnant. When Mary arrives, she describes her joy to her cousin: "My soul magnifies the Lord . . . (in Latin, "Magnificat anima mea, Dominum"). Each in her own way, Mary and Elizabeth express the power of expectancy, service, and legacy. They recognize their capacity to do good and be good through love, beauty, prayer, and truth. The "Magnificat" is one of religion's great utterances, a woman's recognition of her capacity to fulfill destiny. Mary and Elizabeth share faith, humility, and dedication to humanity as they recognize the value of each individual. In the ideal of their interaction resides the soul of the CNDS. Outreach and loving service characterize the order's mission.

The CNDs undertake community decisions intended to fulfill the order's mission at an annual "chapter," when delegate sisters from all over the world—wherever CNDs live, work, and serve—meet in

Montreal. They function with democratic procedures. When young women enter the order, each experiences several months as a "postulant," a time for mutual consideration. "Am I suited to this life?" is the question for the postulant. "Is this order suited to this young woman?" is the question for the CNDs. Postulants who decide to stay accept the more disciplined attire and behavior of the "novice," and the word "novitiate" refers to the religious home of both the postulant and novice. At the end of a term as novice, a young woman who decides to accept the religious life takes vows, usually temporary for some years until professing permanently. In the CNDs when Carolyn joined, there were six years of temporary vows after the novitiate and before permanent profession.

The crucial scriptural moment for the CND is the visit made by Mary, the mother of Jesus, to her older cousin Elizabeth, the mother of John the Baptist, represented above by an anonymous late medieval European artisan.

As Carolyn became a CND in 1953, the order opened the first American novitiate in Bourbonnais, Illinois, near Kankakee. There Carolyn began her life as a sister, first as a postulant for six months and then as a novice for eighteen. Hers was the first group to go through Bourbonnais. They were the first United States novices to profess vows.

After their arrival at the convent, the postulants made a general confession, a review of their lives. Two lines of young women in the chapel waited to enter one of two confessional boxes, telephone-booth-like wood structures with doors of frosted glass. As Carolyn entered the confessional, she closed the door and the priest slid open the small partition separating them. Kneeling, she made the sign of the cross to begin her confession. Suddenly, the unsecured kneeling bench fell over, spilling her out and smashing the door. Sprawled at the feet of the waiting girls, Carolyn laughed so hard that she couldn't get up. Both rows of girls gasped, and then the whole chapel began rocking with laughter. Had the priest thrown her out? To this day, Carolyn's friends from her convent days remind her of how she burst onto the scene. They still wonder what she had to confess that was so explosive.

In 1953, the CND sisters lived much as nuns lived in the middle ages. Each woman's room was a small alcove furnished simply with a dresser, a chair, and a bed. No pictures decorated the walls, bare except for a crucifix. Carolyn got up at five-thirty and had a half hour to get dressed. By six, she was in chapel for morning prayer. Then there was a half hour of guided meditation during which a sister read a text from the Bible and asked the novices to reflect on how the words had meaning in their lives. Mass followed meditation, then breakfast, and then classes in literature, education, and moral theology leading to a bachelor's degree. Most sisters also had a household task, which they referred to as a "ménage," and had to keep their personal rooms in order. After dinner, eaten in silence, there was common recreation time when conversation was allowed. Otherwise, the nuns kept silence except for talk necessary to study. There were prayers and meditation in the evening, and then to bed at nine. Because it was a teaching order and not contemplative, common prayers occurred only at matins (in the morning) and vespers (in the evening).

At first Carolyn was so busy she had no time to be homesick. She did everything with the postulants, eating, praying, and attending classes. They soon began to feel like family. One night, though, unable to sleep, she heard a train in the distance. She missed her home and family and slid out onto the back stairs to look up at the moon. One of the older sisters, Sister Anna MacDonald (Sister Saint Anna), the sub mistress, saw her. "You know," she said, "it's the same moon that is in Connecticut." Somehow the kindness gave Carolyn comfort, and, like anyone setting out on a personal adventure, she reconciled her fear of the unknown with the wonder of its possibilities.

For Carolyn, the CNDs were a constant source of musical inspiration. She still uses Sister Reine's techniques and strategies when she directs choral groups, and her musical life at Waterbury Catholic was the highlight of her high school years. But the new American novitiate in Illinois had no music program for its first class. The sisters in charge were determined to fill the gap as soon as possible. Immediately they began to develop a program so the postulants could learn to sing the liturgy. But they had no organist. On the first day of choir practice, the superior asked if anyone could play the organ. Carolyn and another postulant raised their hands. Carolyn still has no idea why, but she was chosen. Once again music steered the course of her life. She became chapel organist.

Sister Frances McManus (Sister Saint John Joseph), superior of the novitiate, did not, however, expect Carolyn to take on this responsibility without help. Immediately, she arranged for Carolyn to have music lessons. The order brought a teacher, Mary Rita Partlow, from DePaul University in Chicago, fifty miles away, to give her piano lessons. Carolyn remembers her as "a beautiful Texan gal with great talent." Carolyn's advanced music education had begun.

After six months, Carolyn and her class became novices. Of twenty-two girls who began with the class, eighteen decided to continue. For Carolyn, the decision was relatively easy. She conferred with Sister Frances and made up her mind. She simply hoped she was doing the right thing:

> I liked silence and I liked prayer. I wanted to be a Notre Dame sister. It was the right decision at the time.

Carolyn had been drawn to the life of prayer the convent offered. Like more experienced sisters, novices meditated and developed their interior lives. They studied the writings of mystics and saints.

> In the convent, you develop a consciousness of being dependent on a higher power, of not being alone in the world. While you acknowledge your humanness, you lift up your heart to God in the hope that you will be filled with truth.

A few things changed when Carolyn became a novice. As a postulant, she had worn a simple habit and veil, but novices had to wear a more complicated habit and head covering. The nuns had to construct their head covering for themselves. Each sister was given two pieces of starched linen that she learned to fold and attach to her hair with wire pins. Carolyn's fingers can still remember how the folding went. The head covering originated as part of the attire that many women wore in seventeenth-century France.

Carolyn had to make one other change when she went from being a postulant to a novice. She had to accept a new name, one by which she was expected to be known for the rest of her life in the convent. The administrators of the order made the final decision, but they asked Carolyn and other postulants to make a list of names they might like to take. They encouraged the young women to choose family names as well as others of interest. In the mid 1950s, there were more than four thousand CNDs, and each nun's name had to be unique in the community. On the day she took part in the transitional ceremony, Carolyn heard her new name for the first time: Sister Saint Roselyn of Jesus. Her sister Roselyn and her mother Rosalene were delighted.

Sister Frances McManus (Sister Saint John Joseph) was the CND mistress of novices when Carolyn professed her vows and throughout her time in the convent. Sister Frances asked for (and was given) Carolyn's music, "O, Praise Ye the Lord," at her funeral in 1999. "She's the one who provided me piano lessons in the novitiate," Carolyn explains. "She was a good friend. Really a good friend. All her life—and she lived long—she was like a centering factor in our lives, for all the ex nuns, all the CNDs. We'd go back to see her. She loved Dick. 'Where'd you get him?' she asked me. She stayed at Lake Mattawa one time when we first had the cottage. When those figures in your life go, you miss them. When they go, you really miss them, because they're so important to your own foundation."

For two years in the novitiate, Carolyn was absorbed in playing and studying music. She wasn't the official music teacher. Sister Claudette Chevrette (Sister Saint Andre Marie), a CND from the next town, filled that role, but whenever she was not there, Carolyn carried on. It wasn't easy. She needed time to practice despite other responsibilities. Every morning there were academic classes, followed by lunch and more classes. She played the organ every morning for the gathered community at Mass and practiced in the afternoon when the other young women were sewing.

Because of her schedule, she often she got out of doing some chores. The sisters were usually responsible for sewing their own habits. Carolyn says cheerily, "I was always dreadful." Lucky for her, Sister Cecilia Labrecque (Sister Saint Mary Achille), the sewing teacher, understood she needed time to practice and took on the stitching of Carolyn's habit. It was their secret.

Although she had had no training in composition, Carolyn wrote her first piece of music in the novitiate. During the Marian year declared by Pope Pius XII in 1954 to honor Mary, the mother of Jesus, the CNDs planned an evening program in the novitiate, a pageant. It was for the feast day of the Annunciation, a commemoration of the archangel Gabriel's announcement to Mary that she would give birth to Jesus. Taking that as her inspiration, Carolyn put music to the Latin words the angel said to Mary, "Ave Maria, gratia plena, Dominus tecum (Hail, Mary, full of grace, the Lord is with thee)." Carolyn added music for Mary's answer. Both melodies are sung simultaneously. She calls this composition "The Pageant Song."

Soon after Carolyn wrote "The Pageant Song," her sister Joan visited Bourbonnais. She and Carolyn walked around the grounds of the convent, an elegant old building surrounded by fields and orchards. Carolyn clowned around with Joan, who took a picture of her hanging upside down from an apple tree. Joan had come to tell Carolyn she was getting married. When Joan heard Carolyn had written an "Ave Maria," she persuaded Carolyn to give her a copy, and Bill Lawlor sang it at Joan's wedding.

While in the novitiate, Carolyn also wrote music for the sisters to sing, including a musical setting for the Mass, the central Roman Catholic liturgical celebration. It includes a "Kyrie," "Gloria," "Credo," "Sanctus," "Benedictus," and "Agnus Dei." The convent provided Carolyn time and opportunity to nurture a talent that might have gone uncultivated if she had entered nursing or been married as a young woman. Carolyn was encouraged to explore her gifts.

Hoping to get an analytical explanation, I often ask Carolyn why she began writing music. Music is so natural for her, however, that it's hard for her to explain why. She searches for an answer. "It's a way of expressing something I feel." It seems that something mystical happens. The closest she has gotten to an explanation is a story about one of her compositions. Once she was out walking in the snow. Clouds drifted slowly across the sky and the whole scene reminded her of Psalm 103 / 104 (depending on which version of the Bible one consults), "Thou makest the winds thy messengers—and the clouds thy chariot." She was moved to set the text to music to express what she felt. When she had done so, she added a second verse of her own words. Experiences of nature inspire her as can poetry, including scripture. Music usually starts with words searching for a melody, although she says there are times when a melody bubbles up in her head waiting for the right words.

When her two years at the novitiate were over, Carolyn was sent east to Villa Maria Academy, a school run by the CNDs in the Bronx. Although she had completed only two years of college, she was assigned to the elementary school and immediately given a first grade class. But after only three weeks, the superior general called the principal to say that Carolyn was not to be a classroom teacher. Instead she was to teach music and continue her music education. The CNDs assessed Carolyn's talents and did not hesitate to make decisions for her. Carolyn's CND service always turned on learning, teaching, and making music.

11/10/54

This belated note is a confession -

I know Nuns do not hear confessions, but you will have to hear this one. When you were here I thought you had a very high nuisance value with your baseball, tree climbing, kitchen orchestras etc., but I was very wrong, very wrong, you were very undisturbing compared to your sister Joan.

This wedding thing is something - I came home one night and found Joan very blue - no rents - no house to live in, etc. Got to thinking,- should never do that- well got to thinking Moriarity's wife owned a house that was idle - called Mae, presto, she has a house.

Then the fun began - painting, papering - scrubbing - you should see Ed McElligott look at me. He never scrubbed or painted in his life before but boy-oh-boy he is an expert now - The more he scrubs the more he stares at me - just wondering how I went through thirty-five years of this --

You know I thought for a while that the wedding breakfast was going to be held in our kitchen couse your Ma sure went to work painting and polishing that kitchen when she got the news that we were going to have a wedding - a fly lit on the wall the other day and slipped and broke his leg. - Pretty slick I'm telling ya... Between painting Joans house and this house everything tastes of paint - everybody is covered with paint - everybody Kay, Eddie, Joan, Ma, but me is paint crazy - green paint - white paint - brown paint - I just hate paint. While they are painting, I sit home and tend the phone. I sure found out that all the cuckoos are not in clocks - jokers trying to sell pictures - television, jewelry-furniture etc, ring this thing every five minutes. What I tell them I will confess to some broad minded Priest.

I am a little mixed up on this thing as I always thought, what the bride wore was the whole show... Not this wedding honey, not this one. They have been to New York, Hfd., New Haven, Middletown to get a dress for your Ma - boy the tension over Ma's dress was terrific. In fact, when she finally got it, I called N.Y., Milford, etc. and told them "O.K. kids the wedding is going to be for sure."

Now don't you go asking what color it is, that is a deep secret, and I don't give away secrets. It's not white or red or blue or pink or black or brown, and it is none of your business how it is made, but we sure will look like Maggie and Jiggs that day.

I have already collected my trousseau which consists of a pair of black shoes and a suit that I will rent for six dollars from a Mr. Imbimbo who is very disturbed as to how I shall look. He should look in one of his mirrors. Mother Nature sure had her mind on something else when she made him. Ha' think I was Adonis.

Then there is the shower thing. That is just Jesse James without his gun. You ask Joan what night she wants, who she wants at it - what she would like as gifts etc., and then you puss the seitch on the big show and Joan walks in so surprised... works swell though - the place is loaded with loot. I can get into one side of my bed now till after the wedding.

Carolyn corresponded by letter and telephone with her family. Her father typed his letters to her, and they often revealed his wry humor, as in one, above, he mailed her in 1954.

Immediately, the CNDs enrolled Carolyn in the New York College of Music.

> When I began my higher education, the institution where I would study was chosen in the main by the education supervisor in the community. If a sister was talented in language, for instance, she might be guided to LaValle University in Canada. If her talent was in mathematics or English literature, it might be Columbia or New York University or somewhere else, depending on where she lived and worked. The CND sisters have degrees from many colleges and universities, all encouraged by the order. We would meet with the education supervisor periodically, and she would guide us in obtaining materials we needed for applications. CND schools were stronger because of the diversity of our educations.

She taught music to elementary and high school students at Villa Maria for part of the day and then took a subway from the Bronx to Manhattan, her black habit and white headpiece a symbol and a curiosity. When she arrived at the college, a brownstone building on East Eighty-sixth Street, Carolyn heard music pouring out of the windows. Students were draped on the stairs and hanging over the window sills. Carolyn entered the small lobby and could hear students practicing violin, oboe, and piano in a cacophony that was heaven to her ears.

> I was thrilled to be entering the college of music. Oh, God, I thought. I'm going to be studying music in college.

She didn't realize she had to audition in order to take piano lessons at the college, so she hadn't prepared for the adjudicators. While she waited, she could hear the students before her playing concerti. She hadn't even brought music. She moved to the piano and played portions of pieces she had once memorized: Chopin's "Etude, Opus 10, Number 3" and "Etude, Opus 25, Number 1" called "The Harp"; Beethoven's "Sonata, Opus 10, Number 1" and "Sonata, Opus 14, Number 2"; and Poulenc's "Mouvements Perpétuels, Number 1" as far as she could remember them. Then with her usual directness, she told the team of listening teachers that she hadn't been able to practice but was ready to move forward in her music education. The judges must have heard something in her playing, because she was admitted to the school.

She took classes in ear training, harmony, counterpoint, pedagogy, and piano. She was six weeks late in starting school, but in the cooperative spirit of the order, Sister Lena Mastroiani (Sister Saint Paul) at Villa Maria helped her catch up. Quickly the students at the college realized that Carolyn was conscientious. "Hey, Sister," they called. "Did you do your homework?" Although some of them were more experienced than she was, they didn't hesitate to ask how she had analyzed or harmonized a passage. Then they copied her notes.

The first year was busy. Carolyn not only commuted by subway from the Bronx to Manhattan for college, but she also lived the community life, did homework, practiced piano, and taught piano lessons. The Villa Maria superior made all the financial arrangements, collecting fees for lessons, paying Carolyn's tuition, and providing money for school and transportation expenses. If her funds got below a certain level, Carolyn asked for more. She was exempt from the usual convent rule that required that sisters travel in pairs.

> Evening rush hour on a New York subway is madness, yet wonderful to behold. En masse, people from all walks of life and cultures sit, stand, play music, talk to themselves, sleep. One evening as I traveled back to the Bronx, a very tired man fell asleep and gradually leaned and leaned in his seat until his head landed on my left shoulder. My veil was his resting place. I looked down at his dark hair and let him sleep. Many passengers had broad smiles across their faces—who knows what they were thinking. I had to wake him up at 125th Street where I transferred to a bus going to Pelham.

There were spiritual readings late in the afternoon when the sisters gathered in community. Dinner and evening prayers followed. It was a large convent, so there were some sisters whose job was to cook. The rest also had rotating chores such as kitchen duty or cleaning the refectory and chapel. In the evening, sisters gathered for conversation and reading. Once past the novitiate, sisters were allowed to talk during dinner, and Carolyn remembers lively dinnertime discussions on theology, politics, and current events. One elderly nun was an expert on astronomy who shared her enthusiasm: "I'll see you on the staircase at two this morning to see Venus." Another was an avid reader and kept "throwing books" Carolyn's way. Education was multi-faceted.

Carolyn was a good student. The next year the CNDs enrolled her full time at Hunter College, City College of New York, on East Sixty-eighth Street in Manhattan. She moved from the convent at Villa Maria to the convent of another CND school, Saint Jean Baptiste on East Seventy-sixth Street and Lexington Avenue, walking distance from the college. At Hunter, she took more courses in theory, harmony, and conducting as well as voice and piano lessons. She also taught some organ students at Saint Jean's. She grins as she recalls that time: "I was like a drunkard. I loved it. I couldn't get enough."

Carolyn sang in the college choir. The director asked her to sing a solo at the upcoming Christmas concert. Her superior, Sister Helen Mullen (Sister Saint Helen) was happy that Carolyn was doing so well. Sister Helen, just coincidentally, had been a piano student of Carolyn's father, so she had even more reason to be pleased. But days before the performance, chancery

---

a red convertible inhabited by two nuns

sensitivity, compassion, interest in others

by Anne C. Leonard, CND

You hear about a person entering a space and lighting up that space. Carolyn Brown Senier always has had that rare ability and capacity. Although she exudes simplicity and is unassuming, her presence is felt immediately. Carolyn has an outer beauty, but more so, it is her spiritual qualities that attract and have an effect on those she encounters. Carolyn has that special quality of being able to engage individuals and groups in an unobtrusive way. It is her joy and the hope she exudes that attract others.

I have memories of sharing a room with Carolyn when we were staff members at Notre Dame Academy, Staten Island and again when we were studying at Boston University. I recall Carolyn sparking groups to sing their hearts out and her creating an atmosphere where all felt themselves a valuable part of a given presentation, program, or whatever because their gifts were accepted and recognized. I recall Carolyn and me renting a car to travel from Boston to Rhode Island. That car turned out to be a red convertible, and when inhabited by two nuns "in habit," it caused heads to turn. I remember our attending liturgies at Boston University where the now famous author, James Carroll, was then a young campus minister.

Above all, I treasure Carolyn's sensitivity, compassion, and interest in others. Her artistry and sense of style have never changed over the years but have only grown and become seasoned, even more attractive.

Anne C. Leonard is the CND North American provincial leader.

authorities for the Archdiocese of New York said no. In 1957, the church hierarchy felt it inappropriate for a sister to sing in a secular choir. Carolyn had to tell the choir director she couldn't sing the solo. She was terribly embarrassed for herself and Sister Helen, but there wasn't anything they could do without disobeying orders.

In the summer, the sisters spent two weeks relaxing at a Rhode Island beach retreat. The CNDs had a backyard garage converted to a chapel. The building had recently been an inn and was perfect for their purpose, with a large dining room, wide spacious porch facing the Atlantic Ocean, and simple individual bedrooms for approximately thirty people.

> People are sometimes curious about what a nun's beach vacation might be like, and the answer is that it was all hopelessly normal. We could read, write, swim, or visit leisurely with family and friends. I remember when one of the students in school asked another CND, "When do you swim?" Without batting an eyelash, she came back with, "At high tide."

Carolyn's third year as a nun began rather haphazardly. She had no idea where she was going to teach or where she was going to live. The CNDs planned to assign her to their new high school in Stamford, Connecticut, but the building hadn't been finished. As the school year approached with Stamford staffing uncertain, she received multiple assignments. On Sunday evenings, the sisters walked from their residence to benediction, a short evening service in the church. Carolyn, however, waved to them as she continued on to the station to board a New Haven train en route to Waterbury, where she taught two days a week at her old high school, Waterbury Catholic. Sister Reine had had a heart attack, and Carolyn taught her former music teacher's classes.

> Sister Saint Reine Marie was wonderful. She ran the entire music program, and I was honored to try to fill her shoes. At first, it was a little intimidating. She had huge choruses—one hundred people—and small choruses. She taught piano and voice. She taught me organ. She encouraged beautiful tone quality from everyone. No throat singing. As students, we sang wonderful music. We sang Bach's "Jesu, Joy of Man's Desiring" and beautiful spirituals. We performed an intricate nursery rhyme suite. She made beautiful, well-considered selections that were good for education and good to hear. She worked very hard to find them. When she died in 2002, I went down at the sisters' invitation and played at the funeral of Sister Saint Reine.

While in Waterbury, Carolyn stayed at the convent attached to the school. Then on Tuesday afternoon, she boarded the train back to Stamford and, in a temporary school building, taught classes in music appreciation, glee club, and piano for two days.

On Thursday afternoons, she took the train to Manhattan for a piano class with Mildred Waldman at Hunter. Carolyn often took her lesson at Ms. Waldman's home, where there was a grand piano in the living room. Then she headed back to Saint Jean's.

At Fordham on Fridays and Saturdays, she took liberal arts classes required to complete her undergraduate degree. On Sundays, the whole round started again. "I never knew which side of the bed to get up on," Carolyn says.

It was an exciting and stimulating existence that left her without much community life. She always had her suitcase packed and always felt ill prepared, whether it was for teaching a class or taking a piano lesson. She learned how to pack light and use every free moment to prepare a class or practice a piece of music, two strategies she came to depend on.

Eddie and Rosalene, c. 1954

She became a regular feature on the Connecticut trains. One conductor held up the train for her a few times, waiting for her to come flying down the stairs.

> Those train rides became weekly adventures. At Grand Central Station, a food vendor would arrive as the train pulled away. He would call in a loud voice, "No dining car on this train. Get your sandwiches, coffee, and ice cream now. Last chance before 125th Street." Then he would see me and, like clockwork, bend and whisper, "Would you like a cup of coffee, Sister? Some ice cream?"
>
> I was too shy then to say yes, but we spoke briefly and away he went, continuing his sales pitch in the upper volume, his good heart beating, his strong voice carrying to hungry passengers.
>
> I had to change trains at Bridgeport. The regular conductors watched for me and often sat with me on part of the journey to Waterbury. They rapidly summarized and reported news of my hometown. The sisters in that convent were always surprised that I knew so much of the town business on my weekly arrival.

An advantage of the schedule was that her father often met her at the station when she went to Waterbury Catholic. He waited patiently for her to get off the train and then drove her to school. For Carolyn, it was a welcome moment when she saw her dad, but there wasn't much time for a visit. Sometimes, too, her sister Roselyn met the train when it arrived in New York.

Eleanor Roosevelt, c. 1958

> My sister Roselyn, who lived and worked in New York City, got together with me occasionally at Grand Central Station during this traveling year. We might have a cup of coffee together and chat awhile.
>
> I saw her waiting for me one day and, as I walked towards her, a tall woman approached from another direction. It was Eleanor Roosevelt, who as First Lady had often chosen Roselyn's late husband Joe to be her pilot. After Joe went missing in action, Mrs. Roosevelt honored him and Roselyn by coming to our hometown for a memorial luncheon.
>
> There in Grand Central Station, Roselyn introduced me to her, and we three chatted so easily. This great woman hadn't forgotten my sister, even though more than a decade had passed.

For the next six years, Carolyn taught music at two different schools. Although she was only twenty-four, the CNDS gave her the responsibility of planning and running the music department at Stamford Catholic, later Trinity High School. She organized the program, taught piano lessons, directed the choir, and conducted other music classes.

The school served a diverse population, and Carolyn worked hard to interest all the students in music. She developed an organizational skill that she was able to use many times in her teaching career. She knew that boys were notoriously absent from school choirs, so she spoke with the captains of the baseball, basketball, and football teams. She encouraged them to exercise their leadership in a well-rounded life and develop all their skills, including music. She coaxed them into joining the choir. She already knew many of them. She and another young sister sometimes played baseball with them in the schoolyard. Once the leaders joined, others followed. The first year in Stamford, she had a hundred in the choir, forty of them boys. Between other assignments, she taught on and off in Stamford throughout the 1960s. Once, on their way to a student concert, Sister Carolyn and her mom walked down a school corridor. Following at a discreet distance were jovial boys from the select chorus singing a Herman's Hermits tune just loudly enough to be heard: "Mrs. Brown, you've got a lovely daughter . . ."

My students at Stamford gave me a gift I will always treasure: a ticket for me and the friend of my choice to hear Vladimir Horowitz in concert at Carnegie Hall. Horowitz is one of my idols. My father played his piano recordings to us. His monumental technique at the keyboard defies description.

Horowitz had not been heard in concert for nearly a decade before his comeback in the late sixties. My Stamford students asked if I would like to hear him. I did, with my friend Barbara Arnesen. We sat in the orchestra within the first eight rows. For hours after the performance, I was speechless. Very moved by his playing, I decided to tell him by writing a simple note thanking him for playing again. I told him I was glad he was in the world. Having no address, I mailed it to Carnegie Hall, New York. I didn't know if he would even receive it. A few months later, I received a gracious note from him and an autographed copy of one of his recordings.

I heard him several more times once I moved to Boston, even though it was very difficult to get tickets.

Sister Carolyn directs a Stamford Catholic High School choir, c. 1966

> For a concert in Boston shortly after we were married, my husband Richard surprised me with tickets on my birthday. He wrote and told Horowitz how we met and married, how I heard him play years before, and that together, we would hear this concert. Horowitz wrote to wish us a long and happy life. In our music room, we have hung my framed memories of him.
>
> I learned that those who are truly great make time for others. Richard and I managed to attend every recital of his in Boston even though a whisper of his coming to play would cause a ticket sellout within hours.

Like teachers everywhere, Carolyn also learned to be flexible. At Stamford, they needed someone to teach commercial law. Remembering her days on radio when sometimes you have the solo and sometimes you just have to bark, she took on the task.

> You learn how to survive. Whenever the supervisor came around, I set up a union / management debate with the students, and the supervisor loved it.

In 1959, Carolyn's father died. When she attended his wake, it was the first time she had been home since entering the novitiate in 1953. She suffered conflicting emotions. Walking through the rooms where she had grown up, she was overcome, reminded of her childhood there and saddened by the loss of her father.

> If there is one regret I have about entering the convent it's that as an adult I didn't get to know my father. Losing my dad took the wind out of my sails for a long time. He died in June, and I had never experienced such sadness and loneliness before. I was in a place of heart that I barely recognized. I came to know it as grief, a place where my smile couldn't reach my sad eyes.
>
> Soon after the funeral, honoring a long-standing commitment, I registered for the summer at Pius X School of Liturgical Music in Purchase, New York. It was emotionally difficult, and I tried to stabilize my sadness and loss through study.
>
> Time gradually exercised its healing powers until the following year when my sister Roselyn died of cancer. While she was traveling with my mother in England, she took ill and

Carolyn's dad at the piano at the family home in Waterbury: he had a lot of arthritis but nevertheless continued to play. Eventually, Carolyn's mother gave her the piano. She found a mover going to Boston, and they charged her a little bit to move the piano from Waterbury. Carolyn says she'd have thrown a couch out to make room for the piano.

underwent several surgeries. It shocked our family when she succumbed. Not being there and not being able to say goodbye was very hard on all of us. My last visual memory of her was her long wave to me from the stern of the HMS *Mauritania* as she left New York Harbor. Since then, Dick and I have visited her grave many times in the beautiful village of Chipping Campden in the Cotswolds of England.

I witnessed my mother's dreadful sadness over my dad's death and my sister's death and also the death of a young niece. Her grief was probably deeper than anyone's, and she seemed very fragile for a long time. Sadly, I wasn't available to her much during those days, but the rest of the family was near her. However, my mother visited me when she could at whatever convent I was stationed, and we talked and reminisced for hours.

In 1960, the CNDs decided that Carolyn was needed in their Notre Dame Academy on Staten Island. She was put in charge of elementary and secondary school music. Carolyn got along well with the popular former music teacher, but their styles were quite different. Carolyn

Carolyn visiting Roselyn's grave at Chipping Campden, England, in the Cotswolds, 1977. Her husband Dick took the photo. Roselyn died in 1960.

was laid back and liked teaching small groups in different settings, but the former director was much more organized and regimented. Changing things was a challenge. "But this time," Carolyn laughs, "the Beatles saved me." She learned their music from sixth graders in their harmony classes, and she used songs from the Beatles to relax with the students during breaks in secondary chorus rehearsals.

Carolyn developed the program in much the same way as she had in Stamford. Before the end of the year, she had her glee club in good form with all the parts well represented. Teaching so close to New York City provided Carolyn and her students with many musical opportunities.

> When I was teaching on Staten Island, my students and I had unusual musical outings in the city, where there is always opportunity. Leonard Bernstein presented his Concerts for Young People at Philharmonic Hall. He was a brilliant teacher, conductor, and pianist. After the concerts, we would go to the green room, where he welcomed us all.
>
> One day, Sister Gail Charron and I had tickets for one of his morning rehearsals. We had no students with us. We went to the green room and were the only ones there. Evidently, since it was a rehearsal, no one was expected. However, a New York Irish policeman on duty there told us to wait. In a few minutes, Bernstein arrived in a terry cloth robe. He spent about fifteen minutes with us. He described his plans to conduct Mahler's *Sixth Symphony* in Europe the following season. He asked what we did and where we taught. He was so gracious. Finally, his friendly wife Felicia Montealegre arrived to move him along, as wives do, to the next appointment, leaving us with marvelous memories.

It was a period of great hope in the church and the country. Priests and nuns were active in the civil rights movement, and Carolyn read, attended lectures, and went to meetings. She organized musical collages, inspired medleys of folk songs illuminating meaning through juxtaposition of sound and word. The winds of change were in the air, and Carolyn felt herself awakening to once-masked truths.

During her tenure on Staten Island, Carolyn directed her students in many performances.

One was a program of American folk songs. Sister Margaret Giroux (Sister Saint Patricia) of the art department and some of her students developed a large scrim, a storyteller's map of the United States as a backdrop. As the chorus sang each song, stage lights shone on the state of its origin. She was preparing the show when she heard of President Kennedy's assassination. She cancelled the concert and then rescheduled it with a dedication to JFK.

Sister Carolyn's boys choir at Stamford Catholic High School, c. 1959, above, performing on risers, accompanied by the school band, and wearing identical white dinner jackets with bow ties, cumberbunds, and tuxedo trousers in the semi-formal style of the day. Carolyn rehearses the senior boys, top left, c. 1963, as part of the select choir, the boys who once followed Carolyn and her mother through a school corridor singing "Mrs. Brown, you've got a lovely daughter . . . "

The student body was rehearsing Peter Wilhousky's arrangement of "The Battle Hymn of the Republic" when news of President Kennedy's shooting reached us. We didn't tell the students at first, and the principal asked me to keep rehearsing. I remember so clearly the third-verse words we sang: "As he died to make men holy, / let us die to make men free . . ." The prophetic admonition has deep meaning even today, and I always relate the words to those hours of tragedy.

There had been such a sense of hope and optimism. Kennedy was leading the United States, and Pope John XXIII was leading the Roman Catholic Church. There was a feeling that we could do anything and that we were headed in the right direction. And then Pope John XXIII died in June and Kennedy was assassinated in November.

> ### a pair of red sneakers while vacationing at the beach
> ## *delighting in little things, sensitive to others*
> #### *by Barbara Arnesen*
>
> Carolyn Senier and I have had many good laughs together over the past fifty years. Carolyn, as a friend, is loyal, concerned, present when needed, and fun to be with. She is sensitive to others' feelings and concerns. She is gifted musically and handles it with simplicity. She delights in little things. I especially remember her appreciation of red sneakers my father bought her while we were vacationing at the beach.
>
> She is a person who almost always is reaching out to someone in need. Carolyn and her husband Dick have taken many into their home in Boston over the years. I think, particularly, of Gary Maceoin. He lived in their small third floor apartment for a number of years. Gary was a reporter, author, and human rights activist. He was a specialist in the politics and poverty of Latin America and well-known and respected in many countries.
>
> While Carolyn and her husband were living in Boston, there were celebrations in their home and music was central to the festivities. Carolyn has been composing music most of her life. All of it is reflective of her beliefs and priorities.
>
> *Barbara Arnesen is a former CND.*

Despite a full schedule, Carolyn managed to find time to compose while she was at Staten Island. She wrote a series of Christmas carols. Not long after her father's death, out of the depth of her grief came "O Praise Ye the Lord," a song based on Psalm 150, "Let everything that has breath praise the Lord!" She tried this one on the custodian, who was closing windows in the auditorium where Carolyn worked at the grand piano. "What do you think of this?" she asked him. She played it. He shrugged and, underwhelmed by his response, Carolyn reworked and finished the piece. Her student choirs performed it, and the CNDs encouraged Carolyn to have it published. McLaughlin and Reilly, a Boston firm specializing in religious and educational music, produced the song on eight- by twelve-inch card stock so that it could more easily be used in churches and for choral groups. It found its way into many church repertoires. Once Carolyn heard some youngsters singing it as they played on swings in her neighborhood.

> I went to see Mr. Reilly, the publisher. He was getting older and felt overworked, yet he listened to me in a small music room on the first floor. When I mentioned to him that I had another song, "Thou Makest the Winds Thy Messengers," he asked me to sing it for him. When I finished, he groaned, "I wish you hadn't done that. Now I have to publish this one too." And he did, along with others.

During a series of early 1960s summers on the campus of Manhattanville College in Purchase, New York, Carolyn delved into the intricacies of Gregorian and Ambrosian chant with liturgical musicians from around the country.

With nuns, priests, and seminarians, Carolyn took classes at Manhattanville's Pius X School every summer from 1958 through 1964. The school was founded in 1916 to implement strategies among musicians for making ancient forms appealing to worshipers. Pope Pius X, head of the Roman Catholic Church from 1903 to 1914 advocated the reform of church music and the revitalization of Gregorian chant. Pius X School was in a beautiful setting, an imposing Gothic building that everyone called the Castle. Each participant had a small private room in a nearby dorm. They took courses in voice, piano, history of music, conducting, and Gregorian chant. Professionals from around the country and abroad taught classes. Dom Baron and Dom Gajard came from Solesmes, France, a Benedictine monastery and center for Gregorian chant.

The students were working musicians: organists and choir directors. Besides attending classes, students practiced liturgical singing four days a week, analyzing texts and the relationship between music and meaning. On Fridays, the week-long practice culminated in singing the Mass, a prayerful liturgy that Carolyn found intoxicating.

I adored the Pius X School. It was an unbelievable combination of study and music. I also managed to swim there. They have an Olympic pool in the Kennedy Gym next to the Castle.

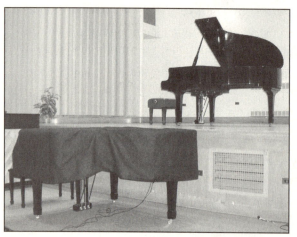

The Manhattanville recital hall where Piux X students performed and heard ancient music

When my classmates saw me walking in the evening towards the pool building, they would tease me: "What classes are you going to, Sister?" I would tell them I was studying breath control. Then I would swim laps.

One summer while Carolyn was at Pius X, Richard Rodgers, who at the time was composing *Sound of Music,* came to visit. His musical is the story of Maria, an exuberant young nun who leaves the convent and marries the man she had worked for as a governess. Mr. Rodgers wanted to hear the sisters singing Gregorian chant and to see what their habits looked like. The Pius X chorus, led by Theodore Marier of Saint Paul's Church in Cambridge, Massachusetts, sang selections. Then Marier led the choir in a rendition of "Oh, What a Beautiful Morning" from Rodgers's *Oklahoma*. Carolyn sat quite near Rodgers, whom she remembers being in tears. "You have no idea the sounds that are going around in my head," he told the chorus.

The next day, Carolyn was leaving the chapel where many had gathered for prayer. As she passed a sister escorting Trude Rittman, Rodgers's choral arranger, a bell sounded. Ms. Rittman asked what the sound was, and learning it was a bell providing a tone to begin the sisters' morning chant, she exclaimed, "There's the opening of the show!"

> When the stage show finally opened, I was really impressed that there was no overture as in most musicals. Instead there was a bell or gong and then a chant sung by nuns. It seems that Trude Rittman really did get her inspiration that morning in the chapel corridor.

In 1963, the CNDs closed the novitiate in Illinois where Carolyn had spent her first two years in the convent. They opened a new novitiate in Ridgefield, Connecticut. Carolyn was appointed music director in 1964. She taught music history and appreciation, piano, organ, choral singing, and guitar to the postulants and novices. The novitiate was located in an old mansion, on a large estate. The grounds were beautifully landscaped. The chapel had been a ballroom with a graceful balcony. Carolyn's room was in former servants' quarters. A new structure had been built to house the dormitories and classrooms. In that beautiful setting Carolyn worked, taught, played, sang, and composed.

> The organ at Ridgefield was an Allen organ. Early on, while we were postulants, our parents organized the Company of Mary, a support group for people whose daughters entered Notre Dame. They often traveled together and shared stories. Sometimes, they gave each other financial support. They helped finance the Allen organ for the Ridgefield Chapel. My father was president of the organization then, and it gave me joy to play an instrument dedicated to "Mr. Edward G. Brown and the Company of Mary." I wouldn't have known music or that instrument if it weren't for him.

By all accounts, Carolyn was a creative, innovative, and inspiring teacher. Gently expecting the best, she "drilled" notes and worked on rough spots with sections of her choirs before joining the parts. She provided time-honored and up-to-date reading and listening in the traditional classroom. She also took students of all ages outdoors to learn to listen by hearing the natural symphonies of forest or field. She came up with imaginative approaches to experiencing traditional music. For example, she used colored scarves to represent musical themes, assigned each theme to parts of the group, and asked members to wave the scarves and dance when they heard their theme. By listening, reading, pondering, and practicing, she prepared diligently to teach. Some former students attest that not only did she transfer joy and love of music, but she also led them into it as a career.

Throughout the year, Carolyn directed music for Christmas, Easter, and other holy days as well as ceremonies of profession when novices took vows. She visited other convents to help young CND musicians. There were other frequent events, including the dedication of a school or a seasonal concert. She wrote music for such occasions, but much of it has since been lost or buried in some stack of papers. While at Ridgefield, she wrote a Mass in honor of Marguerite Bourgeoys, the CNDs' founder.

Sister Carolyn's massed choir at Stamford Catholic, c.1959. The girls' mothers made the dresses in various pastel shades—just like those worn by the Mellotones (see Page 24) fourteen years earlier.

Although Carolyn had taught and studied music for ten years at many levels, she did not have an undergraduate degree. Finally in 1964, the CNDs sent her full time to Manhattanville for a year. She had more than enough credits, but she needed to fulfill the requirement of one year of full time work. She commuted the twenty miles or so from Ridgefield to Manhattanville and graduated in 1965 with a bachelor of music degree. She had 170 undergraduate credits, far more than the required 125. She was offered the prestigious Cardinal Spellman scholarship to study in Italy, but her commitments to the order prevented her from accepting it.

Carolyn's convent years had been busy and productive against a backdrop of change in the Roman Catholic Church. The Second Vatican Council convened in Rome from 1962 to 1965. The council concluded that the institution needed to modernize. It saw the Latin Mass as an obstacle. Many in the clergy focused on making the music of the Mass, sung mostly in Latin, more accessible. In the tradition of Pius X, the church tried to encourage churchgoers to take an active part. Furthermore, in a departure from Pius X's emphasis on Gregorian chant and Latin, they wanted to introduce the vernacular.

Whenever there was an important musical event or ceremony, the CNDs in Connecticut and New York called on Carolyn. In the mid-sixties, following Vatican II mandates, the Archdiocese of Bridgeport established a liturgical commission to encourage observation of church directives. In many places, for the first time in centuries the priest faced worshipers. The church relaxed fasting and abstinence rules. Great Protestant hymns resounded in Catholic cathedrals. The language changed from Latin to English. Ecumenism prevailed.

When the CNDs were asked to suggest someone for the commission, they recommended Carolyn, who at thirty-two became the only woman on a panel otherwise made up of priests and lay representatives.

The new liturgy was due to be phased in between the first Sunday in Advent in early December, 1964 and the first Sunday in Advent, 1965. The commission planned to introduce the new practices when

The "Glory to God" section (see p. 369) from Carolyn's mid 1960s English language Mass in honor of Marguerite Bourgeoys, founder of the CNDs (see p. 366).

© 1964 by Carolyn Brown and © 2005 by Carolyn Brown Senier

the Confraternity of Christian Doctrine, the religious education arm of the American Roman Catholic Church, held its New England Congress. That year's congress was planned for a late

The liturgical commission of the Roman Catholic Diocese of Bridgeport, Connecticut, c. 1966. Carolyn served with clergymen and laymen to elevate worshipers' experience of traditional ritual and prayer. She was thirty-two years old. The photo is reproduced from an old newspaper clipping.

Carolyn saved clippings (but unfortunately not their dates) from the Ridgefield Press, *left, and the* Bridgeport Post. *The articles, written in the mid 1960s, describe Carolyn's pivotal involvement with liturgical change in Connecticut from 1965 to 1968, when the Bridgeport Liturgical Commission, of which she was a member, showcased English language Masses with music she composed. The commission undertook the mandate of the Second Vatican Council, convened by Pope John XXIII to revitalize the Roman Catholic Church. The caption for the* Post *article by Elizabeth Leonard says: "As an expert in liturgy commissioned to glorify the role of music in the Mass, Sister Saint Roselyn plays one of her compositions on the organ"—likely the Allen organ donated to the Ridgefield Novitiate at West Mountain by the Company of Mary when her father was president of the organization. It's a sign of the times that the two articles refer to Carolyn by different names as orders of religious women like the CNDs underwent transformation—The* Ridgefield Press *refers to her as Sister Carolyn Brown. The* Post *article explains about workshops the previous fall on the Sacred Heart University campus in Bridgeport dealing with " . . . theology of music in church, studying hymns, and the practical application of what was learned." Bridgeport Bishop Walter Curtis had asked the commission to prepare Jubilee Masses the previous spring, organized by Carolyn in fifty churches with an evolving choir that traveled especially for the occasions, according to the* Post *article.*

summer's day on the University of Bridgeport campus. Because there was no place big enough to have Mass for thousands of young people and clergy, the commission scheduled twenty-one simultaneous Masses in classrooms and lecture halls. They asked Carolyn to organize and direct the music.

It was an enormous task. Carolyn contacted nuns, priests, and Catholic Youth Organizations throughout the diocese to help identify young people interested in music. She invited student groups and encouraged them to bring guitars. She asked them to share their own music and then moderated a discussion that emphasized reverence, liturgical meaning, community expression, singability, and beauty as criteria for acceptable music. Together, they chose the repertoire. Some of the students were more musically advanced than others, and Carolyn cultivated them

Rehearsing for the New England Confraternity of Christian Doctrine religious education conference on the campus of the University of Bridgeport, Sister Carolyn, right, circles with the group. After a picnic during weekly rehearsals throughout the summer, Carolyn went from group to group, teaching songs and having leaders also circulating. "That's always the key to organizing large groups," according to Carolyn. The photograph appeared in the August 11, 1968 edition of the Bridgeport Post.

as leaders of groups that would be part of the simultaneous Masses. They rehearsed together for several weeks and were enthusiastic about the possibilities. Choruses formed as the summer progressed.

Carolyn felt that guitar accompaniment for people unaccustomed to singing at Mass would be preferable to no accompaniment. However, when traditional instruments were available, she preferred them to the guitar. It was a challenge for her. She played and taught folk guitar and had spent years learning and polishing her skills at Gregorian chant, which she loves. She also understood the church's emphasis on bringing the laity, especially younger people, into more active roles.

The day was a smashing success. She led one of the choirs while the smaller groups confidently led themselves. During the morning, before Masses were offered, Carolyn encouraged the musical groups to mill around campus practicing, tuning, and warming up. She wanted the participants to recognize the music when they heard it later. Then, well-rehearsed small groups of students played and sang outdoors or in classrooms as pairs and small groups of priests faced the congregation and concelebrated twenty-one separate Masses in English. It was a dramatic presentation of possibilities for a rejuvenated church.

Some Roman Catholics and others familiar with the church have come to regret the abandonment of Latin and the disappearance of Gregorian chant. Changes have increased parishioners' participation without necessarily elevating the quality and spiritual potential of music sung and played. Carolyn was concerned that much good traditional music with Latin words was being replaced by music that had English words but not much else. Often, musicality was missing from the songs. Carolyn believes that people should be open to beauty and learn to appreciate hymns that have stood the test of time.

Liturgical commission work was not Carolyn's only assignment. During her residence at Ridgefield, where the CNDs had a school, they decided to have a concert and invite the local community. She organized it.

> We wanted our neighbors to realize we were highly educated women well qualified to run a school. We were new in the area and decided to invite the neighbors in to offer them a concert.

Carolyn spent the summer choosing music and invited other CNDs to join a choir for the concert. More than 120 sisters responded. Sisters from all over the Northeast gathered at the Ridgefield conference center every other week for several months for all-day rehearsals.

> Liturgy, lunch, and large choral gatherings were part of the program as well as small part gatherings. Each day had breaks. Other CND musicians would do sectionals, rehearsing parts for altos or second sopranos while I worked with first sopranos. Then we would switch sections. I would teach the altos and someone else would teach the soprano parts and so on. During the last hour, we worked together as one choral group.

In the weeks between rehearsals, she traveled to convents in Waterbury and Norwalk, Connecticut, New York City, and Schenectady, New York, for choral workshops.

The auditorium was filled for the concert. The chorus sang pieces by Brahms, Fauré, and Schubert. Carolyn wanted some piano solos to round out the program, but no other sister was willing to perform, so Carolyn played solos by Brahms and Liszt. Her mother loved one of Liszt's études and had urged her to include it. Her brother Don vividly remembered the concert:

> Carolyn conducted a concert when she was in the convent. It featured choral music and her piano solos of Liszt and Brahms pieces, both technically difficult compositions. There was a very formal and tense ambience. It was a concert-hall feeling with an audience of parents, musical peers, and friends. Carolyn emerged from the backstage darkness dressed, of course, in her religious garb with starched white chest bib and white headdress peak. She seated herself at the long, black coffin-like grand piano. The audience became hushed. As Carolyn placed her hands on the keyboard and took a breath, the next sound was of a horse fly attacking the keyboard with a loud, buzzing sound. It kept bouncing off the keys and hitting the backboard for what seemed an eternity. She whisked the fly away with her left hand and started in again to recompose herself. This time the fly came back and was louder still, buzzing in and out like some kind of green hornet. As she composed herself again, the silence in the audience was like the mother of all silences. Then Carolyn turned to the audience and said, "Maybe I should play 'Shoo Fly, Fly.'" The audience cracked up. The music poured out, and the concert was wonderful.

The music pouring out was the Liszt her mother had requested. With virtuosity, she played it from memory. Many of the sisters who sang in that concert remember the music—and the fly. At Sister Reine's funeral in 2002, Carolyn led some of them in a choral tribute to her mentor, directing music from the same program.

After the concert, Carolyn's mother was overjoyed and bursting with pride. Also in the audience was Mother Josephine Morgan, director of the Pius X School. She wrote Carolyn,

> I congratulate you as a first-rate conductor and organizer. Mother [Catherine] Carroll and I were very proud of your work and wished that every novitiate in the country could have this musical experience. Unfortunately, first class conductors are lacking. First class accompanists are unheard of and the cooperation you have received from your own order is extraordinary.

The CNDs put the concert on the road, and the 120 singing sisters with their piano soloist director filled the house at CND auditoriums in Bridgeport and Staten Island.

Carolyn remained busy with school teaching and diocesan work while she was in Ridgefield. She taught several days a week at Stamford Catholic, where she had been assigned before her tour on Staten Island. At the same time, the late fall of 1968, Bishop Walter Curtis of Bridgeport planned a celebration to commemorate a jubilee. Instead of having a giant gathering in the cathedral, he planned to celebrate Mass in parishes throughout the diocese. There was concern, however, that local choirs would not be able to provide a suitable level of music. Carolyn was asked to train a choir to travel from church to church. The churches were within an hour of each other, so the distance was ideal. But she also wanted to encourage parishioners to participate actively in the Mass and not listen passively to a choir, however well rehearsed. She felt it

Carolyn, family members including her mother at Carolyn's own left, Carolyn's brother Dick behind Rosalene and his wife Lorraine at Carolyn's own right, Joan's husband Ed McElligott holding a toddler, right, and friends at the Ridgefield, Connecticut, novitiate, c. 1964

lyrical voice and magical hands

sharing sorrows, celebrating successes

by Margaret Mary Chiara

Carolyn Brown was an itinerant musician when our paths first crossed in 1960. Scores of students were engaged by the lyrical voice and magical hands of Sister Saint Roselyn of Jesus. Notre Dame Academy (NDA) on Staten Island was the venue that launched forty plus years of friendship between the vibrant young nun who was a mere seven years older than I when I was NDA President of Student Council.

During the light years when I shared Carolyn's affiliation with the Congregation de Notre Dame, I became aware that many were in awe of her lovely persona and considerable musical talent. For me, Carolyn's enduring sense of fairness and goodness were and are her most attractive attributes.

In the ensuing decades, we shared sorrows and celebrated successes. After taking our leave from the religious community, Carolyn and I were nearly neighbors when she lived in Waltham and I, in Cambridge. This was our opportunity to enjoy one another within the context of ordinary, everyday life.

I recall the entrepreneurial escapade early in the revitalization of Faneuil Hall. Tams and scarves metamorphosed into Celtic Weavers. I remember festive events often accompanied by Dick Senier's fabulous carbonara.

I wear a claddagh ring purchased by a friend from Carolyn's original shop. You do know that one must be gifted with a claddagh, don't you? This symbol of Gaelic culture with its heart, hands, and crown, is an apt image of Carolyn whom I have known and loved all these years. One should be oh-so-kind-and-careful of who or what is the subject or object of your affection (the heart) hence, the loving and protective hands while always being fearlessly faithful and loyal (the crown).

Carolyn Brown Senier, the musician, is only one manifestation of the loving, faithful woman who has accompanied me (and many others) on life's journey. She is a friend with whom I intend to rendezvous in eternity.

Margaret Mary Chiara is United States Attorney for the Western District of Michigan.

would be an excellent opportunity to educate local choirs in the new liturgy. She invited anyone interested to join a choir to learn and practice the liturgy. She directed, and they practiced every week for eight weeks. Then the choir went to parishes where the bishop was celebrating Mass. The traveling, experienced choir joined local choirs and had rehearsal time with new music. Consequently, the traveling choir got larger as more singers joined the core group. The choir, pioneers in post Vatican II music and the English language Mass, sang compositions by Brahms and Woollen as well as by Sister Carolyn Brown.

> Sheer beauty results from combining the strength and power of congregational singing with the more refined offerings of a trained choir. That was the secret of the jubilee

Masses. The choir handled more polished and difficult parts while the congregation sang the less difficult but equally beautiful passages.

The Catholic Church instituted changes beyond the liturgy after Vatican II. CND nuns and those in most congregations worldwide began to wear less restrictive habits, more like uniforms. Gone were the stiff headdresses that had been tradition for three hundred years and gone also were the long skirts. The church opened windows and doors to new ideas and fresh perspectives. And Carolyn did, too.

> I began to think beyond my horizons.
>
> Introspection and self-examination were an integral part of the church and religious communities after the Vatican Council. The 1960s were a demanding time for our country as well. The civil rights movement gained strength. We were experiencing the Selma marchings and great heroes. There were riots and unrest. Folk singers of the day like Joan Baez, Bob Dylan, and Peter, Paul, and Mary uttered powerful words to us through music.
>
> Signs of personal change became apparent to me but did not show externally. Even though I was very busy and seemingly very successful, I was keenly sensing a movement toward some deeper waters of my life.

Then in 1968, Carolyn's health began to change. She lost weight and often felt tired. Her superior at Ridgefield worried about her. Hoping to "build her up," she ordered a case of Guinness Stout so that Carolyn could have a pint a day. While it helped, it did not restore her. The community arranged for necessary medical attention and gave her a generous recuperation period. Nevertheless, when her brother Bob visited, he was alarmed at how pale and thin she had become. At his urging she requested a leave, which was quickly granted. Her mother had long been asking Carolyn to accompany her on a vacation, and Bob felt the time had come.

> My mother rented an efficiency apartment at Shamrock Village in Fort Pierce, Florida. She cast her spell of practical wisdom by cooking and serving stuffed bluefish and other catches of the day, by bringing me to concerts, by letting me rest late into the mornings. This three-month hiatus had more vitamins and healing power than one can imagine.
>
> Sunshine and the Indian River were my constant companions, and slowly my strength returned. I met a lovely family there, Dr. and Mrs. Carbonara who, with several children, lived at the end of the road. They taught me to water ski.
>
> It was thrilling to be on the water again. However, as I had learned before, deep water is not without danger. I remember falling off the skis one day. The speedboat kept pulling me, the driver not realizing my foot was caught in the rope handles and towing me under the surface. When I disappeared, the boat stopped. I surfaced and shouted that I had hurt my foot. The driver started up again to rescue me, but instead again pulled me under the surface, catching my foot even more tightly in the rope handle. I felt brief moments of panic under the water, my leg out awkwardly in front of my body, my body yanked forward.
>
> When the speedboat crew realized what was happening, they stopped, paddled towards me, and lifted me into the boat—bruised, but not broken.

During the Florida vacation, Carolyn went on a cruise with her mother. An old friend of her late sister Roselyn, Dorothy Haight, lent Carolyn formal attire, *de rigueur* for cruises in that day.

Carolyn had been pondering whether to leave the convent for about a year but was determined not to make up her mind too quickly. She wanted to be sure she was embarking on a new life for correct reasons and to decide in wellness and not in illness. After returning from Florida, she called her oldest sister Kaye to ask for advice. Kaye took Carolyn to lunch and later wrote and told her that maybe it was time for her to dive into the water, to take the plunge or get back off the diving board. "Dear Sister," she began:

> If you have come to a point where you cannot go on as before, do what your good common sense tells you to do . . . We will all be glad to know you're available for us to enjoy being with. We are so proud of you and have been since the moment you were born and we always will be, too.

Carolyn's conversations with Monsignor (later auxiliary bishop of New York) Austin Vaughan solidified her decision. He taught at the novitiate and was quite conservative. Carolyn recognized his deep commitment to the priesthood. The laxity of the sixties was in the air, and she was afraid she was being too easy on herself.

Carolyn learning to waterski in Florida, c. 1968

> Weighing the matter took several years before I came to a final decision. A few members of the community to whom I spoke, including the superior general, couldn't have been kinder or more understanding. My superiors gave me time to rest, and the long vacation with my mother in Florida helped. I was fortunate to have a good friend, then Monsignor Vaughan, who, for all his conservative ideas and strong logical mind, helped me to believe in and trust myself. I did not want to be yessed to death. I needed someone to battle ideas with me. He was the right person. After many such skirmishes, he surprised me by telling me to trust my instincts.

She wrote to the superior general, the nun in charge of CNDs worldwide, and spoke to the provincial, the sister in charge of CNDs in the Connecticut area. Despite the investment they had made in her education and their hopes for her musical future with them, both nuns respected her doubts.

During her years in the convent, Carolyn had found the rules and conformity of the CNDS had not gotten in her way. She had done what she loved. By providing her with an education, time, and the serenity she needed to develop as a woman, a composer, and a musician, the Congregation had nurtured her. Now, however, she felt she would no longer flourish in the Congregation.

Despite her recognition that it was time to leave the convent, Carolyn knew she would miss many of the women with whom she had lived for years. She took time to visit individuals as plans were made for her departure. "You're not going to marry a priest, are you?" asked Sister

The SS Bahama Star *captain with singer John Raitt greets Rosalene and Carolyn (in borrowed clothes) during a cruise, c. 1968*

Mary Roberts (Sister Mary Roberts), an elderly nun. When Carolyn smiled and shook her head no, the nun looked relieved and exclaimed, "Then go, go, go: life, love, and hope!" When Carolyn found a sweatshirt many years later with those words on it, she bought it as a remembrance of the warm wishes of her companion at Ridgefield. Many of the women are Carolyn's friends today, some still embracing religious life and some not.

> Moving from the life of a sister to the unknown ahead of me was not a negative move. It was positive. It may sound strange, but I left the convent almost for the same reason I entered.
>
> I wanted to embrace a meaningful life. It is not easy to assess one's gifts or one's meaning, but at that crucial time, I found certainty only in the basic, deep realization that I had been given the gift of life. Granted, I was ill, and I needed medical advice. I was extremely fatigued. But I also felt a certain interior dying, and I decided not to let that happen to me. I did not have that right.

When the day of her departure arrived, the Ridgefield nuns lined up to say good-bye. In Florida, Dorothy Haight's husband Paul had given her Pepe, a miniature poodle. Juggling Pepe and a sign that said "Hug a Warm Puppy—One Cent," Carolyn moved along the line and exchanged hugs with each nun in turn.

Carolyn was granted "exclaustration," a year's leave of absence. But Carolyn tells me,

Sister Carolyn, c. 1968, making music with, from left, her brother Don and nieces Kathleen and Tricia

---

"We were all thrilled with Carolyn—"
Mother prayed her child would be a girl

by Kaye Brown Mark

I remember Mother praying that her child would be a girl. We were all thrilled with Carolyn. She was beautiful, joyful, and musical always. But she could play baseball, throw horseshoes, skate, ski, and dance—outdoing her four brothers, usually. When she was two years old, she learned to swim.

At home with Dad, she began piano lessons. It wasn't long before she was playing the church organ and then singing on the radio.

After high school, she joined the CND community, and through many phases in many states and schools, her music kept developing.

Now she shares her joys and pleasures with us just as Dad did in our home with pupils and friends. We had wonderful Sunday nights of music. We know she loves Mattawa. Perhaps the songs will tell us how.

Her move to Boston after leaving the convent brought her back to us.

Kaye Brown Mark is Carolyn's older sister.

I knew as soon as I went out the door that my decision was the right one.

In the summer of 1969, Carolyn left a religious life where, as her sister Kaye quipped, she had been "on ice" for sixteen years. The world welcoming her roiled with change. It was a momentous, turbulent time for the country and for her. Woodstock, New York, hosted its famous rock concert, Neil Armstrong walked on the moon, inner cities boiled with decades of suppressed rage, and people demonstrated in the streets against the war in Southeast Asia.

A place to live was her first priority. At CND expense, she enrolled in summer classes at Boston University where she could live in a dorm and continue her education. She had attended the university the two previous summers and was well on her way to a master's degree in music education. She needed a mentor, a program requirement for advanced students. She approached the chair of the music education department, Dr. Jack Lemons, who looked at her, puzzled. "I don't remember you," he admitted.

"Well," Carolyn informed him, "I look different."

"What's your name?" he asked. "Well, that's different, too," she replied. Carolyn had started out at B. U. two summers earlier as Sister Saint Roselyn of Jesus in garb straight from the Middle Ages. The next summer, thanks to modernization in the church, she wore simpler clothing and was known as Sister Carolyn Brown.

"Now," she explained, "I'm just Carolyn Brown." The different clothes were obvious. He threw up his hands and advised her not to take her tale of changing identity any further. Calling her his hippie nun, he said, "Don't try to tell this to anybody else. I'll be your mentor."

Carolyn smuggled Pepe into the dorm at 700 Commonwealth Avenue and took a full load of summer courses. The CNDs continued paying the bills and lent her two thousand dollars.

Carolyn had few friends in Boston and understandably felt lonely. But she kept herself busy studying and often went to Waterbury to reacquaint herself with her family. She purposely avoided joining one of the groups in Boston dedicated to helping former nuns and priests ease back into the mainstream. In the back of her mind was her sister's advice—jump into life

Sister Carolyn Brown studies with Prof. Leon Tumarkin.

When she left the CNDs in 1969, Carolyn continued a masters of music program at the Boston University School of Fine and Applied Arts, where she studied piano with Professor Leon Tumarkin. In the summer of 1968, the Boston University Magazine *offered an account of her work in liturgical music. The photo, above, appears with an article and headline: "Sister Carolyn Develops New Liturgy Styles." Observing her appointment to the Bridgeport liturgical commission, it also mentions her organization of the traveling choir to assist with Bishop Curtis's Jubilee Masses. "Her efforts already have added a lively and active participation by the congregation in the Masses," the article says. "The choir handled the more polished and difficult parts, while the congregations sang the less difficult but equally beautiful passages which required volume." The article observes that Sister Carolyn believes that folk music "is a valid medium, but it must be used with understanding of music and liturgy." Finally, the article explains that, "wherever possible, Sister Carolyn urged, children should be exposed to religious music. 'Children are our hope. Give them good music because we are training the future adult church choir right now.'"*

and swim. She took advantage of all the activities provided for summer school students and found she enjoyed meeting new people and being independent.

Carolyn found an apartment in Waltham. She shared it with her cousin Elizabeth Crichton, who had also recently emerged from the CNDs. Carolyn's brother Don picked up a 1960 blue Plymouth Fury for her. Monsignor Vaughan visited occasionally to see how she was doing. She was a little low on money, and he must have taken note of her near-empty refrigerator. Telling

During her first summer as "just plain" Carolyn Brown, she took full advantage of the student activities program at Boston University. "It was only five dollars, but only about fifty people out of thousands took advantage of the offerings. On weekends, we went by bus to attractions all over the Greater Boston area. Anybody enrolled at BU was eligible, but only we few benefited." Among the excursions was a Boston Bay Shoreline cruise organized by the Hub's famous old salt and storyteller, Edward Rowe Snow. One tale of the islands involves the famous, ghostly "Lady in Black." In preparation for the tale, Mr. Snow took Carolyn aside and asked her if she would play along. She agreed and was spirited away from the group by one of Mr. Snow's assistants. Escorted to a large pine box, she was invited to step into the coffin of the "Lady in Black." She lay there for some time: "I was thinking, 'No one knows where I am. I'm all alone in this coffin.'" Eventually, Mr. Snow led the others in her tour to her resting place where, on cue, he lifted the top and she emerged to startle the others. One snapped her picture. She is "entombed," below. All the way back to the dock, she harmonized with another passenger, and Mr. Snow autographed her program.

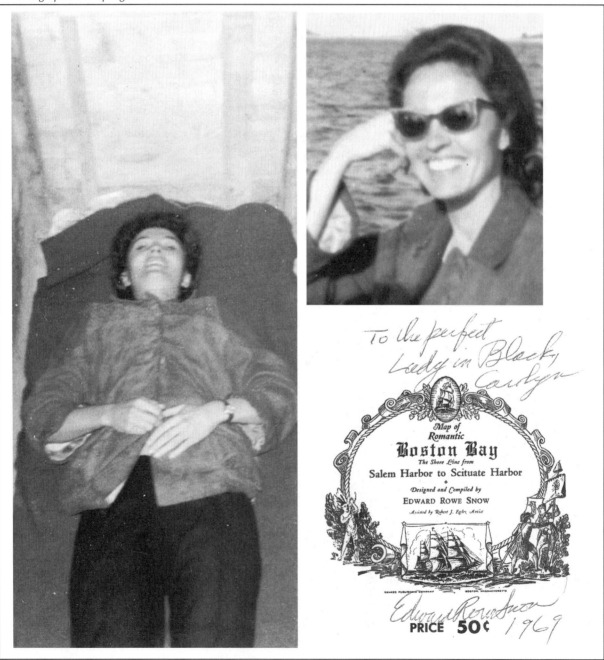

opportunities to participate in outstanding productions
providing an excellent music education program

by Samuel A. Turner

I first met Carolyn Brown Senier in 1969 when she applied for a position as music teacher at the Oak Hill Elementary School in Newton, Massachusetts.

It was a sultry June afternoon, just before the close of school for the year. Oak Hill was to share a music teacher with another elementary school and, therefore, the two principals met to interview candidates. Looking for that special individual who would serve the needs of both our schools, we reviewed applications. I was struck by the fact that Ms. Brown had sixteen years of teaching "under her belt" and realized that the sixteen years was in a convent. My curiosity was aroused, and it was my belief that, if this woman had enough courage to leave the convent after sixteen years, she must be a person of conviction and one willing to take a risk. For Oak Hill, this kind of teacher would be a perfect fit.

The school was located in a section of the city that would be difficult for even Sherlock Holmes to find. We waited and waited until we received a call that Ms. Brown had become lost but would soon arrive. A secretary eventually ushered in a stunning woman in a gorgeous orange dress. All I could think was, "And she was a nun?" She took a seat, and it didn't take me long to determine that she would be our new music teacher.

My assumptions proved correct. Carolyn Brown was hired full time as the music educator for our two schools and, in this position provided an outstanding music education program for all the students. In addition to the regular curriculum, she gave the students opportunities to participate in outstanding productions like *Fiddler on the Roof* and a wonderful, fun-filled, original program that highlighted the music of George and Ira Gershwin. The Gershwin program included students, faculty, and parents. George and Ira would have been truly proud.

This soft-spoken, talented, engaging woman has won the hearts of many and brought joy to thousands of students—and others—who have been fortunate to know and work with her.

Samuel Turner was principal of Oak Hill School in Newton, Massachusetts.

her to "pass it on" when she was able to, he sent her some money. She was on her way.

Carolyn looked for work doing what she loved and was trained for—teaching music. Her search took her to Newton, Massachusetts, a progressive, upscale Boston suburb. She arrived for the end-of-June interview hot, late, and flustered. Unused to driving in the city, she had trouble finding the Newton school. When she got there, she found the position was for two schools, both housing kindergarten through sixth grade. She met Sam Turner, the principal of Oak Hill, who hired Carolyn almost on the spot. He persuaded the other principal, Olive Eldridge of Memorial School, that a former nun would be an asset. Co-workers insisted that the bright orange dress Carolyn wore to the interview also helped.

Like her predecessor, Carolyn taught music in grade groupings. But at the beginning of her second year in Newton, Carolyn approached

Principal Turner with an idea. She asked that music be made optional and immediately began developing classes in keyboard, recorder, guitar, glee club, orchestra, and special choruses. She had been nervous about teaching in a public school after years in parochial schools and directing novitiate and diocesan choirs. But her music training and experience gave her confidence, and she knew what to do to make a music program work. Principal Turner was willing to be creative with scheduling, and immediately the music program took off. In the six years she taught in Newton, she directed her elementary students in *Fiddler on the Roof*; *Wizard of Oz*; *You're A Good Man, Charlie Brown*; *Oliver*; and a Gershwin revue with students and faculty performing together. She remembered the fun she had had in elementary school musicals and was happy to give that experience to hundreds of students in her classes:

> The faculty collaborated on the productions. Other teachers at Oak Hill always helped, particularly Ann Burns Macqueen, whom the students respected and loved. Having her in the same room during rehearsals made work with lively students much easier.

At Boston University, where Carolyn had been working on her master's degree for three years, Dr. Lemons assigned Dr. Robert Choate to be her thesis adviser. Carolyn tried valiantly to organize her notes.

> I had stuff all over the place and was overwhelmed at the thought of putting it into order. My friend, Sister Mary Ann Foley, helped me put my notes into piles and advised me to write everything out on a long roll of shelf paper. Then, I had a meeting with Dr. Choate.

---

shows she directed had a professional quality
responding with a personal touch for each friend

by Ann Burns Macqueen

I first met Carolyn Senier in 1969 when she came to Oak Hill Elementary School in Newton, Massachusetts as our music teacher. For a variety of reasons, our music program at that time was badly in need of a "lift."

Carolyn's approach, combining an infectious love of music and a policy of including all middle grade children in choral programs, quickly produced a positive attitude in the children. Shows she directed and produced, such as *Oliver* and *Fiddler on the Roof* with children aged ten to twelve, had a professional quality that delighted parents and teachers alike. A spirit of unity abounded in the school.

On a personal note, Carolyn has been a true friend for more than thirty years. During a difficult period in my life, she seemed to sense when a last minute invitation for dinner or a planned visit with her family provided the help I badly needed. I have seen this same quality shown many times with many people. The circle of friends is large. However, each of us feels a special connection with Carolyn, and she responds with a personal touch for each of her friends.

There is no doubt that Carolyn is multi-talented musically. In addition to her teaching ability, she has a beautiful singing voice that her friends have enjoyed at many musical evenings at the Seniers'. Of particular pleasure to me has been her rendition of classical selections that she has kindly played when asked.

Ann Burns Macqueen is a retired elementary school teacher.

He asked if he could see a first draft of my thesis. I gulped and said, yes, I could bring it in the next day. When I arrived at his office, I suggested we should move some of the furniture first so that we could roll out the shelf paper. Good-naturedly, he realized what I held under my arm. We moved some furniture. I rolled out twenty feet of shelf paper on which I had taped referenced index cards and a written text along the sides. We crawled up the thesis on our hands and knees, master and apprentice, side by side. This elegant gentleman, a true educator, there on the floor of his office, gave me the first reader approval to type it up and present it formally.

Carolyn's 1973 thesis discusses post Vatican II changes in Roman Catholic liturgy and echoes her work with the Bridgeport diocese. She argues for a variety of good music in Latin and English.

> Diversity of style need not be at odds with the spirit of unity among God's people. The ability to be open to new ritual and new music, to be ever searching for fresh insights and new attitudes toward liturgy is a sign of life and excitement in our liturgies.

Carolyn's thesis also acknowledges Christianity's role to remind man he has a cause for rejoicing and then to offer him the means to sing his joy. (She comments thirty years later that she might have written in gender neutral language if the practice had been more prevalent.)

As a member of the Massachusetts Teachers Association when she taught at Oak Hill School, Carolyn traveled to Europe on summer tours the group organized. She spent time in Seville, above.

Most of all in the thesis, Carolyn emphasizes the role of music in the prayer and celebration of the Roman Catholic Church:

> Genuine liturgical music shares the threefold orientation of the celebration that it serves: it reflects the faith that the composer has lived; it stimulates faith in those who participate in its execution; it is itself prayer, praise of the One in whom we believe. For the Christian who cannot even say, 'Father,' unless the Spirit move him (Romans, 8:14), all genuine praise is the surging of the spirit. For the sound of the voice of God is too great for human words to contain and therefore at times it must be expressed in song. The man who praises, whether in silence or in song, actively yields to the Spirit of God, which moves throughout creation. He is able to understand the Indian poet Tagore who translates his own Sanscrit poetry into English, a poet "whose song is but a plaintive little strain mingling with the great music of the world."

Thou has made me known to friends
whom I knew not.
Thou hast given me seats
in homes not my own.
Thou hast brought the distant near.

from *Gitanjali*
Rabindranath Tagore, 1913

Carolyn, clockwise from top left, in c. 1969, c. 1970 in a photograph by her friend, the professional Boston photographer Ira Kaye; c. 1973, c. 1982 with her dog Farley in a photograph taken for the catalogue for Celtic Weavers, her Boston retail clothing store; c. 1992 in Lake Como, Italy; c. 1978

Carolyn and her husband Richard Senier in Tenerife, c. 1978

an interesting life with music at its heart
keeping shop in Boston's Faneuil Hall Marketplace

Carolyn met her husband, Richard Senier, in 1970. She had been out of the convent for about a year, had been dispensed of her vows, and was living with her cousin Elizabeth Crichton in Waltham. She had enjoyed her "defrosting," and whenever she was invited to a party, she went. She kept bumping into Dick, first at an acquaintance's house and then at a couple of parties. She hadn't taken much notice of him except to remember that he was rather self-confident. But Richard had noticed Carolyn.

Once they happened to be at a party on Commonwealth Avenue in Boston. At the end of the evening, when he realized that Carolyn was walking to her car alone, Dick offered to accompany her. She was surprised and grateful for his kindness and consideration. Together they walked the several blocks back to her car. When this happened again at another party, Carolyn began to take notice of the tall, good-looking man with sandy-colored hair. When he phoned her at Thanksgiving to invite her to join a group of people not planning to spend the holiday with family, she was genuinely sorry to refuse, but she already had plans to go to Waterbury for the holiday.

Finally, Richard called Carolyn to invite her on a date.

> It had just snowed. I was dying to take a walk in the fresh winter air. When Dick called to see if I wanted to go out that evening, I said yes.

I decided he was the man I wanted to be with for the rest of my life.

He arrived to pick her up, and he teased her about being so easy that she was ready to go out at seven with someone who called at six. She wasn't at all uncomfortable with his teasing. After all, she had grown up with four Irish brothers who sometimes rolled her into Hitchcock Lake in a tire. When he complimented her on her dress, she came right back at him with,

> Well, I always wear this dress when it's not an important occasion.

Already smitten with the beautiful soft-spoken woman, Richard found her self-confidence and banter a pleasant surprise. On that first date, they went to hear piano player Eddie Watson at Novak's, a popular jazz bar. Dick, who grew up in the city, knew where to go.

From the beginning, music was the recurring theme in their romance. Like Carolyn, Richard is a musician. He plays classical pieces but also has a cabaret and dance hall background. His repertoire is endless, and he is willing to play at the drop of a request. On one early date Richard sang the entire score of *Pirates of Penzance* from memory, while they walked through Boston Public Gardens. Carolyn recalls another evening when they listened together to a Chopin piano concerto with the volume turned up and the lights turned down.

> I almost reached heaven. That's when I decided that he was the man I wanted to be with for the rest of my life. Listening together was so wonderful.

Richard has an amazing memory and vast resource of stories and jokes. He can always find a connection with people he meets. If he doesn't find one right away, he keeps searching until there it is—a distant cousin of his was married to your hairdresser's uncle. But what endeared him to Carolyn—and still does—is his steadfast friendship. She explains this to me:

> If Richard is your friend, he is your friend for life, and he will not abandon you.

Richard also brought Carolyn a renewed sense of Irish heritage. When she was growing up in Waterbury, being Irish was important to her family but not crucial. Her mother's people had been United States citizens for several generations, and her father had been born in the U. S. For Richard, however, being Irish was a fundamental aspect of his persona.

The Senier family was still growing in 1935, above left, where Dick is front left. Carolyn likes to point out that his mother definitely has her eye on him, probably to be sure he doesn't get into mischief. Bridget (Delia) Connolly, Dick's mother, grew up in the stone house, top right, on the Atlantic Ocean in Ballyconneely, County Galway, Ireland. Dick took the picture in 1977. He is at right in the middle picture, c.1940, and eighth from left, next to his father in 1965, in the picture of Dick's parents with ten of their eleven sons (one had died) in the picture above right.

His father and mother had arrived in the states in 1926, and although Richard was born in the U. S., four of his brothers were born in Ireland.

Richard's father, Tom Senier, brought his trade as a weaver of Irish woolens with him. When Dick and Carolyn visited Dick's father, Carolyn saw the cloth. She thought it was beautiful.

Richard Senier, c. 1973, snapped by Carolyn across a restaurant table during their honeymoon

> Mr. Senier had a great eye for color and texture. A lot of the cloth was heavy, made especially for coats and jackets.
>
> He experimented with different threads. In the basement of his Dorchester home were four looms, and although with retirement he had cut back on the time he spent weaving, he nevertheless enjoyed making his cloth. I wanted Dick to have a jacket, at least.

Mr. Senier was also a fiddler and accordion player. He led local Irish bands. Whenever Richard met someone, he was greeted with "Oh, you're Tom Senier's son," something that could be said of quite a few young men, since Richard had nine living brothers.

When Richard met Carolyn, he was an independent television producer. Soon, he moved to Los Angeles. Dick phoned Carolyn every day, and they had long talks on the phone. They wrote often, and it soon became obvious that L. A. was not in his future.

Dick and Carolyn honeymooned in New Orleans and, courtesy of friends Joan and Larry Page (who went along), the Bahamas, where Carolyn took a spin on a moped, left; she and Dick relaxed in the sun, above: in Carolyn's album, the photo is captioned "Lovers"

countless variations and improvisations
a belief that good outcomes are always possible

by Joan Page

For this special book, I've reminisced through three decades of experiences with Carolyn. With considerable nostalgia and affection, I've selected some small slices of life that bear Carolyn's trademark: a positive response to life with the belief that good outcomes are always possible.

When our friend Richard Senier introduced Carolyn Brown to my husband and me thirty-two years ago, we were charmed immediately but moved to Florida before the "possibilities" of their relationship were realized. When they married, we felt overjoyed and invited the newlyweds to Miami for a cruise. What must have shocked them was learning that we would be cruising to the Bahamas with them. Not long after the ship docked in Nassau, I came face to face with Carolyn's adventurous self. She coaxed me onto the back of a rented motorcycle and roared off down the road. No helmets back in the seventies and no conventional bus tours for Carolyn. Instead she gave us both a sightseeing trip around the island that we talk about today.

During another Florida visit, we decided to try our luck on a deep-sea fishing adventure. There wasn't much excitement for the first hour or so until Carolyn felt a sharp tug on her line. I remember thinking that she couldn't be strong enough to battle a thirty-two pound barracuda (which we later gave to the people at the dock), yet she hung in there and eventually won the fight. Watching her reel in that prized fish was fun. Even better, however, was the fourteen-pound grouper Dick caught. We ate that barbequed à la Carolyn on our patio that evening.

Often, it seems that the kitchen has been an ideal place for Carolyn's creativity to express itself, using countless variations and improvisations. Through the years, she has taught me about freshly made crab cakes, paella, exotic mushrooms, and homemade ketchup. The ketchup is a story in itself, ideal for showing how this woman can "create" her way out of a mess. Carolyn wanted to prepare ketchup using her mother's special recipe. One gallon of simmering sauce was nearly finished cooking when the taste test revealed a disastrous problem: We had added five tablespoons of pepper instead of two tablespoons. It was hotter than Tabasco. After a good laugh at ourselves, Carolyn went into "correction-mode" asking for more cooking pots and adding tomato juice until sheer volume had diluted the pepper. We made enough ketchup that night to go into business; the only hitch was having a house that smelled like tomatoes for weeks afterward.

Here is an incident that typifies Carolyn's way of responding to a situation. She and Richard were ending a visit with us, all set to leave on a 10 PM flight when word came from the airline that the flight was delayed until 2 AM. We sat around discussing what to do for awhile. Then Carolyn got up, walked across the room, sat down at the piano, and proceeded to turn our living room into a concert hall, playing her favorite pieces and our requests. Those waiting hours were filled with music, laughter, and camaraderie as the years of our friendship have been.

Joan Page is a retired registered nurse.

Dick had spent six years in the seminary. At length, he decided not to become a priest and then took a variety of jobs, from teaching philosophy and classical languages to reporting about the Second Vatican Council in Rome. In 1963, he was diagnosed with cancer and was still living under its shadow when he met Carolyn. The ordeal had made him very angry: it had been impossible to make reasonable plans while serving what seemed to be a death sentence. Carolyn was the antidote he needed.

In November of 1973, they were married. Their honeymoon was typical of their future life together, full of travel and friends. They went to New Orleans first

Carolyn, right, with her friend Joan Page at a fountain in Rome, c. 1974

and then to Florida where their good friends Joan and Larry Page gave them a surprise weekend cruise to Nassau. Of course, Joan and Larry went along, and since the only room left had four single bunks, Richard and Carolyn spent part of their honeymoon sleeping with friends. "We never stopped laughing," Carolyn remembers.

Carolyn and Richard moved to an apartment in Brookline. Carolyn still taught in Newton, and Richard had television projects. One, a documentary film, took them to Italy in 1974. Carolyn took a leave of absence during the fall, and they spent three months in Rome. Dick was able to introduce Carolyn to the city he loves. They have returned more than twenty-five times.

Their relationship was mutually nurturing. Full of good humor and always ready to take the floor or offer a quip, Dick also supplied Carolyn with emotional support and encouragement. He was dependable.

> Dick has been the strong harmony in our duet. He gives me strength in many ways. I developed a lump on one of my eyelids shortly after we were married. Dick sent me to Dr. H. Freeman Allen at Massachusetts Eye and Ear Infirmary. Dr. Allen was a grand specialist. He was also a vestryman at Boston's famous Trinity Church in Copley Square, a volunteer to the Sioux Indians, and a pianist.

Thinking I had a cyst, he operated on my eye. He said that almost always, this type of lump was a cyst. I was awake during the surgery; only my eye was anesthetized. Early in the procedure, he realized it was a tumor, not a cyst. Dr. Allen and his assistant tried to decide what to do in case of malignancy. Should they remove the tumor and other parts with the eyelid? If it were cancer, would it spread? Would they have to do something that might be disfiguring? He put down his instruments and said to his assistant, "Let's pray over this." A few minutes later, he said, "We'll just remove the tumor, get a biopsy, and if need be, proceed later." In the early 1970s, even at one of the most prestigious hospitals in the world, it took at least three days to get a biopsy report.

As we waited anxiously, Dick and I knew we could be heading to a dark place. I tried to pretend that the "what ifs" were not possible. I'll never forget the way he looked at me and said, "You've got to prepare yourself. It could be cancer. If so, it would probably be fatal." He certainly didn't want to lose me, but he had been through his own cancer and had learned to look it straight in the eye. By the end of the week, we discovered there was no malignancy. I had also discovered Dick's deep strength, there in our home.

On a business trip to Italy with Dick, who was shooting a documentary film for his production company in 1975, Carolyn saw Rome. She had a pretty good view, too, straight from the robes of the statue of Saint Peter overlooking Vatican Square.

Rosalene often visited Dick and Carolyn at their apartment, sometimes for extended periods. She and Carolyn's husband hit it off from the start. Dick says,

When I met my future mother-in-law in 1971, she was seventy-six years old, widowed, and very attractive, good humored, and welcoming. We soon discovered similar interests: music, family, travel, and (of course) Carolyn. She lived in senior housing behind the Immaculate Conception Church in downtown Waterbury.

After our marriage, Rosalene often spent extended visits with us at our Brookline apartment and fit in with our expanding group of friends. She loved nothing more than a good party, especially a musical one, and we had plenty of those. When we were ourselves invited to the homes of others, she was usually included.

Whether it was over a cup of tea and her apple pie or when I drove her back to Waterbury, I found it easy to talk with her. I am more loquacious by nature than she, but she always loved a chat and could spot a phony a mile away. She was what we would call a good sport.

I dislike turnpikes and highways, preferring the side roads which are always more interesting. Give me the Merritt Parkway any day instead of Route 95. My circuitous driving always baffled my mother-in-law. More than once she would look at me and say, "Where the hell are we?"

Like her daughter, she was ready to go at the hint of an invitation. Consequently, we took her everywhere—to Cape Cod, to Florida, to the Metropolitan Opera, even to Sicily where she insisted on going to the top of Mount Etna, no easy feat. Hers was a life full of giving. Her homemade apple pies and fruitcakes were legend, as were her chili sauce and her very own cookbook. If you want cooking of that sort these days you nearly always need to have a mother-in-law. Lucky for me, her daughter Carolyn carries the torch.

She had nice friends, mostly widows, much given to card playing. On my visits to Waterbury I would put on a show for them, telling Irish jokes and singing the odd song. I couldn't have picked a better audience or a better way of worming my way into Rosalene's heart.

Carolyn was enjoying life, but she was ready for a change of pace in her career. She had taught music for more than twenty years and had already reduced her teaching load to part-time at Oak Hill. Then, in 1976, Carolyn read about plans to rehabilitate the two-hundred-year-old Quincy Market next to historic Faneuil Hall in downtown Boston. For months there had been teaser ads in the *Boston Globe*, ". . . coming soon . . . "

The inner-city "festival" market was a new concept in the United States. In the sixties, suburban strip malls and shopping centers had become popular. Shoppers abandoned inner cit-

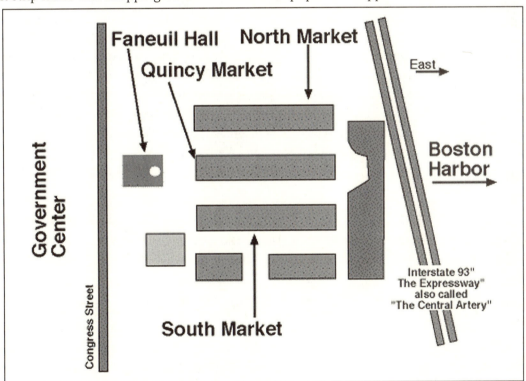

A schematic map of Boston's Faneuil Hall Marketplace, above. On the strength of reading a cryptic ad in the Boston Globe *and the purchase of cloth for fifteen hundred dollars from her father-in-law with money unexpectedly given by the CND "in fairness and justice" to former sisters, Carolyn began her eventual million dollar, five-city business on a Quincy Market pushcart in 1976.*

In the nineteenth century, Quincy Market was a vibrant place of commerce and exchange with pushcarts and vendors working in the shadow of historic Faneuil Hall. By the mid twentieth century, it was well past its prime. James Rouse of Baltimore imagined rehabilitating by creating the first festival market in the United States. There was a lot of hype in the 1976 Declaration of Independence bicentennial year. Looking for a change of career, Carolyn signed up for a pushcart in the to-be-gentrified marketplace. Within a year, Dick joined her fulltime.

ies for outlying areas where they could park easily. James Rouse, a visionary city planner from Baltimore who developed the model towns of Reston, Virginia, and Columbia, Maryland, had a different idea. He conceived Faneuil Hall Marketplace as a reiteration of a model with inner city small businesses located close to each other and accessible to public transportation. Faneuil Hall Marketplace was a perfect location, situated adjacent to Boston's North End. Home to scores of Italian immigrants and their descendants, the North End had an outdoor Saturday market near the waterfront where vendors sold fruits and vegetables from pushcarts rolled away at the end of the day. Made up of three long two-story buildings, Quincy Market dated to the early nineteenth century when it housed vendors of meat and produce. Originally an architectural tour de force, it had fallen on hard times and in the 1960s, many of the stores were closed or in disrepair. The historic market was in danger of demolition. Rouse planned an area that would have small individually owned businesses interspersed with restaurants and food stalls.

Carolyn was intrigued by the prospect. She had recently paid her father-in-law fifteen hundred dollars for a quantity of his hand woven Irish cloth. She cinched the deal after receiving a surprise check of two thousand dollars from the CNDs for some property they had sold.

> That year's CND chapter voted to divide the money among former nuns. They sent us a letter with the check and said the money was sent "in a sense of justice to their own."

Carolyn wanted to do something special with the money. Without telling Richard, she asked his father if he would sell her some of his cloth. Mr. Senier was pleased that someone was interested. After they struck their bargain, he rolled cloth generously off the bolts. Richard found out about it when Carolyn got into a minor car accident while carrying the cloth home. He came to pick her up and saw it in the back seat. Her intended surprise was exposed.

She saw possibilities for business. One morning on a day off from school, she went to Faneuil Hall Marketplace offices to inquire about pushcarts. The central market building had opened in August of 1976. The pushcart idea was one of Rouse's pet projects. He was determined to fill the market's outer halls with small businesses in kiosks that resembled North End pushcarts. He was so dedicated to the concept that, the story goes, on opening day of the market when no

Thomas Senier, Dick's father, with bolts of his Celtic Weavers cloth. Mr. Senier was a well-known Boston figure not only for his gregarious personality that lent itself to easy political connections but also for his music. And his cloth was beautiful. The Boston Sunday Post *presented a full-page article on his business, called Celtic Weavers, in June, 1947. Working with Mr. Senier at that time, according to the article, were his sons Bobby, James, Leo, and William. Carolyn's husband Dick was named for his own grandfather, Richard Senier, the master weaver, who also appears in the* Post *article. By 1973, Thomas Senier had retired and was weaving cloth as a hobby in his basement. Carolyn saw a legacy and approached her father-in-law with a plan to bring it to life.*

Carolyn had a fashionable palazzo pants outfit sewn from Thomas Senier's cloth, c. 1976, above. Whether she intended it or not, with the Boston Public Gardens as a backdrop and wearing hand-woven Irish fabric, she combines the ambiance of Brahmin Boston with the pride of immigrant Boston. Developer James Rouse added the zest of the "new Boston" to the mix as he invested himself in creating a fresh way of perceiving Quincy Market at Faneuil Hall Marketplace.

pushcarts had yet been rented, he stocked one of them himself and sold baskets to shoppers.

From Tom Senier's cloth, Carolyn had wide palazzo pants, a fitted vest, and a doughboy hat custom-tailored. Hoping to persuade them to accept her as a pushcart operator, she wore the outfit for her interview with the Faneuil Hall Marketplace management, which was selective about merchandise. Her strategy was successful. She leased a pushcart for fifty dollars for the weekend after Thanksgiving, the beginning of the holiday shopping season, the busiest of the year.

Carolyn needed inventory quickly, and she knew she needed enough to last the weekend. She decided on doughboy hats like those worn by the cartoon character Andy Capp, big floppy tweed caps each with a visor and a large button in the center of the top like the one she wore to the marketplace interview. She contacted people who could sew—friends, teachers in her school, her sister Kaye, her niece. She gave them some cloth and paid them three dollars an hour, then more than minimum wage, to make hats from patterns she herself made by taking apart a favorite hat. Soon she was cutting out hats on her dining room table and about twenty people were doing the same on theirs. She also asked them to make scarves and aprons. She hated sewing as much as she had in the convent, so she left the sewing to them.

Her cadre of workers was industrious, and on the Friday after Thanksgiving, the pushcart was well supplied. Carolyn donned one of the caps, and business took off. She sold caps, scarves, and aprons, and before the weekend was over, they were gone. Carolyn's profit was one thousand dollars after paying for cloth, rent, and all her workers. She then rented the pushcart during the slow season after Christmas. Her workers kept making hats, and people kept buying them. All over Boston, Carolyn saw people wearing the thirty-dollar doughboy caps. It wasn't an

Carolyn, top, selling hats from the Faneuil Hall Marketplace pushcart, c. 1977, while people try them on, bottom

inexpensive purchase in the late 1970s, and Dick and Carolyn realized they had a success. The hats were warm, had an elastic band for adjustability, and were limited editions made in vintage cloth. Sales began to outstrip their supply, so Richard phoned the Irish Export Board. They directed him to a couple in Bronxville, New York, who were overstocked with big blocky Irish walking hats. They were willing to sell theirs for a dollar over the wholesale price they had paid. Carolyn and Richard bought the lot and added them to their stock.

One afternoon as Carolyn and Dick sold from the pushcart, a tall man approached with his wife. They handled the hats, looking at the fabric and how they were made. "So who makes your caps?" the man asked. Watching the couple, Dick figured they had an experienced interest and before long, Dick and Carolyn realized that standing before them was one of the last of Boston's old-time cap makers, Abraham Barron, who had learned the skill from his wife Gladys's father.

What would be more promising for sales in the spirit of the pushcart than an old-time Boston cap maker who himself worked on sewing machines? Abe agreed to supply Carolyn with his line. He and Gladys

---

mutual feeling of good vibes, enduring friendship
interfaith celebrations and rousing musicales

by Gladys Barron

Abe and I met Carolyn and Richard Senier in 1977 at the Quincy Market in Boston. As we browsed through the merchandise, Abe commented on their hats and praised the material but felt the workmanship was inferior. Richard questioned him about his background and was delighted to learn that Abe was an experienced hat and cap manufacturer. We agreed to meet for coffee later that day, and there was a mutual feeling of good vibes that led to an enduring friendship.

Abe had been designing and creating headwear for most of his life, and he suggested patterns and styling changes that Carolyn immediately agreed to. We soon found that we could relate to each other on a very spiritual level that transcended most relationships, and in a short time, we were adopted into the Seniers' family.

Carolyn and Richard joined us for Passover Seders in our house, and we went to Christmas Eve in their home. We observed many occasions together and celebrated birthdays and anniversaries—usually at the Seniers' home with a rousing musicale.

When the Seniers retired, they chose to live in a country setting in Orange, Massachusetts, where Carolyn enjoys a wonderful affinity with nature and all her surroundings. Her garden is a creation of flowers and plantings that reflect her desire to have beauty all around her. Not only can she name all the flowers and many of the trees around Lake Mattawa, but she can also identify most of the birds that visit or dwell around the lake. It is all part of the music that is the essence of Carolyn's being.

Gladys Barron lives in retirement on Cape Cod.

hit it off immediately with Richard and Carolyn, and the two couples became friends as well as business associates.

Now the pushcart offered a variety of hats and caps. People began to seek out the stall, and Carolyn and Richard spent most afternoons and weekends at Faneuil Hall Marketplace. Her family in Waterbury had no idea what she was doing.

> They thought I was literally pushing a cart through Boston selling hats like Molly Malone with her cockles and mussels.

Tom Senier, however, knew what she was doing and was very pleased to see his cloth being used and the caps selling. He recognized Carolyn's appreciation for his fabric and offered to give her the rest of his inventory—"Once," Carolyn tells me with a grin, "he saw that my check had cleared and I was running an honest-to-goodness business." Carolyn and Richard called their fledgling company O'Seanora Products. O'Seanora is Irish for Senier. But with Tom's generous gift and his blessing, they also assumed his trade name, Celtic Weavers. As a child, Richard had sold his father's scarves as he worked his paper route through the streets of Upham's Corner in the Dorchester section of Boston. Now he and Carolyn were selling them from a gentrified pushcart in Faneuil Hall Marketplace.

Carolyn was having fun. She enjoyed business. At the end of their first summer, the marketplace management invited her to open a shop in the newly renovated South Market adjacent to the food court. She decided not to go back to her job in Newton and said goodbye to teaching music in order to become a full time shopowner. She and Richard rented space on the second floor of South Market—a relatively small shop of 330 square feet—for two thousand dollars a month. The market management wanted her to keep the pushcart, too, but she and Richard said no, deciding against overextending themselves.

When they applied for a start-up loan, two banks turned them down. Then they applied to a bank where the loan officer, an Italian American from East Boston, was the son of a tailor. When Carolyn explained to him that she had a roomful of hand-woven Irish woolens, he understood its value. He let them use the cloth as collateral. Carolyn and Richard paid off a good part of the fifty-three-thousand-dollar loan in the first year.

Carolyn never bothered to balance her checkbook ("I still don't," she remarks). But years in the convent had taught her how to organize people, and common sense and understanding of style helped her to know instinctively what to buy and how to display it. In 1978, Richard gave up his work in TV and joined the business full time. From then on, Dick provided optimism and drive, and Carolyn provided a sense of fashion and practicality. The business, however, was always in Carolyn's name and, although they consulted, he left final decisions to her.

The shop became one of the busiest in the market. Quality hats and caps, Irish wool sweaters, capes from England and Ireland, and silk scarves from Italy became the backbone of business.

> Everything has important details: where to order, when to order, who to call, when to call, what to buy, when to buy. When you're working internationally, there are other important details: what costs are added with shipping and duties, the fluctuation of the dollar against international currency, the sheer distance if things aren't right. We wanted our business to be about quality and service, and we wanted people who came through our shop to enjoy the experience.

Carolyn and Dick in their first South Market shop: 330 square feet upgraded from a pushcart c. 1977. Along with Irish merchandise, they sold a full line of Scottish tartans and offered custom-made clothing. Carolyn says it is a challenge to display in limited space, so ingenuity was important. After retirement from Celtic Weavers, Carolyn placed the oval standing mirror in her music room at Lake Mattawa.

Keeping a shop was more than a full time business for both Carolyn and Richard. Celtic Weavers opened at ten in the morning and didn't close until nine at night. Initially, they both stayed all day, but as they developed a staff, Carolyn spent time at home keeping accounts and paying bills. Carolyn called European vendors early in the morning, right after she took a walk or worked in her garden, because of the five- or six-hour time difference. Although the Seniers were advised to carry Irish knickknacks and souvenirs, they never did, instead stocking their shelves only with high quality products.

When she was at the shop, Carolyn spent her days with customers, keeping an eye on the merchandise and helping young men pick out just the right gift. When they were there at the same time, Richard took over the cash register. His way with words and Irish small talk kept customers in the shop. They were fortunate in having loyal employees like Mary Bigge, whose low-key, quiet approach cinched a sale more often than not. Aine Graham, the "heart of the store," according to Carolyn, worked for them from the early eighties. Aine started as an enthusiastic customer and easily moved into the shop as a saleswoman. She stayed on until they sold Celtic Weavers in 1998 and remains a trusted friend.

Richard and Carolyn often worked different hours, and lunch was usually a snack taken on the run, sometimes from one of the vendors in the food court. But in the evenings, no matter what time they got home, one or the other or both of them cooked dinner, and they enjoyed a leisurely candlelit meal.

Rosalene came periodically for pleasant, extended visits. The Seniers' friends readily took her into the fold. Often, she came laden with goodies, especially pies, but as she aged, she seemed tired of making them from scratch but unwilling to admit it. Once, after Dick drove her to Boston from Waterbury, she allowed him to bring her luggage to the guest room. Back from her work at Celtic Weavers later in the evening, Carolyn spotted a paper bag at the foot of the stairs. Unsure whose bag it was, she peeked in and saw a package of Jiffy Pie Crust Mix.

> My mother had started bringing store-bought pies to family gatherings, and once, when she brought *Mrs. Smith's Homemade Pie*, we asked her what had happened to Mrs. Brown's homemade pies. I think she was pleased that we liked her pies better, but she really wasn't

Carolyn modeling a Celtic Weavers outfit in a Quincy Market fashion show, c. 1978

Celtic Weavers: a happy, lively place to work
beautiful clothing in soft shades of heather and green

by Aine Graham

My little cottage in Ireland is miles away from the nearest town with no access to computers or typewriters. I'm sitting by the sea, jotting down often lovely thoughts of Carolyn.

Celtic Weavers was a warm friendly name for Carolyn's shop, such a happy, lively place to work. Customers would pop in for a laugh and hum along to the classical and Irish music we played. Carolyn selected beautiful clothing in soft shades of heather and greens to match the landscape in Ireland, as soft as the moss on the rocks in Connemara: everything hand-woven to perfection. She modeled the outfits so well, her posture enviable.

One day, she was called to a meeting. Her dress was too casual, so we promptly changed outfits. She looked stunning in my dress, but her dress looked a pity on me. That day, I ducked into more doorways on my way home. We laughed hysterically for days.

Her humility is a joy. When I sit beside her at the piano while she composes and she starts to sing, I am reminded of the dawn chorus I hear from the larks and song birds outside my cottage window in Ireland. I experience the same peace, joy, and blessings.

Evenings spent in Carolyn's home were the best. Herself and Richard cooked delicious dinners. We would retire to the music room and sing the night away. Farley, her red dog, sat quietly and listened. He has gone where the good fairies go. His nature was as gentle as Carolyn's.

Carolyn is a beautiful thought in my heart.

Aine Graham worked side by side with Carolyn and Dick for eighteen years at Celtic Weavers. She refers to Carolyn with the Irish honorific, "Herself," idiomatically used as the subject of the sentence.

about to bake pies from scratch. I was bemused when I looked in the bag at the foot of the stairs and saw the pie crust mix. She was determined to trick me, and I wondered how it would play out. I quietly told Dick about it and asked him to get some blueberries. He brought them in with a bit of a flourish.

The next day, I mentioned the bag at the foot of the stairs. She identified it as hers, and I didn't let on that I knew about the Jiffy Mix. I asked her if she would like to go to work with me the next day, maybe see the shop, look around the marketplace, and have lunch. She readily agreed. The next morning, she was ready for the outing. Dick and I were discussing the day, and he commented that he would be upstairs all day in his study working on the computer. My mother immediately perked up, and I could see the wheels turning: "Oh. He's going to be away and she's going to be away . . ." I knew what she was going to say next: "Carolyn, I don't think I'll go to Faneuil Hall after all. I'll stay here for the day."

I went upstairs where Dick had already started working and asked him to make her some soup. "Today's the day," I said. He laughed. We had already exchanged a little chuckle over the contents of that bag. Then, I was off to work. Dick called me at noontime. He had made her some lunch and, yes, she was making pies.

That day, I didn't bother to have lunch. I arrived home around three. "Have a piece of pie," my mother said. I had glanced in the wastebasket, and there, shredded, was the Jiffy box. I didn't laugh or even let on I knew she had used that mix. I didn't want her to think I thought the pie she made from the mix was as good as her own, yet I wanted to let her have the pleasure of fooling us into thinking she had made the pie crust from scratch. I sat

A page from Rosalene's recipe book and Rosalene stirring up a batch of tomato catsup, right, above, c. 1980. Carolyn says her mom wasn't especially enamored of writing out the cookbook and she doesn't recommend trying the pie crust recipe (which isn't really for pie crust). The ketchup, however, says Carolyn, is very good.

with her and had some. "How's the pie?" she asked. "It's good," I said. "But the crust is a little softer than usual." I think I outfoxed her.

Carolyn kept the day-to-day accounts for Celtic Weavers. Her mother's shrewd management of household finances had made an impression on her, and she knew how to schedule payments when money was tight so that each creditor got something. Although she hired a bookkeeper, Carolyn signed checks and made decisions about who would get paid and when. Six months after the shop opened, Carolyn and Richard went out of town to a trade show over Christmas. Their dog Farley was so annoyed at being left behind that he went into Carolyn's home office and completely tore apart every piece of paper on her desk. When Carolyn and Richard returned, six months of records were strewn in pieces on the floor. Carolyn scooped up the papers and threw them into a large carton. She remembers saying, "I have no time for this. If I'm ever audited, I'll worry about it."

A year and a half later, a Faneuil Hall accounting firm audited her. By then, she had a proper accountant so that everything was in good order except for the first six months. When the auditor arrived, Carolyn started him with the most recent records. He was impressed with her business and her organization. When she then handed him the carton full of the mess from the first six months, she told him, "You won't believe this, but my dog ate the receipts, and I haven't wanted to take the time to piece this together." The startled auditor said "This will take me weeks to do" and took the carton with him. When he wrote his report, he praised her for her record keeping, making the observation that everything was appropriately done, even though, initially, records were in poor order because "Mrs. Senier was just learning the business."

Carolyn and her dog Farley, c. 1979

Carolyn is sure he didn't even check the carton.

It wasn't long before Celtic Weavers outgrew the first small space. Carolyn's larger items, such as bulky Irish sweaters known for their style and warmth, took up a lot of room. Dick wanted to move to a larger shop. After a bank refused to lend them money to move, Carolyn considered the possibility of financing from the Small Business Association (SBA). She went to them for advice and told them she had to have a bigger shop if she was going to succeed.

She waited weeks, but nothing happened. Carolyn and Richard decided to take the risk anyway. The owner of the space they were considering needed an answer. Carolyn leveled about not having the cash and asked him to sell the lease on the promise that he would receive the first twenty thousand dollars the store made. He agreed and, on a handshake, they moved. In the meantime, she went to the SBA again to ask about the loan. Four men and one woman on the committee were hesitant to lend to Carolyn because of her inexperience and also because of difficulties small businesses had at the marketplace. "Why do you want to move?" they asked.

"Look," Carolyn said, "I have to tell you. I'm not asking you if I can make this move. I couldn't wait for you. I've already done it. Now I'm asking you to help me succeed at it." They were amazed. The woman on the committee was delegated to visit the shop. When she arrived, it was jammed with people, and scarves and hats were flying off the shelves. She was convinced that Carolyn had a going concern, a bank's description of sufficient business to warrant a loan. The woman told Carolyn she thought they could lend her the twenty thousand dollars she needed to buy out the lease of the larger shop. She said she would call in a few days.

Carolyn felt considerable stress from the uncertainty of it all. She was home in her robe and nightgown, suffering from a migraine headache when the call came. The loan had come through and more besides. Agreeing to lend her money to pay off earlier loans, something rarely done, the SBA also approved thirty-three thousand dollars more so she would have cash flow to succeed. Carolyn thanked the caller. Her niece Joan, who was living with Carolyn and Richard at the time, was amazed at her aplomb. "Aunt Carolyn," she laughed, "whoever that was will never know he was talking to a woman in her nightgown racked with a mind-numbing headache." In

two nuns dancing the Irish jig in the kitchen
positive attitude, delighting in beauty—lucky streak and all

by Joan McGrath

How can I possibly describe my Aunt Carolyn? There are so many roles that she has embraced over the years.

My earliest memories of Carolyn are visiting her in Ridgefield, Connecticut, at the CND convent. When I was a child, our family would drive over on Sunday afternoon to see her. Her traditional habit never detracted from her bright, beautiful smile. Her laughter and smiles made these visits very joyful.

I came to know her much better during my college years. She was starting her business, Celtic Weavers, in Boston, and I helped her with some sewing. This is when I came to realize that Carolyn has a lucky streak. We were trying to prepare enough inventory to open the shop for longer periods of time. It was in January, and Carolyn was busy teaching school during the day. On cue, it began to snow. School was cancelled, so she had two extra days for the project! Who else would be so lucky?

One of the luckiest things to happen to her was meeting her husband, Richard. If ever two people were soul mates, Carolyn and Dick are the perfect example. They share similar values and complement each other musically.

Carolyn's positive outlook extends to people. She delights in the beauty, talent, and strengths of others, always complimenting and reminding them of their own wonderful attributes. I think it is why people love to be around her. She makes everyone feel special.

After college, I lived with Carolyn and Dick for three years. Their door was always open. They could throw an impromptu party at a moment's notice. On any given night, guests would be gathered around the piano and dining room table. One evening, I came home to find two nuns dancing the Irish jig in the kitchen!

Carolyn is a marvelous hostess. She loves to prepare wonderful food and then enjoy it with her guests. She does so with a casualness that makes it seem easy. She is very carefree about things that would rattle another hostess. For example, one winter she had a party after a concert featuring music she had composed. It was snowing all day, and the roads were hazardous. It didn't prevent a single guest from attending the party. That week was particularly cold, and the Seniers' pipes were frozen. The toilet situation was difficult. The kitchen sink defrosted just hours before the party. (There is that luck again!) There were buckets and mops in the clogged tub, and you had to cross your fingers to use the toilet. Amid all this, Carolyn was serving caviar! A lesser hostess would have crumbled.

Joan McGrath is Carolyn's niece.

the late eighties, one of the men on the committee came into the shop with his grandson. "I'm so glad to see you're still here," he said. "I'm proud to say I voted for you."

As an advertising promotion, when Carolyn and Richard had been in business only about a year, Faneuil Hall Marketplace hosted the mayors of what the management identified as "The

Possibly as an outcome of stress, Carolyn developed rheumatoid arthritis simultaneously with the growth of Celtic Weavers. Her hands show the effects of arthritis, above, c. 1978. Playing piano and guitar kept her fingers active, although by the end of the 1990s, Carolyn gave up the guitar because of arthritis pain.

Great Cities of the World." The management wanted the mayors to see the opportunities the market provided for international merchandise. Fergus O'Brien, Lord Mayor of Dublin was among them, and Celtic Weavers was the natural host for his visit. In Irish Boston, it was a high profile event. Richard convinced Irish suppliers to provide appropriate food and drink. Carolyn and Richard invited two hundred people—special customers, friends, and relatives—for high tea in a beautiful function room named for and restored to the design of Alexander Parris, architect of the original Quincy Market. At nine in the evening, the doors were opened to the entire city. More than a thousand people came to the party, and Carolyn and Richard's reputation for throwing the classiest of parties was secured.

They had been at Celtic Weavers for about two years when Carolyn felt it was time they learned something more formal about the business world. As a teacher and choral director, she had developed strategies to coordinate music programs in schools and churches. She was now determined to learn strategies that make a business succeed. She approached SCORE, the Service Corps of Retired Executives, a program that enlists retired business people to advise novice entrepreneurs. They assigned her a mentor, Leon Margolis. He advised her how to anticipate seasons and trends, to bring in winter coats in July. He knew, for example, that Canadians vacationing in Boston in the summer would be tempted to spend money on winter clothes when the Canadian dollar was strong, as it was then. Tempering his advice with her own dependable intuition, Carolyn continually reinvented her business to keep it fresh.

Eventually, developers from Hartford, Philadelphia, and Providence approached the Seniers with deals to persuade them to open shops in markets there. By 1982, they had a catalogue business and operated five shops.

> We fell into the classic trap of the small business—overextension. We opened Celtic Weavers at the Civic Center in Hartford, at the Bourse Building in Philadelphia, at the

Carolyn and Dick mailed a catalogue to thirty thousand recipients, c. 1980. Dressed in merchandise from Celtic Weavers, they were photographed with their dog, Farley, in their Roslindale backyard, top. Wooed by developers of festival markets around the Northeast, they expanded to five locations, including one in Hartford described in a 1980 article, above left. When Fergus O'Brien, Lord Mayor of Dublin, visited Boston in 1980, Celtic Weavers hosted him, above right. Carolyn presided at a catered party for fifteen hundred in the Quincy Market Alexander Parris room.

"We instituted the custom of barging in on each other . . . "
hospitality, music, great conversations, good food

by Pat Morris

After going to television classes for teachers in 1973, I went to a gospel concert at the Paulist Center, a Catholic Church in Boston. Carolyn was at the concert with a friend, Jim Morris. Dick arrived late because he was producing the television courses I was attending. During the concert, Jim pointed to me and told Carolyn he would like to meet me. Carolyn responded: "You already have; she was at the New Year's Eve party."

After the concert, a few of us went to the European Restaurant in the North End for pizza. It was my thirtieth birthday and the beginning of my love affair with Jim Morris and my love relationship with Carolyn and Dick.

The four of us spent a lot of time together laughing, talking, and enjoying music and good cooking. When Jim and I decided to move into a house that had not been renovated in fifty years, Carolyn and Dick came every weekend during the fall to scrape, paint, wallpaper, and give encouragement. Then one Saturday, Dick decided they should go and enjoy the foliage, but Carolyn made Dick turn around and come back to Dorchester to help us. She called it "the autumn we lost." When they decided to move into their ten-room house in Roslindale, we were thankful it didn't need any work.

As Carolyn was learning her business, getting financing, and choosing stock for the next season, there always seemed to be one or more guests living in their house. Dick's brother Bill moved in. An Irish cousin needed a safe place. Carolyn's niece, Joan, wanted to work in Boston for a while. Gary Maceoin, in his eighties, made their home his home. Hospitality, music, great conversations, and good food were always available, and the dinner parties never stopped. Carolyn and Dick were the chosen godparents and family for our children. They agreed to raise them should anything happen to us. Michael and Cara were surrounded and drenched in love, gentleness, and music because of them.

Blessings heaped upon blessings have come to us because of Carolyn and Dick. At a wake, they heard of a house for sale in Brookline. We made an offer and again, after much fixing up, we moved 2.7 miles away from them. We instituted the custom of barging in on each other, that is, showing up unannounced around dinnertime and amidst much laughing, expecting to be taken care of and fed. They came in the middle of the night when my father died, and when our kitchen was being remodeled, we moved in with them.

Whenever our friends meet Carolyn, they inevitably say: "She is soooo beautiful." To this day, I always respond, "And she is as good as she is beautiful." She has always been a model of gentleness and grace, of thoughtfulness and deep ethical thinking. She has always been a wise woman who nurtures relationships. Most recently, she has stretched my heart. With patience and diligence over many months and with some difficulty, she has taught me the real meaning of forgiveness and compassion. I am enriched, inspired, and very lucky to be one of her love relationships.

Pat Morris is a retired Boston Public School teacher.

> Arcade in Providence, at a small shop in Wellesley, and we produced a catalogue. We became jugglers of time, of merchandise, of money, of health.

> Warning signs of financial trouble appeared gradually. We kept on an even keel, but with great difficulty. I took inspiration from my mother who used to parcel out money to the grocer, the electric company, the bank. During periods of financial stress, everyone got a little of what the money pocket contained. The country's economy had several downturns that did not help our situation.

After a while, long distance managing took its toll. In 1983, Carolyn realized she was having more trouble than she should paying bills on time. When the quarterly accountant's report came, it corroborated her fears. Richard answered the phone, and the accountant told him to sit down. He broke the news to Carolyn in the evening as they were getting ready to go to dinner at the home of Jim and Pat Morris. They were in significant financial trouble.

Carolyn was despondent. After six years of hard work, she saw everything disintegrating. They cancelled dinner with their friends. About a half hour later, over the kitchen table, Carolyn heard these words from Dick:

> Look. Anyone can succeed when things are going well, but it takes guts and smarts to succeed when things are not going well. Dry your tears, go upstairs, and do yourself up. We're going out to a fancy restaurant.

Carolyn and Dick stopped at the Morrises to tell them they were going out on the town. Jim and Pat and their other guests were astounded to see them. They knew the Seniers were upset. They were all worried and talking about them when Carolyn appeared in an eye-arresting red dress and Dick in his best suit. Paying homage to Katharine Hepburn in *The Lion in Winter*, Carolyn announced, "This is how we register despair."

They went to the Bostonian Hotel overlooking Faneuil Hall Marketplace and had a fabulous dinner. Fortunately, Carolyn says, their MasterCard was paid up. In time, the bank restructured their loans and spaced out payments. They got back to business.

> There comes a point where a business can be too big for your smallness. Wisdom finally caught up with us. Although bankruptcy loomed over our heads, we were able to cut back and reduce our business ventures and overhead early enough. We studied our business, concentrating harder on our home location at Faneuil Hall.

While Carolyn was working hard at Celtic Weavers, she had no time for composing music or leading choral groups. But in 1985, she received word that one of her early compositions, "O, Praise Ye the Lord," was going to be sung at Saint Peter's, the most important Roman Catholic basilica, at the Vatican. The Congregation of Sisters of Christian Charity wanted to sing "O, Praise Ye . . ." at the beatification Mass for their founder, Pauline von Mallinckrodt. Richard immediately decided they had to be there for the ceremony.

The Sisters of Christian Charity must have sent the music to members worldwide, because they arrived in Rome ready to sing. When Carolyn introduced herself to their superior general, she asked Carolyn to accompany the choir of nuns on the Saint Peter's organ. Carolyn reluctantly agreed, but only if the organist would set the stops. She had no time to practice, and she had not played an organ for more than fifteen years. Fluent in Italian, Dick worked quickly with the accommodating organist, a Franciscan monk, translating Carolyn's sense of where the stops might be set. Allowing the familiar feeling of keys and pedals to pull her back into the instru-

A Celtic Weavers window display, c. 1982

ment, she began to play. The sisters' voices swelled through the basilica.

> There were prelates in high regalia, and there could have been cardinals. I'm just not sure. I remember that it was springtime, and I had dressed in layers. I was getting very hot, and I was perspiring profusely and kept peeling off layers of clothing—a cape, a sweater, a scarf—while I played. They all fell to the floor by the organ bench.

Later, the official organist played "O, Praise Ye, the Lord" as an interlude, and Carolyn loved hearing her hymn played by an organist whose command of the instrument was so superior.

Playing the organ at the Vatican was a bright spot in an otherwise trying time. As Carolyn grappled with financial difficulties, her mother battled heart disease.

> Although I never really got to know my dad through adult eyes and mind, I did get a chance to know my mother. I was lucky to have her twice as long. After I left the CNDs, she helped me buy clothes and find lamps, beds, dishes, and other necessities for my apartment. She emptied drawers of silverware and searched the attic for items to give me to ease my transition. I visited her often, driving to Waterbury for weekends and holidays.

A busy springtime day in Quincy Market at Faneuil Hall Marketplace, flagship site of Celtic Weavers

Carolyn and Dick—Herself and Himself—keeping shop at Celtic Weavers, top, c. 1991; Carolyn with Aine Graham, "the heart of the store" and Carolyn's good friend, above left, c. 1996; the late Abraham Barron, the capmaker, c. 1997

When Dick and I married, she often visited us and became involved in our life and with our friends. We took lovely trips with her. She instigated an excursion to the top of Mount Etna when she, Dick, and I were in Sicily together with our friend Pat Moylan. "I always wanted to do that," she said, and so off we went together to that volcano in the sky. She was in her eighties by then.

Once at Martha's Vineyard, she and her childhood friend Anna Grimes, Dick, and I rented a cottage in Oak Bluffs. We toured, swam, and ate, but my fondest memories are evening songs with Dick playing the accordion and Anna singing old fashioned tunes for Mom, who hummed along.

She enjoyed receiving phone calls. I spoke to her almost daily. During our business trips we would call her periodically from Dublin or Donegal or Australia—from wherever we happened to be. She enjoyed being able to say to her card club, "I heard from Carolyn and Dick. They called me from . . ."

Rosalene cruising Long Island Sound on her son Don's boat, c. 1980

When we decided to add a dining room onto our house at Mendum Street, her first question was, "Why do you want to do that? Isn't your house large enough?" I told her I had been saving the money to build and that we wanted a dining room—we enjoyed sharing meals with friends and wanted more seating space than the kitchen provided. She thought about it, and the following day, she said to me, "I've been thinking about this new room of yours. Go to the bank and borrow the money. Don't cut yourself short. You may need your money for an emergency." She should have been a CFO.

Once she made a wedding cake for my friend Pat and enjoyed the after-the-wedding party at our house long into the night. She loved a party. However, she was developing heart trouble, and I was concerned that she was over-exerting herself. About eleven, I whispered to her, "When you are ready to go to bed, let me know, and I'll help you upstairs." "No, no, not yet," she refused. At half past midnight, I whispered, "Are you ready to retire?" "No, no, not yet," she said. At two in the morning, somewhat worried, I whispered. "Do you think you should go upstairs to bed?" She finally said, "Yes." I helped her up the stairs and said, "Good night, Mom. I'll see you in the morning." Over her shoulder, she answered, "Like hell you will." And she slept well into the afternoon.

In 1983, my mother's eyes closed after a long, adventurous, loving, and generous life. Her death was peaceful. She died in her sleep. Her enlarged heart, which contained us all, stopped beating, but the beat goes on in her family.

I'm sure I'm not alone in feeling that, with both parents gone, an even more sacred part of my journey had begun. The cord was severed, the physical touch gone . . . and yet, I know that they are never gone.

Dick remembers Rosalene's final illness:

> She had a heart attack when she was 85. We were all at her daughter Kaye's house in Vermont, and I had to drive her back to Waterbury because she was insistent on having her own doctors. Carolyn held her mother for the entire journey, fraught with worry because my old station wagon burned oil at a furious pace, and I had to stop every fifty miles or so to fill the thing up. Somehow, Rosalene survived.
>
> Another, more serious attack followed, which left her comatose. When she regained consciousness, she had lost speech. She lay in bed and stared at all of us, expressing nothing at all, although her eyes followed us. One afternoon I sat on the edge of her bed and began to tell the latest news from Boston, followed by a joke or two. She was so attentive. Suddenly, after a punch line, she let out a solid laugh and started to talk again. There were relapses, and she reemerged from one while listening to a recording of Carolyn playing Liszt.
>
> Among her great joys was Carolyn's playing, especially of Chopin and Liszt. I instead regaled her with ballads and songs of her own youth, much as her late husband had done. Maybe that is what led her to tell Carolyn (but not me), "He's a lot like Daddy!"

During her mother's final illness, Carolyn developed rheumatoid arthritis. "Everything was hurting," Carolyn says. Her doctor warned that stress aggravates arthritis and advised her to reduce its causes. She and Richard cut back and slowly divested of their many shops, keeping only their flagship store. In 1986, with solvency returning, they moved their store to the first floor of North Market near Durgin Park, the famous old-time meat-and-potatoes restaurant where tourists flock to eat at long tables on a sawdusted floor. They had plenty of merchandise from other stores to fill it. Business was good.

In the late eighties, Richard organized a trip to Scotland for the North American Buyers Association, a group he helped found to assist people who were going overseas to buy products. Independent of the group, Carolyn and Dick also flew to the Orkney Islands off the northern coast of Scotland. There, they met the knitters of their bulky sweaters and the artisans who handcrafted the thick wedding bands they sold. They toured the islands and got to know artisans who made their wares. Making connections with manufacturers and crafts people became a cornerstone of their business success.

> It was the best way to predict what was new, to be on the leading edge of Irish and Scottish fashion so you weren't like every other shop. Also you could help the artisans by letting them know what the American market wanted so they could keep that in mind when creating their products.

Celtic Weavers, a stone's throw from Faneuil Hall

On one of their early trips to Ireland, Richard took Carolyn to meet Fergus O'Farrell and his wife, Maire. Richard had met Fergus through a mutual friend on a trip to Italy and Ireland in 1959.

Walking through Ireland with Fergus is an experience. Fergus *is* Ireland. No matter where you go, there is something he made.

Fergus is a woodworker, painter, restorer of monuments, sculptor, and skilled artisan. A shopkeeper like Carolyn, he has had a store for more than fifty years. He sells his own crafts as well as those of other artisans. In 1986, Fergus designed the layout and fixtures for the Seniers' shop and then came to Boston to implement his design. Maire came, too, and, experienced at selling Irish goods to the Irish, pitched in as a sales person at Celtic Weavers. Carolyn and Richard have Fergus's paintings and metal sculptures in their Mattawa home. Carolyn admires him as much as Richard does. Carolyn and Dick went to Scotland one springtime with Fergus and Maire, and Carolyn kept a bit of a travel journal.

Carolyn plays the organ in the home church of Dick's mother in Ballyconneely, County Galway, Ireland, top; Dick's brother Leo, above, shows Carolyn how to set a loom during the same trip

> . . . . We hired a car and headed west to Greenock and took the ferry to Duncan. We drove up the coast of Loch Fyne to Inverary and, exhausted, we registered at The Great Hotel, christened "not so great" by Richard. The next morning bright and early we drove along the coast of the loch, enjoying snow-covered mountains and autumn colors.
>
> Scotland has waterways everywhere in the west. We would cast an eye to the left and see boot-clad men and women collecting periwinkles after the tides receded. On our way toward Craigan, blackberries were still being picked (at least those berries that hadn't been touched by the Pooka, fairies that sometimes look like white horses and have mischievous reputations). On this route north, Fergus gave marvelous lectures about alignment stones way out in the fields, memorabilia of ancient civilization. On this vast expanse of scenic Scotland, a manor house appears in the distance and sometimes a nearby

equestrian trains his horse to jump hurdles.

Again and again we came upon mighty views of mountains with waterfalls in abundance. From the distance, they look painted onto the sides of the hills. Only as we neared them did we feel their force and see their movement.

On we drove to Armandale Pier where I purchased gorgeous and unusual jackets for the shop. They also carried garments of fine wool combined with cotton chenille like the ones I sell.

We lunched in Portree, where rows of pink, blue, and white homes line the wharf. Still, moored fishing boats filled the harbor and in places where the tide was low enough, collectors of periwinkles placed their catch in orange bags for later use.

In a manor on Skye, I discovered a classic book called *Ring of Bright Water* by Gavin Maxwell. A charming story with an otter at its center, it was such a good read for this kind of holiday, which makes excellent use of our "running away money."

Business meant travel, because most of the Seniers' wares came from other countries. Elements of fun were often part of the plan.

Usually, we traveled to Ireland to buy our merchandise. Occasionally, we went to New York where fashion shows had a Celtic contingent of manufacturers and craftspeople. My friend Pat Morris wanted to join me on one of the buying excursions so she would understand what "buying" entails. We flew to New York, where we had reservations in the Essex House Hotel on Central Park South. They misunderstood our arrangements for two single beds.

like a bright star on a clear night
hurtling across Rome at midnight
by Fergus O'Farrell

We are lucky if in our lifetime we find an exceptional person who comes into our circle of friends and illuminates our life like a bright star on a clear night. When we are lucky enough to meet such a one, we treasure our good fortune and life takes on a different meaning with the knowledge that we rejoice in the friendship of this paragon.

About thirty years ago an American friend brought into my store in Dublin just such a ray of sunshine who has been a friend since then. My wife Maire and I, Carolyn and Richard, her husband, have spent many holidays in Italy, France, England and Wales, and in the USA. Maire and I have the good fortune to have blended perfectly with them, which is a difficult thing to do; this is possible only because of the good nature and calming influence of Carolyn's presence and the music that flows from her fingertips. How lucky Richard is to be married to such a person of virtue!

Every year while Carolyn ran her store, Celtic Weavers, Richard and herself spent a hectic time in Ireland at the annual Craft Fair buying for the next year and arranging styles, colors and sizes for that year. The stallholders and the salesmen of the various merchants were always delighted to welcome Celtic Weavers, in the person of Carolyn, to their stands; I have never heard from any of them a crooked word about her, but only praise for the pleasant way she did her business.

No matter how well we dined, Carolyn always finished off with a large ice cream! Of course, she is slightly mad, which helps a good deal! Imagine stripping off and diving into a lake to wash her dog! The lasting image I have of Carolyn is of her perched on the pillion of a Vespa scooter, her cape flowing behind her in the wind, hurtling across Rome at midnight.

Fergus O'Farrell is an Irish artist.

When we objected, we were given a very small room on the sixth floor. Someone had made an error. However, much to our surprise, our tiny room had a door opening into a huge living room. We investigated and found another huge bedroom with a king-sized bed and yet a second living room and then another bedroom, a kitchen, and a dining room. We realized we were in someone's condominium, all somehow attached to our tiny, crowded room. All the rooms were connected to outside corridors. We had an entire wing of the Essex House, and we were the only ones who realized it.

We did what anyone should do. We locked and chained the doors to make them inaccessible to anyone else, silently thanked the hotel for such splendor, and invited my nephews Mark and Christopher, who were living in New York, to come over for a party. We had wine and cheese from the refrigerator and a jolly good evening.

I highly recommend these accommodations.

Carolyn and Richard sometimes turned pleasure trips into business. Once, they toured near Lake Como in northern Italy. Carolyn realized they were near the Saldarinis, the manufacturer of Carolyn's favorite scarves, wool challis woven in subtle colors and shadings. Carolyn and Richard stopped in and were treated graciously by Signora Saldarini. When Carolyn found out that Saldarinis no longer made a particular pattern, she asked if they would make them if she bought three hundred. The answer was a resounding, "Si!"

We traveled that time to Italy with Lola McGrail, Dick's elementary school teacher, who initiated his interest in languages. She and I have become friends over the past decade and often enjoy the Boston Symphony together. We went to New York for opera binges and to Quebec for music festivals. She was with us and Madame Saldarini when I realized that I had a bond with Madame not only in business but in music. Madame had performed in piano concerts in Siena as a young musician and described romantic, open-air

---

traveler, plumber, painter, poet, sportswoman, gardener

despite disparity, adding a new dimension to life

by Lola McGrail

Musician, composer, teacher, gourmet cook, gardener, businesswoman, traveler, plumber, painter, poet, sportswoman, five-star hostess, and best of all, friend.

I met Carolyn several years ago. Richard, her husband, had been a pupil of mine when I was a teacher of Spanish in the Mather School in Dorchester. He was ten years old at the time. We met again in the early nineties at an anniversary celebration at the school.

Shortly after that, I met Carolyn, and a new dimension was added to my life. Despite the disparity of our ages, we have so many interests in common.

She is a hostess without peer, and I enjoy her hospitality. She is a musician and composer, and I listen and learn. She is a teacher who often answers my questions by singing or playing the response over the phone. I heard some of the Mattawa songs that way, too.

And then we traveled—to the opera in New York and Milan, to favorite restaurants and gardens in Quebec City, to interesting sites at home and abroad and, best of all, an unforgettable trip through northern Italy.

She is a woman of many talents and has earned many titles, the greatest of which is "friend."

Lola McGrail was Richard Senier's elementary school Spanish teacher.

performances there. I had mentioned Siena to her because we planned to meet Cara Morris who was studying there. Cara lovingly adopted us as her godparents years earlier and met us as planned the following weekend in front of LaScala in Milan. There we were, a multi-generation quartet: Dick, Cara, Lola, and me, equally anticipating the excitement of opera in that famous opera house.

Inveterate globe trotters, Carolyn and Dick love to travel. The world is their oyster, especially Europe, and they have seen wild corners as well as halls of culture and commerce. Carolyn's nieces address her as Auntie Mame in deference to her adventures. By themselves or with friends or family, Carolyn and Dick have often toured the British Isles, especially Ireland, where just as in Italy they feel very much at home. Australia, New Zealand, Tenerife, and South America have been among their destinations. They have traveled both luxe and spare, sometimes enjoying the lavish accommodations of a grand hotel like Alvear Palace in Buenos Aires or climbing into Peruvian hills to explore the ruins of Machu Pichu.

The Seniers often travel with family or friends. Carolyn is with Lola McGrail in Rome, c. 1997, top; Gladys and Abe Barron faced Carolyn's camera with Firenze in the background, c. 1996, above.

Theatre and opera are never far from their minds, whether they go to performances by nearby groups or take in the world's finest in a majestic venue. They travel for fun, they travel for excitement, and they travel to learn. Carolyn acknowledges that it is one thing to hear Vivaldi and it is another to have Vivaldi's Venezia live in you as you hear Vivaldi. Ultimately, whether they travel for business or pleasure, music is never far away.

By the early nineties, Celtic Weavers was a preferred United States showcase for clothing and crafts from Ireland and Scotland. The Industrial Development Board of Northern Ireland was developing a program to help weavers, goldsmiths, and other artisans promote their handcrafts.

Cara Morris in Carolyn's shoes, c. 1978

Two years in a row, they invited Carolyn to present a workshop to young entrepreneurs in County Down in Northern Ireland. She stressed the importance of being confident.

> I told them when you approach a banker for a loan, you don't beg. You tell them, "I'm going to do this. Do you want to be my banker?" You must always keep your word. Don't promise what you can't deliver. And I told them from my own experience that you can come back from financial difficulty.

For twenty-three years, Carolyn sustained a thriving business. Celtic Weavers was a mainstay of the marketplace.

> While selling clothing, I learned things like texture, merchandising, color, how to project what tall or short or fair or dark-skinned customers would buy, foreign exchange of the Irish punt and English pound and Italian lire and German mark and how the dollar exchange and duties affected the price of everything. A fringed garment, for example, had a higher customs rate than an unadorned one.

She can get a grape into my father's mouth from clear across the table.

gifted eye for design, impeccable taste in the finest products

by Cara Morris

Carolyn's role in my life has been profound. My earliest memories are preceded by photographs of Carolyn and me: holding me when I was an infant, playing the guitar at my baptism, taking care as I balanced in her stylish pumps, sharing the piano bench at Christmas; dancing on the edge of the Arboretum. There is not one piece of my life I have not shared with Carolyn.

Carolyn has been a friend and teacher who helped me appreciate life's joys and eased life's pain. She inspired me to learn the Mozart "Sonata in C Major" on the piano and even to compose on my own. It's the only song I still know by heart. When I thought I had lost the love of my life, Carolyn instructed me that "to smile and be happy is the best strategy." She was *so* right.

I have always loved watching Carolyn and Dick love each other, laugh, learn, and work every day. At Lake Mattawa, where Carolyn and I swim across Lake Mattawa together, there are butterfly stroke lessons and sunset rowboat rides over to the "big lake."

At Christmas time when I worked at Celtic Weavers, Carolyn was a tough but inspiring manager with a gifted eye for design and impeccable taste in the finest products from Ireland. Meantime, at home, Carolyn and Farley the dog communicated in a language all their own. Carolyn also has a very special talent. She can get a grape into my father's mouth from clear across the dinner table.

Because Carolyn is all of those things and more, I chose her as my godmother. It bonds you for life with a person who, like a mother, offers unconditional love and support and teaches you to be better. Carolyn has inspired me to be kinder and more forgiving and to have fun every day of my life.

Cara Morris is Carolyn and Richard's goddaughter.

> We tried to make Celtic Weavers a happy place to work and to shop. Dick's story-telling and Aine's Irish wit and common sense were linchpins of our business. We wanted everyone who came to us to have a good time, whether or not they bought anything.

Success, however, did not buffer them from the politics and machinations of the larger business world around them. After Rouse died, his original vision of small individually-owned businesses underwent a transformation. Larger chains moved in and began to squeeze out the smaller businesses. Disney and Warner Brothers had deep pockets. The market management raised rents and reduced services, and there were rumors that management was not properly using tenants' advertising budget and other charges. Richard became active in the merchants association and spearheaded a class action suit against the landlord, demanding to see the merchants association's books, which the landlord, a member, had withheld.

In 1996 their lease expired, and Carolyn and Richard began to think about retirement. Never before had they had trouble renewing a lease, but management refused this time. The Seniers felt it was retaliation for their activity with the merchants association. They had planned to sell their business. Without a lease, Carolyn and Richard knew they would be out of business and have nothing at all to sell. In twenty-three years, they had gone from a pushcart to a thriving business as a main player in Boston's first festival market. So, when the lease was officially terminated, Carolyn and Richard simply refused to move. They continued to pay rent, and management was hesitant to evict them. Business was fine, but Carolyn wasn't sure how much inventory to buy, and she continued under a cloud of worry and concern.

Eventually, management began to settle the lawsuit with individual merchants. A marathon meeting took place. All day, management stressed its trustworthiness. Most of the board of the merchants association was ready to sign off on the suit. It had been four long years. Carolyn listened quietly to the whole discussion and

---

calculated risk came naturally
talent for product selection and display
by Diane Sweet

Carolyn Senier first met with me in Boston concerning her Celtic Weavers retail business. Her physical beauty completely concurred with her inner beauty and strength. I was immediately impressed with Carolyn's lovingly powerful personality.

Her shop was beautifully arranged and the staff seemed so pleasant and happy in the midst of a fairly chaotic business environment. Success seemed to come naturally to Carolyn; calculated risk seemed to be natural to this woman. Carolyn's talent for product selection and display was evident from beginning to end but it was also quite clear that her customers came back because of Carolyn and her influence. What a happy place to shop.

We worked happily together for years but I had mixed feelings when Carolyn decided to change her life style and sell her business. I was glad for Carolyn and her husband to be relieved of the great stress that a retail business can bring but it was clear that our friendship would continue. Selfishly, I was most concerned about that. I had become accustomed to having a bit of this beauty in my life and have been thrilled to continue our friendship.

Diane Sweet represented Nicholas Mosse Pottery to Celtic Weavers.

Dick, c. 1997, president of the Faneuil Hall Merchants Association, welcoming the crowd in many languages

then, toward the end of the day, she spoke up. She said she would not sign off until management agreed to renew her lease. "What are you going to do for me?" she asked. "It's my business. I'm a sole proprietor, a woman. You are unjustly depriving me of my retirement by not allowing me to sell my business. I'm not going to let you do this to me without a fight." She wanted the right to sell her business with a lease that offered fair market rent. She stressed her trustworthiness. Other members of the merchants association supported her. But by seven in the evening, after nine hours, there was no agreement. Carolyn rose and said, "I'm sorry, but my friend and I have tickets for the symphony." Carolyn joined her friend Bonnie Kelly at the symphony that night, but the marketplace was very much on her mind.

The next morning Carolyn met with the landlord's vice president, and to her surprise, he told her they were prepared to offer her the deal she wanted, the right to sell her business with a lease at a reasonable rate. In addition, he promised to help her with the sale of her business. It would all be in writing.

> I asked him what changed his mind. He answered that, after a sleepless night, he realized we all needed more trust and he would trust me.

For her part, Carolyn said she would keep management informed of how their efforts to sell the business proceeded. They would keep Celtic Weavers open and flourishing. "I give you my word," she promised. "If I can't sell it, I'll tell you."

> To give him his due, Paul Latta, the landlord's vice president, kept his promise. He shepherded the sale and instructed management to help us.

After several years of uncertainty, Carolyn sold Celtic Weavers in 1999 to Pat Sullivan. He had run a pushcart at the market for many years and was ready to move on to the larger shop. Carolyn is pleased that the shop flourishes. The new owners report that people often come in asking for Carolyn or Richard.

On a sunny Saint Patrick's Day in 2004, I accompanied the Seniers to Faneuil Hall Marketplace. I had never been to Celtic Weavers when Carolyn and Richard owned it. Whenever I went there in the nineties, I was chaperoning middle school kids on a field trip. I never took time to find their shop, because the kids wanted the food court. But since I was writing this book, I wanted to see where Carolyn had spent twenty-three years, so they took me along.

Although it was cold outside, the inside was warm and vibrant with color. People were shopping and buying souvenirs. Dick excused himself to visit cronies in the South Market. I followed Carolyn into the main hall under the central dome filling with the early lunch crowd. Almost immediately, a diminutive woman looked up from her job sweeping around the tables. "Hello," she said warmly, her accent Haitian. "How are you?" Carolyn briefly introduced us and stopped to converse. It was obvious they had often chatted before and that the woman was glad to have Carolyn back, if only for that short, nostalgic encounter.

We traversed the central market en route to North Market where Carolyn showed me her first two shops. Men moving crates, security people, and other merchants waved to her, some of them stopping to exchange pleasantries, many asking about her new life in the country. We strolled back to South Market and Celtic Weavers where we met Richard. The shop was bustling. Patrick's daughter Tarin was happy to see the Seniers. "People keep asking for you," they said. With the proprietor's permission, Carolyn gave me a bit of a tour. As the shop busied and Tarin was taken up with customers, Carolyn welcomed visitors to the shop, offering assistance and deferentially turning them back to the owner.

Finally the call of lunch was too loud to ignore. We headed over to Durgin Park, an old standby for tourists and a longtime habit for the Seniers. We joined those filling the second floor dining room, a place seemingly always in motion. As we scanned the familiar menus and ordered corned beef and cabbage in honor of the holiday, an animated and stylish young woman approached the table. It was Shana Kelley, the owner. She was not at all what I pictured, but I soon learned she is the granddaughter of the founder. She sat with us for a while during lunch, excusing herself to attend to myriad details.

Sometimes when we leave a job or a home, we feel like a pebble that sinks unknown to the bottom of the lake after the ripples subside. It was obvious to me that Carolyn had made her

---

a shrewd buyer, purveyor of high quality

catching a herring red-handed

by Joseph Moylan

I first met Carolyn Brown at a party at my house in Boston given for one or another of Richard Senier's political associates. Richard told me he had invited a young lady to meet the crowd. I knew that she had been a nun, but my knowledge of nuns was limited to teachers at a Catholic grammar school. I was certainly not prepared for the sight of this beautiful, leggy woman with whom Richard was enthralled. Her quiet, unspoiled manner and striking beauty caught the attention of all the men and the notice of all the women.

Richard did not take long to realize that he could not live without this beautiful, talented woman by his side. Richard and Carolyn were married within a year. Our friendship continued, and we shared Carolyn's triumphs at teaching music in a Newton public school and in business. She became known as a shrewd buyer of fashionable goods in Ireland and a purveyor of high quality goods in Boston.

Another facet of Carolyn's character is a propensity for spouting mixed metaphors. One that stays with me happened when my wife was in the hospital and Richard came with Carolyn for a visit. After having spent the day on Cape Cod at the time when the herring were spawning, Carolyn, still excited from her day, gushed, "Guess what I did today. I caught a herring red handed!" Carolyn grinned. "What had he done?" my wife asked.

I leave the unraveling to you.

Joseph Moylan is a longtime friend of the Seniers.

mark among people who work as well as shop at Faneuil Hall Marketplace. They had not forgotten her. As for Carolyn, she knows what she and Richard created.

> Celtic Weavers grew from an original fifteen hundred dollars worth of hand-woven fabric, through a busy twenty-three years full of good, interesting people and exciting travel to retirement where we reap its benefits in beauty, in a generally simple and occasionally devil-may-care way of life. All the work made the music possible.

The Seniers lived in Roslindale almost from the beginning of their marketplace business. In 1977, the year they opened Celtic Weavers, they moved to Mendum Street, where their house was perfect for parties and guests. Carolyn and Richard had plenty of both. Although it wasn't the best time for them to buy a house, opportunity knocked and they couldn't say no. For years they had admired the Mendum Street home of friends. When the Moylans' neighbors mentioned they were going to sell their house, Joe told them about the Seniers. The woman telephoned

Richard and said, "We think you want to buy our house." Both Carolyn and Richard were not really interested in buying a house—opening a business was enough—but they liked looking at houses. When Richard got off the phone, Carolyn said, "Let's go look."

After fifteen minutes in the house, two doors down from the Moylans', they fell in love with the place. Right then and there, they said yes, shook hands with the owners, and sealed the deal over a glass of sherry. They moved in during a December storm. It took two huge moving vans that held their grand piano, dining room table, and a loom they had acquired but never used.

The Seniers' Mendum Street house, top left, and their backyard: Harvard University's Arnold Arboretum, above

Mendum Street is in a quiet Roslindale neighborhood in Boston, on the north side of Arnold Arboretum. Designed by Frederick Law Olmstead, the Arboretum is nearly three hundred acres of grass and flowering trees and shrubs. In spring, rhododendrons and lilacs bring out strollers and garden enthusiasts. The Seniers' large house sat above the street up thirty-six steps flanked by azaleas, dogwood, heather, and forsythia. On the first floor was a spacious living room, an eat-in kitchen, a dining room, and enough space for the piano. Four bedrooms were on the second floor. One became Carolyn's office. And on the third floor was an apartment with two large rooms and a sleeping alcove. It was a perfect place for them, with room out back in the Arboretum for Carolyn to walk with their dog Farley.

Carolyn loves animals, and it is clear that Farley and she had a special understanding. A golden retriever, Farley watched over her protectively, and many of their friends speak of Carolyn's conversations with the dog. Carolyn enjoyed taking care of Whitney and Shamrock, Pat Morris's dogs, and at Lake Mattawa there is inevitably a neighbor's dog or cat accustomed to Carolyn's attention. Friends have heard her call to birds and have heard the birds respond. No one is surprised that she would like to make a good friend of an otter at Lake Mattawa.

Carolyn with Farley, c. 1988, in a photograph taken by her friend, the Connecticut professional photographer Georgia Breithaupt Sharon

When she and Dick lived on Mendum Street, she insisted one afternoon that a neighborhood cat named Sammy release a bird he had caught. Carolyn helped the small bird, a fledgling woodpecker, and shooed Sammy. She and several neighbors, including Sammy's owner, discussed what she should do with the not-quite-lifeless bird. She placed it with some milk-soaked bread in a clear plastic bird feeder hanging in her garden. The next morning at five, an adult woodpecker made such a commotion it woke Carolyn. She hurried outside to the feeder, and there was the fledgling, hopping up and down. "You made it," she said. Evidently, its mother was watching overhead. Carolyn put Farley indoors and went to Sammy's owner to ask that the cat be kept in for a while. Then, she took the little bird to the Arboretum wall.

> By now, I was talking to the bird. "Come on, Woody," I said. "Let's see if you can fly." The first time, it just arched over the wall and fell into some dry old sticks and leaves. I found it and tried another lift-off from my hand. It went farther and fell into poison ivy a distance away. As I retrieved it, I said, "Look, Woody. You can do it." This time, the bird seemed to anchor itself in my hand. I can feel it standing there digging in, getting its bearings. It wasn't afraid of me any more. At last, it pressed its feet into the palm of my hand and launched itself into the air, high into the tree where I had heard the adult woodpecker.

Carolyn enjoys cooking, and she has the epicure's knack for recognizing the essence of the food she prepares as she improvises and offers wonderful things to eat, c. 1980, right, and c. 1983 with Dick and Michael Morris on Mendum Street, above

Thereafter, for weeks, Sammy made a point of ignoring Carolyn. Then, one night Farley was missing. Sammy showed up outside Carolyn's bedroom window in the middle of the night and made a big racket. She went downstairs, opened the door, and picked him up. In a moment, he wanted to get down and walked away, pausing every few steps to look back at her as if to encourage her to follow. But she didn't. The next day, however, Farley was still missing. She began to search for him and found him over the Arboretum wall, badly injured. She is certain that Sammy was trying to let her know.

Dick and Carolyn made friends with many of their Mendum Street neighbors, including Arthur Robb, a man in his eighties who lived across the street.

> Dick and I often looked in on Arthur after his wife died. He had every tool anyone would ever need for fixing cars, lawnmowers, and sinks. We often shared a cup of tea and a chat. He talked about money and the stock market most of the time, but he also taught me how to plant trees with hay at the bottom of a deep hole, giving it winter warmth. He passed many flowers from his yard to mine over the years.
>
> When he became ill, Dick found a doctor for him, and soon we realized he would not live very long. He moved to a nursing home where we visited him. Dick made soup to bring him, and since he was very fond of our dog Farley, we would take our beautiful shaggy beast to see him. We brought his wheelchair out into the sun. He was bedridden most of the time.
>
> One day I experienced something extraordinary. I went to see Arthur, and he seemed very anxious, talking about money and what legacy he was leaving his distant relatives and what they would think of him.
>
> I went home and looked for something to read to give him comfort. I found a Hebrew prayer book in our library. So this former Catholic sister brought Hebrew prayers to read to her old Congregationalist friend who had abandoned religion. He was still rambling about money. I said, "Arthur. Forget about money. Try to find peace. You're dying." He grew very

quiet. I said, "I'm going to read to you. If you want me to stop, just let me know." I began to read: "The Lord is my Shepherd . . . " Within a moment of listening to the psalm, Arthur's old body found his young heart and became a single, strong voice. I stopped reading as he continued the psalm from memory, his voice growing louder and stronger. Then he recited the words, "Now I lay me down to sleep . . . ," and after that, he uttered all the prayers of his childhood. I witnessed a mysterious reaching in him, some deep wellspring of life opening up in him shortly before he died.

Like her father, Carolyn loves to host large Christmas Eve dinners. Dick admits to disliking Christmas before their marriage, but Carolyn's memories make it a special time for her. Long ago she succeeded at making Richard as much a fan as she is. One Christmas Eve, she and Dick came home late from their shop. They had been so busy they didn't even have the tree up yet. With an exceptionally busy holiday season, there had been no time to trim it. They hadn't been able to get it to stand up, anyway, so they leaned it against a window at its own crooked angle. But sixteen people were coming, so they swept into the house and began to get ready.

Richard and Carolyn got the roast and Yorkshire pudding in the oven. People started to arrive. Abe, the cap maker Carolyn and Dick met during the pushcart days, was there as well as his wife Gladys and old friends, the Moylans, the Morrises and their children, and Jim Morris's sister Kathy and her family. They all had a wonderful time decorating the tree with neckties and earrings.

They were relaxing in the dining room when someone noticed smoke coming from the kitchen. The oven was in flames, and the whole house began to fill with thick black smoke. Someone called the fire department, and within minutes firefighters were dragging hoses up the long front

Peace activist and writer Gary Maceoin, left, was among those who lived in the Seniers' Mendum Street third-floor apartment over the years. With Dick and Carolyn, c. 1986, he animates the kitchen conversation.

At holidays, Carolyn made the most of the Brown party tradition, and she has inveigled Dick into celebrating, too. Christmas is always a time for festivity, and there have been some memorable Halloween parties, with Carolyn entirely in the spirit of the occasion, along with the guests, including her brother Dick, c. 1998, top and the Moylans, c. 1994, above.

stairs past evacuating guests. One visiting child said, "Gee. I thought this would be boring!" After the firefighters had extinguished the flames in the stove, the party continued. The food was cold, and luckily so was the fire, but the friends were ready for a good time. Abe joked that it had been a strange way to light the menorah, a Hanukkah custom they shared with Carolyn and Dick when the holidays were close. The evening took up where it left off. In the spirit of the evening, Carolyn flambéed the plum pudding. When she was leaving, Kathy, who had been a nurse in Vietnam said, "This was the most exciting dinner party I've been to since Vietnam."

The Seniers' kitchen table is and always has been a grand meeting place for neighbors, friends, and relatives. Mendum Street was no exception. They also became famous for their parties. Halloween provided a good excuse, and Carolyn exercised her creativity with costume, appearing outrageously hideous or dressed as the sun or some such. Two weeks after she and Dick returned from Sicily with Pat Moylan and Rosalene, Carolyn dressed her mother in black, with plenty of makeup, strings of beads, a wig, and a large floppy hat, an effective disguise. Pat sat next to Rosalene on the sofa and asked, "So, how do you know the Seniers?"

The house on Mendum Street was perfect for guests. For most of the years Dick and Carolyn lived there, they had someone staying with them, whether it was friends, relatives, or visiting manufacturers and suppliers. Carolyn herself is surprised when she realizes that, until they moved to Lake Mattawa, they almost always had live-in guests, some of whom stayed for as long as six years.

They also kept tabs on each other's large families.

Carolyn's nieces and their families at Lake Mattawa with Dick and Carolyn, c. 2002, above, include, from left, Joan McGrath, Erin McGrath, Carolyn, Amy Lamontagne, Dick, Eileen Lamontagne, Richard McGrath, Caroline McGrath, Lauren McGrath, Claire Lamontagne, Paul Lamontagne, Carla Brown, and Sean McGrath

Our family is so large and we live in so many places that we could lose contact with each other due to varied and busy lives. When my mother died, she left us a note telling us that her greatest wish was that we would always make the effort to take part in family occasions and remain in touch with each other. She said that Dad would feel the same way, too. This is why we have an annual family picnic, usually in August.

Bringing food and drink for an army, we gather and greet each other, catching up on lives and stories. We marvel at growth in the younger generations, noticing their talents and development. We welcome the new babies and remember those who have passed on. The kids swim, bicycle, and play baseball or cards. My brothers and I usually have a horseshoe challenge. Something lights up in us during the competition, and that early childhood joy of being together returns to make the game a happy one . . . even if we lose!

And then, there is music. Kaye's son Emil sometimes brings his Dixieland band; Gloria, Ed's daughter, sings, or his grandson Louis plays his clarinet. Who knows? Every year has been a new surprise. Always, there is music.

Family and friends tune up at one of the Seniers' Mendum Street musical evenings. Carolyn's nephew-in-law Matthew Carrano, Dick on flute, Florence Clark on piano, and Carolyn's niece Kathleen Brown-Carrano with guitar are from left, below

special family gatherings

singing, guitar-playing, an inspiration to many

by Claire Lamontagne

When I was little, Carolyn played the guitar and sang sometmes at our house. Holidays and family gatherings were always special when Carolyn played the piano.

Our family would visit Carolyn when she was a nun at a convent in Ridgefield, Connecticut. Nuns taught me in school, but they were never singing, guitar-playing nuns like my aunt. She musically inspired many people in our family. She let my young son Paul borrow her folk guitar, and he has not put it down since.

My mother, Carolyn's sister Joan, admired a hymn Carolyn wrote called "O, Praise Ye the Lord." As she was dying in 1999, my mother asked Carolyn to play the hymn at her funeral. Carolyn was surprised but quickly said, "I will." I know it must have been difficult for her to keep her composure, but she played the hymn beautifully. Her gift of music for my mother was a comfort to us. I admire how Carolyn carefully listens to people when talking with them. My aunt is truly a talented, intelligent, caring person.

I always enjoyed hearing stories about the lake where she spent the summer with my mother and their siblings. The family liked swimming, boating, and music. I am happy she is now enjoying her life on Lake Mattawa doing the same things.

Claire Lamontagne is Carolyn's niece.

> **more famous than the Pope**
> ## *a cosmetic makeover at Bloomingdale's*
> ### *by Kathleen Brown-Carrano*
>
> When I was very young, my Aunt Carolyn, then Sister Saint Roselyn, conducted a choir in Ridgefield, Connecticut, and I thought she was more famous than the Pope. She wore a habit then, and I assumed she had some special pipeline to God. She gave me my first guitar lessons. Through the years she encouraged me to play by ear. She motivated me to write music.
>
> Carolyn has a whimsical, fun-seeking side. She took four of her nieces on a sailboat ride around Boston Harbor one day and to the Boston Esplanade to hear the Boston Pops. Once, she treated my cousin Claire and me to a fancy lunch at Copley Square while a harpist played in the courtyard and then we had cosmetic makeovers at Bloomingdale's, followed by a rowboat ride.
>
> On a more serious note, when Carolyn's mother, my grandmother, was hospitalized in the 1980s and in a coma for a few weeks, I came up with the idea of recording Carolyn playing her mother's favorite Liszt piano piece. We placed the Walkman headphones on Grandma's head. A few minutes into the recording, I slipped the headphones off and asked Grandma if she wanted to hear more. For the first time, she looked straight at me and clearly nodded, "Yes."
>
> Ever since I can remember, when Carolyn walks into a room, everyone stares at her because she is so beautiful. People who really know her say that her spirit is even more beautiful than her looks.
> *Kathleen Brown-Carrano is Carolyn's niece.*

When they started out in Brookline, Carolyn and Richard had music evenings that continued at Mendum Street. Guests came to dinner, and then everyone ended up around the grand piano with Richard playing from his inexhaustible repertoire and everyone joining in. People stayed so long that Carolyn had to resort to Maire O'Farrell's Irish lament, "Have you no homes to go to?"

Whenever Flo and Sam Turner came to dinner, Flo entertained with her luxurious contralto, singing jazz and gospel tunes. Flo brought her young students to the Seniers' house to play their annual recital on the venerable Brown grand piano. The tradition continues at Lake Mattawa.

Although she composed little or nothing during her years as a shopkeeper, Carolyn continued to explore music. There were seasons' passes to the symphony, outings to New York, and trips to Europe for the opera, concerts, plays, and dance performances. For three or four years in the late 1980s, she studied piano at the Longy School of Music with David Bacon. He incorporated poetry and drama in his teaching of music. In some ways, the lessons were therapy for her. Rheumatoid arthritis had caused her hands to swell, and she needed medication for pain. Her fingers are misshapen by arthritis that makes playing the piano challenging, but she has managed through constant use, exercise, and good medical help to keep her condition under control. Despite physical hindrances, Carolyn maintains her facility at the piano and continues to explore the precincts of composition.

You came down from your throne
and stood at my cottage door.
I was singing all alone in a corner,
and the melody caught your ear.
You came down
and stood at my cottage door.

Masters are many in your hall,
and songs are sung there at all hours.
But the simple carol of this novice
struck at your love.
One plaintive little strain
mingled with the great music of the world,
and with a flower for a prize
you came down
and stopped at my cottage door.

from *Gitanjali*
Rabindranath Tagore, 1913

Carolyn, c. 1996, top; the composer Carolyn Brown Senier, 2004, above and right

Carolyn at Lake Mattawa, 2004

going deeper into existence where stars are undiminished by city lights

creating beautiful music in a secluded Lake Mattawa cove

Carolyn and Richard bought their home on Lake Mattawa in 1984. For years they had traveled west from Boston on Route 2 to visit Carolyn's sister Kaye at her vacation house in West Halifax, Vermont. They often noticed the small lake tucked in close to the highway outside of Orange. It reminded Carolyn of Hitchcock Lake and the summer cottage of her childhood, which her father sold when she was in high school. One day as Carolyn and Richard drove home through Erving, a small town west of Orange, their car broke down. The repairman said it would not be ready until three that afternoon, and when they picked it up, they figured anything they had to do in Boston could wait till the next day. "Let's look at that lake," said Carolyn. It was early autumn. There was a hint of chill in the air, and leaves were just beginning to turn.

As they drove slowly along the road, they saw a man working around his house. Richard pulled the car over. He introduced himself and asked if any houses on the lake were for sale. Leo Bessette was his name, and he proved to be a friend. He pointed to a dirt road that leads to a small beach. There, right next to the beach, was a cottage with a "For Sale" sign. Carolyn looked across a cove much like the one at Hitchcock Lake. They wrote down the name and phone number of the owner and headed back to Boston.

> *Birds wake up and add their melodies in a crescendo like no other music. What better symphony to start the day?*

The following week Carolyn and Richard called a real estate agent and made an appointment. They found the lake is called Mattawa. A closer look at the cottage was enough to tell them it was not for them. It was too small and needed a lot of work. Ever optimistic, Richard saw the next door cottage, a small wooden-framed structure with a big screened-in porch a few feet from the water. Though it was not for sale, Richard urged the real estate agent to contact the owner. Success!

Again Carolyn and Richard made the two-hour trip. This time the October sky was a clear blue, maple trees ringing the lake were bright oranges and reds, and the oaks were a golden yellow in contrast to dark green firs and pines. They walked into the cottage, a simple uninsulated basic summer camp with combined kitchen and living room, two small bedrooms, a bathroom with only a sink and toilet, and a seven-foot screened-in porch that ran the full thirty-two-foot width of the place. They stepped onto the porch. Behind them was the tiny cottage smelling of wet wood and damp rugs. In front, reflecting the greens and gold of autumn, was the blue lake. "We'll think about it," they told the real estate agent, but as they drove away, they looked at each other and decided, "Let's do it!" They pulled over, flagged down the agent, and said, "We'll take it." Rosalene had died the year before, and as the down payment Carolyn used money her mother had left her.

Carolyn likes to say that "mattawa" means "a place where friends meet." Richard Chaisson, a local historian, explains that at the turn of the century—the nineteenth into the twentieth—the lake was called North Pond even though it was in the southern part of Orange. Originally, the lake was part of New Salem and since it was in northern New Salem, was appropriately called North Pond. But when town boundaries shifted around 1830, Orange annexed the area south of the Millers River including North Pond. The name stuck for awhile. Then, a group of lakeside residents had a naming contest to address the misnomer. The winning name was "mattawa," which was thought to be Pocumtuck for "a meeting place." Mr. Chaisson says he has found other translations for the word, but this is the one that seems to please everyone.

Lake Mattawa is a glacial pool fed by North Pond Brook and underground springs. It perches on a divide of two watersheds and can, therefore, flow either north as the continuation of North Pond Brook or south as the middle branch of Swift River. The north end valve is closed, and so the outflow spills over the dam near Carolyn and Dick's home, taking the waters of the lake south to Swift River, on to Quabbin Reservoir, and into the water pipes of Boston residents.

Within a few years, Carolyn and Richard turned the place into a year-round home. David Frye, a local contractor, put on a badly needed roof. Carolyn had him enclose the porch, adding three more feet. With more roofline, he enlarged the bathroom to include a bathtub. Carolyn painted the exposed ceiling and walls yellow, orange, and fuchsia. Over the years she put in gardens, first along the shoreline in front of the porch just like at Hitchcock Lake, and then in back.

The house on Lake Mattawa gave Carolyn the chance to return to the physical outdoor life she lived as a child. Every year she swims as soon as the water is bearable—and sometimes before that. Swimming across the cove and into the lake, taking strong easy strokes in a slow graceful crawl, she has gotten back into form. Her niece Claire worried about her swimming alone and gave her an orange bubble that trails behind her in the water as she enjoys her daily morning excursions. Although Richard does not enjoy swimming or boating, Carolyn notices how much pleasure he gets from the lake. There are eagles to watch for and loons to listen to, and he loves the occasional visit from a neighborhood fisherman who drops off an extra bass for dinner. Of their life at the lake, Dick says

Carolyn and Dick in Lake Como, Italy, c. 1992

> In retirement at Lake Mattawa we have new challenges: creating gardens in less-than-fertile soil, building a music room and filling it with melodies and guests, integrating with the community and contributing to it. Things have always fallen into place without catastrophe. We travel and go to theater, concerts, and operas here and abroad. Our home is still a refuge for oth-

ers as well as ourselves, and we are never, never weary of each other.

In general, life has always been the same, whether we had plenty of money or none, whether we lived in an apartment in Brookline or with Arnold Arboretum as a splendid back yard or at the tranquil waterfront of Lake Mattawa. To be sure, we have had our share of difficulties, though they only brought us closer.

Carolyn's persona blesses my life as it has the lives of all who know and have known her. Unlike most of us, who admit to harboring darker feelings than we care to express, Carolyn finds light everywhere: in the flowers and ferns of her garden; at the sight of the great blue heron and bald eagle who tip their wings as they glide in front of our home; with friends and family, and always, with music.

When I first met Carolyn, I recall hearing bells and seeing flashes of red. No joke! She hardly noticed me. So certain was I that she was not going to be in my future that I actively avoided the inevitable. In fact, according to my doctors, I didn't have much of a future because of a couple of surgeries for a very volatile form of cancer that usually proved fatal. To be frank, I was an angry man.

But, in due course, we had a date, and the discovery phase followed. Both of us had been in religious life, both are pianists and guitarists, and we both loved almost all of music's treasury with few exceptions. I abhorred Elvis, she liked him. We agreed on

"In general," says Dick of his marriage with Carolyn, "life has always been the same, whether we had plenty of money or none, whether we lived in an apartment in Brookline or with Arnold Arboretum as a splendid back yard or at the tranquil waterfront of Lake Mattawa." They are together at the piano, top, c. 1977, and in the backyard of friends in Orange, c. 1998, above.

Chopin, Liszt, Debussy, Ravel, and Streisand. We were both from large Irish families, so some of the rough spots had been worn down. We both loved our mothers. Our fathers were musicians.

I made other discoveries, too. She could beat me at swimming, bowling, softball, tennis, ping-pong, Scrabble, and pinochle. About the only thing I was better in was profanity.

Because Carolyn is possessed of extraordinary grace and constant good humor, I found no outlet for my anger, no reason for it. Although it was hard for me to muster up hope for a future, there had to be a reason for meeting Carolyn. In her angelic way, she made me understand, to accept the gift of each day and the power love brings to face the here and now.

Things move slower when you're in your late thirties than when you're in your early twenties, at least where love and romance are concerned, so it took me a couple of years to realize that I had won the lottery of life. We married on a chilly November morning in the company of a few friends.

I introduced Carolyn to Italy, where I had lived and worked. She *taught* Italy to me. Whenever we have two pennies to rub together, she will tell you, we head for Rome. In our thirty-one years we have traveled extensively: to Ireland, the British Isles, Europe, Australia, and New Zealand, virtually all of Canada and the United States, Mexico, Central and South America.

After twenty-three years of successful business, here we are in retirement. There are travel and days filled with friends as well as the routine of life together. I do the heavy lifting, get the breakfast, fetch the newspapers and mail. Carolyn reigns. I go out to my little office about fifty feet from the house where I pretend to write and solve everyone's problems. She goes to the piano.

In summer, we have cocktails on the dock, watch the great blue herons, ducks, and geese; welcome fishermen; sometimes even have our dinner there. When the weather is inclement, we open the fireplace. I have my martini and often serenade Carolyn as she gets dinner. Just as often, she serenades me with her latest opus.

We live among song titles and punch lines.

We are blessed, as they say, in that we have similar backgrounds, similar tastes, and the same devil-may-care attitude. Anyone who knows us also knows which one is the devil. Charlotte Brontë writes a passage in *Jane Eyre* that captures our relationship:

> **I have now been married ten years. I know what it is to live entirely for and with what I love best on earth. I hold myself supremely blest—blest beyond what language can express; because I am my husband's life as fully as he is mine. I know no weariness of my Edward's society: he knows none of mine, anymore than we each do of the pulsation of the heart that beats in our separate bosoms; consequently we are ever together. To be together is to be at once as free as in solitude, as gay as in company. We talk, I believe, all day long: to talk together is but a more animated and an audible thinking. All my confidence is bestowed on him, all his confidence is devoted to me: we are precisely suited in character—perfect concord is the result.**

A bit Victorian, I know, but an ideal I have always felt was ours. We are different, no question. I see the big picture. Carolyn is good on details. In business she could immediately connect the dots between buying and selling, between product and customer, but she was uncomfortable with banks and landlords. Left to me, Celtic Weavers would have had only red hats, red sweaters, and red scarves. But I had no fear of banks or landlords.

Dick and Carolyn have filled the lake house with friends and music. One evening at Lake Mattawa some years ago, Carolyn announced there was going to be a lunar eclipse. Flo and their

a cherished rough piece of driftwood
fast friends through devotion to music

by Florence Clark

Early in my life my parents instilled in me the importance of recognizing good character in choosing friends. There were always spiritual and moral applications in their teaching. Carolyn exemplifies so much of what I was taught. She is, without a doubt, a virtuous woman.

I have known Carolyn for more than thirty years. We immediately became fast friends through our devotion to music.

Carolyn is (and has been for a number of years) my music mentor. I have in my possession a cherished rough piece of driftwood that is about eight inches long and four inches wide. When I received the package from Carolyn, it was wrapped with colorful paper and tied with beautiful bows. I don't recall the occasion, but as we know with Carolyn, there doesn't have to be any more special occasion than simply celebrating friendship. The piece of wood is finished with a very thin coating of varnish. It is not flat on any part of its surface but fairly smooth on the top with a painted fish of yellow, blue, green, and red. Printed words in black paint are, "Lord, if it's really you, tell me to come to you upon the water. Jesus said, 'Then come!'" This apparently insignificant piece of wood became priceless to me because earlier in our friendship, Carolyn had sung the words to me. Her friend Kathleen Deignan, who gave Carolyn the inscribed driftwood, had set them to music. At a time in my life when I was going through a deeply emotional experience, she comforted me with that song.

Carolyn's music will "come to you" from the depths of her soul. That has been my experience. I trust her. I celebrate her smile, her personality, her charm, her faith, and her creative self.

And her choice of a perfect mate, Richard.

Florence Clark is a singer of gospel music.

---

friend Gary Maceoin were there. When Carolyn realized they weren't going to see the moon from the dock because of trees lining the lake, she got into the rowboat with Farley. Flo was next. Then Gary and Richard, who decided they didn't want to be left behind. Carolyn rowed the four of them out through the cove and onto the middle of the lake. The view was perfect, and the group in the overloaded boat was awash in slowly diminishing moonlight. No one remembers who started, but someone began singing "Shine on Harvest Moon," and soon they were singing all the moon songs they could remember: "Moonlight Becomes You," "Moon Over Miami," "Moonlight Serenade." The repertoire went on and on, their naturally good voices enhanced by the water and the night's silence. Around the lake, lights went off, and people came out onto their docks to listen to the moon serenade.

Sometimes, people paddle their kayaks or canoes to within earshot of Carolyn's piano. One is Arlan Butler of Athol, who explains:

> I love to listen to that lady. Her music is so beautiful. I love to take the kayak out and listen to her play. I've met other people who do, too. Sometimes she'll be composing and

play a couple of bars and be quiet and play a couple of more bars and be quiet for a minute. Or maybe she'll just play classical music for a long time and you can listen. It's peaceful. The music just comes across the water, and it's beautiful.

Then there are crystalline spring mornings, when Carolyn likes to steal onto her dock at an early hour. She says

> If there is a choice of hours for wonder, I'd take the mornings any day. The most precious time is spring or early summer during the mating season of the birds. Their songs are so beautiful and lush. I often slip out to the dock at dawn wrapped in a comforter if it is chilly or damp. No one is around. The world is very quiet. I listen to their singing, starting with the highest pitch of the littlest bird. Gradually and surely, the birds wake up and add their own melodies. Sounds get stronger, and what is so unique is the way they echo over the water and around the cove and build to a crescendo like no other music. What better symphony to start the day? Occasionally one of my friends will join me for these morning mysteries—always with a promise to be absolutely quiet.

I met Carolyn and Richard in 1994 when we all took part in a local musical in New Salem. They were introduced to me as the owners of Celtic Weavers, an upscale shop in Boston that I had never visited. But, as usual, Richard wasn't content until he established some connection. When I said I had graduated from Emmanuel College in Boston in 1960, he gleefully told me that he had been a lecturer in philosophy there from 1959 to 1961. I couldn't believe that I hadn't known him. Emmanuel is a small college. But when I looked in my yearbook, there he was, younger and slimmer—as was I—but Richard no less.

Carolyn, Richard, about thirty area residents, and I had all been commandeered into taking part in the musical by its author Dorothy Johnson. *Yankee Spirits* is a light-hearted spoof of the temperance movement of the late nineteenth century. Some years earlier, Dorothy had written

There can be more or fewer depending on who's traveling or who's busy that day, but the core of the Friday "breakfast club" (with Carolyn's visiting friend Bonnie Kelly, second from right), includes, c. 2001, from left, above, Jack Borden, Carolyn, Dick, Mel Wagner, Lee Howe, Jan Borden, Bonnie, and Doris Abramson. Dorothy Johnson, who no doubt took the picture, is also a mainstay.

energy, imagination to rehearsals, performances
"Why couldn't she write a duet for Richard and herself?"

by Dorothy Johnson

The beautiful Carolyn Brown Senier came to the Common Reader Bookshop for the first time in the summer of 1989. She walked through the shop announcing that her husband would love the store and she'd make sure he came to see it too.

The next afternoon she returned with her husband Richard, who charmed us with stories and erudition, and we've been friends ever since.

In the beginning we all were "store" friends, but gradually we shared cocktail hours and meals with Richard and Carolyn. Then we began to meet for Friday breakfasts, a long-honored tradition. By 1994, after extensive conversation and some hilarity, a number of us decided to do an original show at the 1794 Meetinghouse. It was a temperance melodrama, with Richard playing a genial drunk and Carolyn his long-suffering but steadfast wife. She sang a lovely duet with Martha Dodge about patience and hope in a marriage. Two years later she sang a solo as a greyhound in the Meetinghouse musical *DOGS*.

Andrew Lichtenberg wrote the music for those shows as well as for *Home Movies*, *Friends and Neighbors,* and *Mother Goose Lost.* I knew Carolyn had written music, so when we started work on *Home Movies,* I thought, "Why couldn't she write a duet for Richard and herself?" I gave her the lyrics, we made some changes, and the result was "I'd Give You the Moon." Every time they sang that song you could see couples in the audience move a little closer together.

She brings great energy and imagination to rehearsals and performances. She was music director for three of the five shows and spent hours teaching the songs to the performers with grace, style, and humor. Singing was always a serious business, but when she stood in front of the chorus, finding the opening note on the piano to get them started, even the most insecure soprano and reluctant baritone brought forth music together. She made each person in the chorus feel important.

Carolyn can see the humor in everyday life and in herself. Somehow or other, she is capable of malapropisms that belie her education. It's mostly a phrase turned on its ear like when she talked about being in business and said, "the business was a white elephant around our necks." When she was caught at that one she shrugged her shoulders and grinned as if to say innocently, "I don't know how that happened."

It matters little whether Carolyn is dressed in faded jeans or designer clothes; she is always elegant. Hers is an elegance that comes from within, from her sense of self and her real appreciation of others. I might say she has an elegant generosity of spirit that has been a gift to the Meetinghouse performances and a gift to her many friends.

Dorothy Johnson writes and directs original musicals as fundraisers for the 1794 Meetinghouse.

her first musical, *Small Town Life* in conjunction with composer Steven Schoenberg. She decided to write another, this time with composer Andrew Lichtenberg of Pelham, to celebrate the opening of the 1794 Meetinghouse to public performances. Nearly two hundred years old, the meetinghouse had been closed for years and in the late 1980s was given to the Town of New Salem. The town, in turn, handed it over to a non-profit board formed to refurbish the building and revitalize it as a performing arts center. *Yankee Spirits* was an early performance in the newly renovated building.

---

unconditional love, loyalty, honesty
she listens to you when you speak

by Lee Howe

What's to say about Carolyn? What's *not* to say about Carolyn! On top of her serene beauty, she sings, plays the piano, acts, swims in cold waters, rows a boat, listens to *you* when you speak, comforts you, runs a business with great skill, cooks up a mean meal, advises, directs, is married to a charming rapscallion, and loves and lives life to the fullest. Well, that's not all, but I am already overwhelmed with the possibilities.

The Lake Mattawa Association used to meet for an annual picnic down on Holtshire Road. The food was free (well, almost) and a contest for the best dessert followed. One year, we definitely noticed Carolyn and Dick when they came in. The second year, we sat near them and spoke a few words. On the third year, we had decided to invite them over for dinner. They beat us to it. So began a long and thrilling relationship. We couldn't get enough of their company. And still can't.

One year, Dick, Carolyn, my late husband John, and I made an unforgettable trip to Italy together. It was unstructured and casual. We walked around and found many hidden restaurants through Dick's fluent Italian. Everyone loved such a beautiful couple. Carolyn is tall and elegant and always smiling. Once she and I went into an earring shop and, separately, looked around. When we checked out, we had bought four pairs of earrings—two for her and two for me—that were identical except for color. My orange ones are still my favorites.

We learned all the good things from Carolyn, things like unconditional love, loyalty, honesty, simplicity, and modesty.

Lee Howe is a longtime Mattawa friend of the Seniers.

Carolyn and Dick had met Dorothy and her partner Doris Abramson a year earlier. Carolyn's good friends, Lee and John Howe, also summer residents at Lake Mattawa, pointed them to Dorothy and Doris's bookstore, Common Reader, on New Salem Common across from the Meetinghouse. The Seniers were overjoyed to find a bookstore so near with an eclectic, interesting mix of titles as well as two well-read, interesting shop owners. It wasn't long before Dorothy recruited them. She immediately wrote parts into the musical for them. Richard played a drunken piano player, and Carolyn played his wife. I was a silly temperance leader whose hat kept slipping to one side. We all enjoyed ourselves in *Yankee Spirits*.

In 2001, the Seniers sold their home in Boston and contracted with my husband, Tony Palmieri, to put an addition on their Lake Mattawa house. It serves as a parlor and music room complete with two pianos, two guitars, two keyboards, five flutes, and a balalaika. The signature feature is a large stained glass window greeting visitors as they walk through the archway from the old part of the house to the new. We all had great fun watching the addition develop—even Tony who did the hard work. He had never had such a beautiful setting for a project—shade to protect him from the summer sun, a broad picnic table by the shore for lunch, and the cool, clean water of Lake Mattawa for an end-of-the-day swim. I was happy to make any excuse to join them.

Getting to know Carolyn has been a musical adventure for me. I am a singing wannabee. If there is one thing I might sell my soul for, it would be to have a voice like Kiri Te Kanawa or Victoria de los Angeles and a life at the New York Metropolitan Opera. Except for high school chorus and a short attempt at playing the guitar in the 60s, I have no musical training. Carolyn has let me into that world—at least as far as my capabilities can bring me. When she directed the chorus for *Home Movies* and *Friends and Neighbors*, I kept telling Tony that I couldn't believe how good we were sounding. I didn't realize then the wealth of training and talent that Carolyn was bringing to the job of directing us. Andy Lichtenberg's music is wonderfully complex, and Carolyn helped us sing it just right.

She has also been very generous in sharing the process of composing central to this book. One summer morning, I canoed to Carolyn's house from a cottage Tony and I rented on Lake Mattawa. She asked if I would like to hear the latest version of "De Profundis." On the piano stand was her music with what looked like two notes on each page. With that in front of her, she sang and played first one part, then another, explaining where a voice comes in or themes interact. She has helped me listen as I have never listened before.

I love going to a musical performance with Carolyn. She is so attentive. I can tell she is hearing richly, picking out harmonies and shading. No doubt she hears inadequacies lost to me, but she is always easy on the performers. And she will invariably remind me about how beautiful some section was. "Dah, dah, te, dah," she vocalizes, and I nod, mystified.

The music room addition opened new opportunities for Carolyn and Richard to give parties. The kitchen that had been cluttered with more furniture than it was made for became open and functional with a specially-designed counter brought from their Boston house. Carolyn and I have spent quite a few evenings cooking and trying out new recipes on that counter. A while ago, Richard found out how much Tony and I love to cook and eat Italian food. He gave us a subscription to a magazine called *La Cucina Italiana*. Then he suggested we choose recipes from the current issue for an evening of eating. As it turns out, Carolyn and I do most of the cooking while Richard entertains us on the piano and Tony does the chopping. Carolyn and I look over recipes, decide on the menu, and divide up the shopping: "You get the garlic, I have plenty of Parmesan cheese." We snack on pâté and Richard's homemade bread while Caroiyn and I make fresh pasta or ravioli stuffed with goat cheese and the lamb loin or the pork roast cooks in the oven. Tony stirs the berry sauce or chops vegetables for the salad. We drink our share of wine and leave a terrible mess in the kitchen—perfect evenings.

The new room has become the scene of musical evenings. Once, Richard collected lyrics for dozens of songs and copied them for about fifty guests. After eating a delectable meal, we all

a musical moment we will never forget
a friendship leading to many special evenings

by Buck Williams

Our lives have been notably enriched since we decided to restore a small farmhouse in New Salem, Massachusetts. This fortuitous decision brought us, unknowingly, into the wonderful cultural environment of this community. We soon became involved in this activity by exposure to the 1794 Meetinghouse and the many musical productions that are held there each summer. This would, of course, include Quabbin Valley Pro Musica and the bi-annual Dorothy Johnson musicals.

We first met Carolyn and Richard Senier through our daughter and grandson who were involved in the Meetinghouse musicals. On many occasions, Carolyn was most helpful to Jane and Dylan in preparing for their singing parts in these and other musicals where Dylan has been performing since he was six years old.

In one of these musicals Carolyn and Richard played Dylan's grandparents. Carolyn wrote the music for these parts. It was an entertaining and successful evening, and we sincerely enjoyed the loving way Carolyn and Richard portrayed our part in Dylan's life. This was the beginning of a cherished friendship with two very talented people.

Our involvement with the musicals and our interest in the recreation provided by Lake Mattawa soon introduced us to the full extent of Carolyn and Richard Senier's musical talents. This has become a most enlightening and rewarding experience for us. We have become "fast friends." This friendship has led to many special evenings filled with the beautiful music and the enchantment of the combined talents of these two talented people.

I have never met anyone so spiritually charming as Carolyn Senier. She is a beautiful woman in every sense of the word. Her charm affects everyone who is lucky enough to come into her space. While always angelic, she can be lighthearted, humorous, sincere, and / or inspiring as befits the occasion. This spirituality is reflected in the exquisite music she has written and shared with us.

We will never forget our first dinner as guests of the Seniers, in their lovely home on Lake Mattawa. This evening, and all subsequent enchanting evenings there, was largely spent around the grand piano. Their music room features a grand piano framed in a large window overlooking Lake Mattawa, Fortunately we were there as the sun was setting on the lake. It was a perfect setting. I asked Carolyn to play *"Claire de Lune."* It was a musical moment we will never forget. Her consummate playing of this wonderful masterpiece spellbound us. Both Dorothy and I were overcome with emotion as we were so delightfully entertained.

The driving talent in Carolyn's personality compels her to compose beautiful music whether it is for public enjoyment or to be shared only with her friends on a moonlit night on Lake Mattawa.

Buck Williams is a retired Philadelphia contractor who summers with his wife Dorothy in New Salem.

Dick and Carolyn and their friends Tony and Mary-Ann Palmieri (who wrote this profile) share frequent musical and theatrical outings as well as cooking evenings at each other's homes. Mary-Ann, left, and Carolyn present the secondo, *above.*

scrunched ourselves into the piano room and sang for hours. A friend of mine who happened to be canoeing on the lake later told me the house seemed to be vibrating.

Carolyn loves the adventures that come to them on Lake Mattawa and in the surrounding countryside, and somewhat surprisingly—although it is certain he would be happy wherever Carolyn is—so does Dick.

>I thought I married a "city kid" from Boston until we found Lake Mattawa. At Mendum Street, I'd drag Dick out to walk in the snow in the Arboretum. He was reluctant, but he always came with me. I was therefore totally surprised to discover Dick's longing to get back to the cottage each summer. Around about December, I would begin to detect comments or insinuations such as, "In about four months, we'll open up the cottage." Then in February, I'd hear, "I called Dave Frye to see how early we could safely turn on the water at the lake." Or in March, "Just think. In less than a month, we'll be able to spend more time there." Longings I never knew he had were longings that matched my own, and they eventually transformed into selling our Boston home and moving to Mattawa year round.
>
>We absolutely love the natural environment and the people. The 1794 Meetinghouse in New Salem expands relationships and creativity for us. Talent is not lacking in the hills and quiet roads that lead there.
>
>I feel we go deeper into our existence by living here where we see the stars undiminished by city lights. Standing on the dock at midnight, we look at them before a last swim or in winter across a tundra-like expanse of frozen water.

> It is one thing to know that turtles swim and great blue herons and bald eagles fly, but seeing them swim and fly daily is quite another. It is one thing to buy apples for a pie or fresh corn for a picnic, but to go for rides through the orchards and cornfields minutes from our home magnifies and nourishes our sense of awe. Dick and I love long rides in the valley, stopping frequently for local produce and chatting. If you've always lived here, you know what we have begun to learn, that here at Lake Mattawa and its surroundings is a place on this planet filled with beauty, simplicity, music, books, good neighbors, and down home wisdom. I cannot help noticing how it fosters a generous spirit of sharing one's gifts in a spirit of community. We have been here part time for nearly twenty years and full time residents for only three, yet we know we are home surrounded by things we love.

During the summer of 2003, Carolyn and Richard hosted a summer barbeque. Old friends from Boston as well as newer friends from western Massachusetts came. Like her father at Christmas Eve parties, Carolyn made trays of pasta and sausages. One of the guests arrived in his small plane at Orange Municipal Airport and as he flew home, dipped his wings over the lake. The lake is full of such moments. When I ask her, she tells me she doesn't miss the city.

Living on Lake Mattawa has brought many blessings to Carolyn. Among them has been her return to composing music after more than twenty years. "I thought I had no more to say musically," she says, wistfully. For all those years she was a busy, productive businesswoman, music was a major part of her life—listening, singing, and playing. But with retirement on the lake, she has returned to that earlier passion, composing.

In 1997, we were all in a new Dorothy Johnson-Andrew Lichtenberg production: *Dogs, A Musical*. Carolyn played a sophisticated greyhound. I was a Dalmatian. Then two years later, Dorothy created another musical, *Home Movies*. By then, Dorothy knew that Carolyn had composed music, taught music, and led choruses. She asked Carolyn to direct the chorus and also to write music for a duet for herself and Dick. Carolyn was not at all sure she could do it, but there had been a melody floating around in her head, so she gave it a try. The result was "I'd Give You the Moon," a departure from anything she had written. She found the old joy in composing again. It was a show stopper every time.

Writing "I'd Give You the Moon" seemed to open floodgates. Carolyn looked over unfinished music from the past or scraps scribbled hurriedly. Since the fall of 2001, she has sung with Quabbin Valley Pro Musica, a local chorus directed by Geoffrey Hudson and sponsored by 1794 Meetinghouse. Geoff mentioned he had heard she was writing music. She asked him to look over some things to see if they were worth pursuing. During the summer of 2002, Geoff and Carolyn got together, and he encouraged her. He especially liked what she was doing with her choral setting of Psalm 138 / 139, "Oh, Lord, you have probed me and you know me." In January, 2003, on a snowy Superbowl Sunday, Pro Musica sang it in a crowded Unitarian Church on the Petersham Common. Carolyn was thrilled to hear her music sung again.

Just before that concert, she began work on "Song of Abraham" in memory of Abe Barron, her friend the cap maker, who died on January 1, 2003. She started with the Hebrew prayer Abe taught her for celebrating the Passover Seder. She asked Abe's cantor on Cape Cod to help with the text because she wanted to include Hebrew as well as English. She had already finished work on another piece she called "De Profundis," dedicated to North Quabbin Women in Black,

Directed by Geoffrey Hudson, The Lake Mattawa Singers and musicians from New York's Mark Morris Dance Company rehearse for the June 5, 2004, premiere of Carolyn's "Song of Abraham," written in honor of Abe Barron, the capmaker. The music was performed to a sell-out crowd in the 1794 Meetinghouse.

a group of local women and men who gather silently in a weekly peace vigil observed since October 27, 2001. Throughout 2003, she composed new works, including the large and soaring "In Praise of Names," the delicate and dissonant "Summer Days," and her love song for Dick, "When I Knew." "Song of Abraham" premiered under the baton of Geoffrey Hudson at the 1794 Meetinghouse with the Lake Mattawa Singers and musicians from the Mark Morris Dance Company of New York on June 5, 2004. "De Profundis" premiered with Quabbin Valley Pro Musica under Hudson's direction on June 27, 2004. A compact disc of music from *The Mattawa Song Cycle* was released in August 2004.

Living at Lake Mattawa has given Carolyn time, inspiration, and the peace she has sought for so long. Like her years as a CND and her stint as the owner of Celtic Weavers, time on the lake has been—and still is—critical. Nurtured and encouraged by husband and friends, she has rediscovered her music. It spills from her fingers.

In some ways it's not very far from Hitchcock Lake to Lake Mattawa. Mature, creative, and industrious, Carolyn Brown Senier has come full circle back to the lake and the music.

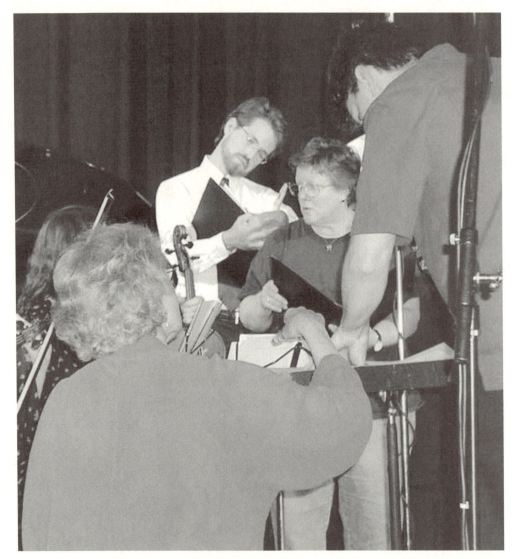

Carolyn Brown Senier, left, 2004, conferring with Geoffrey Hudson, conductor, during a rehearsal for the premiere of her Song of Abraham *in the 1794 Meetinghouse, New Salem, Massachusetts. Matthew Behnke and Lynn Dudley of the Lake Mattawa Singers look over their music or chat with instrumentalists.*

a manuscript page from Carolyn's De Profundis, *2003*

Ancient Song, Modern Harmony
music by Carolyn Brown Senier

Geoffrey Hudson, composer, conductor, and editor of music

an essay from the music editor
sing it bold and strong

by Geoffrey Hudson

"Sing it bold and strong." The climactic words from Carolyn Brown Senier's "De Profundis" could serve as a motto for her work as a composer. But while the chorus in the De Profundis sings "bold and strong" at top volume, almost as a musical shout, Carolyn's boldness and strength are more likely to be evidenced by a seamless pianissimo, or a unison melody. Carolyn's voice as a composer is bold and strong. Sure in that strength, she has no need to shout.

Carolyn's music is economical. The materials she uses are not extravagant; there are few big gestures that draw attention to themselves. With familiar musical ingredients, she builds pieces that combine simplicity and surprise. Carolyn's music accomplishes the difficult feat of making the listener feel sure of where the music is going, even if it doesn't actually go there. With a subtle harmonic twist, Carolyn redirects a phrase and leads the listener somewhere deliciously new.

Carolyn's music is lyrical. Her writing is wonderfully suited to the voice. The phrase lengths fit easily to the breath; the strength of her melodies helps carry the singers. She occasionally makes surprising demands on the voice: a leap that looks awkward on paper, a sustained quiet phrase in the basses' upper range, an unusual voicing of a chord. But when those ideas come off the page and are put into practice, they invariably spring to life. What had seemed at first glance odd or ungainly proves to be perfectly natural in context.

> *With a subtle harmonic twist, Carolyn redirects a phrase and leads the listener somewhere deliciously new.*

In conjunction with the release of this book, I had the privilege of assembling and directing a small vocal group, the Lake Mattawa Singers, to record seven of the pieces in this collection. When rehearsals began, most of the singers had never heard or sung any of Carolyn's music. After our first week of rehearsals, one of the altos approached me during a break. "I love singing this music," she said. "It lets me use my whole voice." Carolyn knows the full range of the human voice—soft and loud, full and frail, high and low—and brings all of it into play.

Carolyn's music is expressive. It has a radiance and urgency to communicate. Carolyn doesn't merely set words to music, she uses music to bring them to life. Perhaps this intensity of expression is a product of the tension between the economy and lyricism of her musical voice. The former eliminates all wasted gestures, while the latter infuses each phrase with beauty. The result is a music in which every nuance supports the entirety. Carolyn's music doesn't sound like a pale reflection of someone else's musical language. It's all her own.

The collection of music in front of you represents a lifetime of work. It is the work of an active church musician, composing pieces that can be rehearsed quickly and used in services. It is the introspective and personal work of a composer writing for herself alone, bringing to life the voice she hears inside. It is the work of a community member, writing songs for her friends and neighbors to sing in local theatricals. As you look through this book, you will find music for many occasions, for many different kinds of performing groups. Hymns, popular songs, anthems for solo voices, and larger works calling for chorus, soloists, and instruments. Pick a piece that catches your eye. Play it through on the piano. If you can, gather a small group of voices around you. Let the music leap off the page.

Geoffrey Hudson, above, with pianist Gretchen Saathoff at a recording session for The Mattawa Song Cycle compact disc featuring seven songs by Carolyn Brown Senier; The Lake Mattawa Singers, top on the facing page, including from left, front, William "Britt" Albritton, Lynn Boudreau, Adam Bergeron, and Brian Stoessel; back, Lynn Dudley, Sarah Metcalf, Sarah Clay, Paul J. Helmuth, Judy Wardlaw, Matthew Behnke, and Elizabeth Chilton; sound engineer Richard Chase of Pleasant Sound is at bottom.

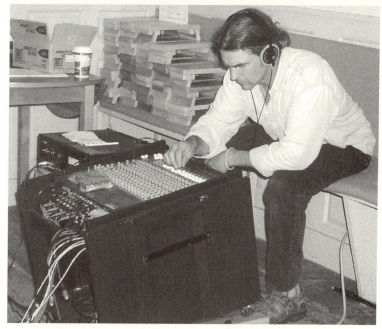

From dawn till dusk
I sit here before my door,
and I know that of a sudden
the happy moment will arrive . . .
In the meanwhile I smile and I sing . . .
In the meanwhile the air is filling
with the perfume of promise. . . .

Many a song have I sung
in many a mood of mind . . .

from *Gitanjali*
Rabindranath Tagore, 1913

The Mattawa Song Cycle

music composed and compiled at Lake Mattawa

by Carolyn Brown Senier

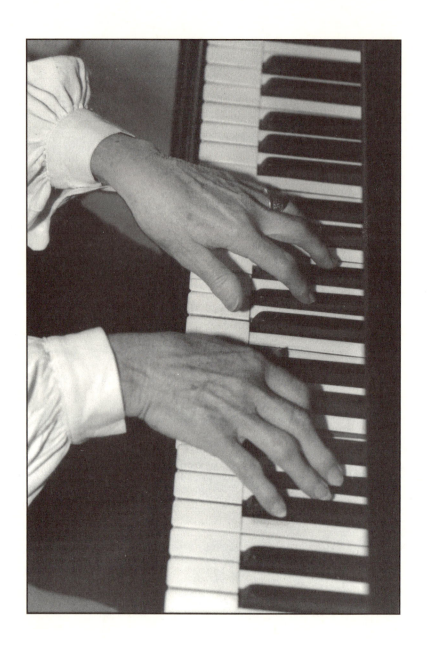

songs for concert
preceded by annotations by Carolyn Brown Senier

De Profundis (2002) • SATB 140

In Praise of Names (2004) • SATB 163

Song of Abraham (2003) • SATB 218

Thou Makest the Winds Thy Messengers (1965) 244
    Thou Makest the Winds Thy Messengers • SSAATB 245
    Thou Makest the Winds Thy Messengers • SSA 251
    Thou Makest the Winds Thy Messengers • trumpets in B-flat 257

You Know Me (1966, 2002) • SATB 258

Four Songs for a Woman of Galilee 273
    Pageant Song (1953) • SA 276
    Respice Stellam (1962) • SSATB 281
    Hail, Mary (1964) • unison or solo 291
    Assumpta Est Maria (1954) • SATB 294

Love Songs 298
    I'd Give You the Moon (1999) • duet 300
    Listen to Your Heart (2001) • trio 304
    Summer Days (2003) • SATB 312
    When I Knew (1996) • SATB 317

Carolyn Brown Senier's lyrics are her own poetry, often combined with portions of scripture. Sometimes she uses other sources. Carolyn cites scriptural references in a traditional language—Latin, for instance. Translations are provided from other languages into English. Carolyn combines layers of scripture with layers of music to expand thought and harmony. In keeping with the style conventions observed in the rest of this book, pronouns referring to God are generally not capitalized, although in deference to the composer, the word "He" is capitalized in the "Creed," a part of her *Mass in Honor of Marguerite Bourgeoys.* Earlier songs employ the universal masculine to refer to people whether male or female. In later songs, the composer uses gender-neutral language. When appropriate, psalms are referred to by two numbers separated by a forward slash: Psalm 103 / 104. The first number locates the psalm in sequence according to ordering in Douay-Rheims and related pre-Vatican II Roman Catholic translations. The second number locates the psalm in sequence according to ordering in Hebrew, Protestant, and post-Vatican II Roman Catholic translations, although some psalms bear the same number regardless of translation.

De Profundis

Dedicated to North Quabbin Women in Black
adapted from Psalm 129/130
words by Carolyn Brown Senier

De profundis clamavi ad te Domine
Domine, exaudi vocem meam
De profundis clamavi ad te Domine
Domine, exaudi vocem meam
Let the winds be still
Let the waves be calm
Domine, exaudi vocem meam
Let the world be warmed by the silent sun
  melting our cold nights away
    Domine—
Exaudi vocem meam
  (De profundis clamavi ad te Domine)
Let our children in ev'ry land know they are free to play
De profundis clamavi ad te Domine
De profundis clamavi ad te Domine
Domine, exaudi vocem meam

Let the storm winds be still
Let the waves be calm
Exaudi vocem meam
Let our children know they are free to play
  (De profundis)
Clamavi ad te Domine
Domine exaudi vocem meam
From the depths we rise rejoicing
Join the waiting world
Give voice to heaven's song
Sing the cry, "Destroy all poisons"
Sing it bold and strong
Now greet the dawn
And stand in silent wonder
And in this stillness
Listen for its quiet psalm
Domine exaudi vocem meam

Translation of Latin words
De profundis clamavi ad te Domine.
Domine, exaudi vocem meam.
From the depths I cry to you, O Lord.
Lord, hear my voice.

Ancient Latin words, "De profundis clamavi ad te, Domine" (Out of the depths I cry to you, O Lord) stirred creativity and combined with sound to join modern meaning. Everywhere during the period just before the Iraq war, I could hear people describing their feelings of being overcome, of being in a storm, of drowning in dark moments of anxiety and worry, of being engulfed by huge waves of terror, of fear for the future and for all children in a broken world. Moved by such reflection, particularly those of Lynn Boudreau, one of the Women in Black, I wrote this music. I hope that it reflects the depths of their silent standing for peace and carries their message through music to other hearts.

"De Profundis" is replete with chromatic melodies: that is, on the words "de profundis," the second syllable "fun-" moves from a B-flat to C-flat back to B-flat, followed by its melodic twin on the word "clamavi." On the syllable "ma-" from B-flat to C-flat to B-flat and its counter answer, "ad te Domine," D-flat, C, C-flat, B-flat, a descending chromatic musical line.

Throughout the entire composition, there is a rising and falling chromatic feeling until the final two measures of "vocem meam," "my voice": E-flat, F-flat, G-flat, G-flat, G-flat, F-flat, E-flat.

De Profundis

dedicated to the North Quabbin Women in Black
for SATB Chorus and Piano

From Psalm 129

Words and Music by
Carolyn Brown Senier

Music © 2002 and © 2005 by Carolyn Brown Senier.
Copyright includes words by Carolyn Brown Senier.

Additional copies are available from Haley's • P O Box 248 • Athol, MA 01331
800.215.8805   haley.antique@verizon.net

In Praise of Names
words by Carolyn Brown Senier

Gaudeamus
Te Deum
Laudamus
Magnificat

We praise those
Who bless our days
Who bless our world
Since dawn began

We praise the ones we know
Who fashioned our dreams
   each hope and plan

We praise every name
We've known
And bind our hearts now
With ancient song

Magnificat anima mea Dominum
(Magnificat anima mea Dominum)
   (Magnificat anima mea Dominum)
   (Magnificat anima mea Dominum)

We now journey through the night
   (Magnificat . . .)
While searching for you in mem'ry's light
The dawn wakens life once more
   (Magnificat, magnificat . . .)
While gathering mem'ries at your door
   (. . . anima mea Dominum)
   (Te Deum laudamus)

The day star
   (Gaudeamus)
Now guides our way
   (Gaudeamus)
Reminding our world
Of you today
   (Gaudeamus, gaudeamus)
   (Laudamus)

We still walk
   (Gaudeamus)
   (Magnificat . . .)
The earth as one
   (Gaudeamus)
While praising your names
   (. . . anima mea . . .)
   (Gaudeamus)
   (Gaudeamus, gaudeamus, gaudeamus)
In day's full sun
   (. . . Dominum)

If ever
   (Laudamus)
Our hearts forget
   (Laudamus)
To speak your name
To speak your name
Your name

We fill the air
   (fill the air)
With your names
To praise

Mothers
Fathers
Sisters
And brothers

Katherine, Roselyn
   (Laudamus, laudamus)
Joan, Tricia
   (Laudamus, gaudeamus)
Edward, Robert
   (Laudamus, laudamus)
Donald, Richard
   (Laudamus, gaudeamus)
Gaudeamus

Speak your names in praise!

(name)
(Laudamus, laudamus)
(name), (name)
(Laudamus, gaudeamus)
(name), (name)
(Laudamus, laudamus)
(name), (name)
(Laudamus, gaudeamus)
Gaudeamus

And now open mem'ries wide
   (Laudamus)
And carry love to names inside
   (Laudamus)
   (Gaudeamus)

Your names we now recall
   (Gaudeamus, gaudeamus)
   (Laudamus)
And honor your lives
Embracing all
We praise ev'ry name we've known
And strengthen our bonds
With praises' song
Gaudeamus

Translation of Latin words
Gaudeamus
We rejoice
Te Deum laudamus
We praise you God
Magnificat anima mea Dominum
My soul magnifies the Lord

While I was reviewing photograph albums for *The Mattawa Song Cycle,* your faces appeared here, showed up there, and nudged a million memories. In a nearly spring March day, love cradled my existence and since then, you have been part of it in one way or another. This composition is my testimonial to all of you, to those whom I remember and to those, sadly, whom I may have forgotten. The opening words are great praises from the body of liturgical chant, and their meaning and melody are its developmental milieu:

   Gaudeamus - We rejoice.   *Te Deum* - We praise God.
   Magnificat - My soul magnifies the Lord.   *Laudamus* - We praise.

With these ancient words surrounding us, the music praises your names. In its opening phrases, the music draws on the spirit of the "Gaudeamus" and "Te Deum" chants found in the *Liber Usualis* and combines with a "Magnificat." Just before the final chorale, you are invited to enter the music and join the names of those you know to this song of praise. Don't be shy about it!

In Praise of Names

for Double Chorus, Soloists (SAAB), and Piano

Words and Music by
Carolyn Brown Senier

Music © 2005 by Carolyn Brown Senier.
Words © 2005 by Carolyn Brown Senier.

Additional copies are available from Haley's • P O Box 248 • Athol, MA 01331
800.215.8805   haley.antique@verizon.net

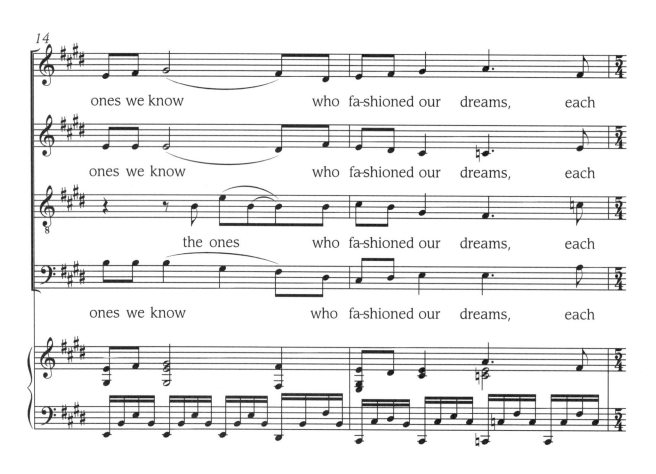

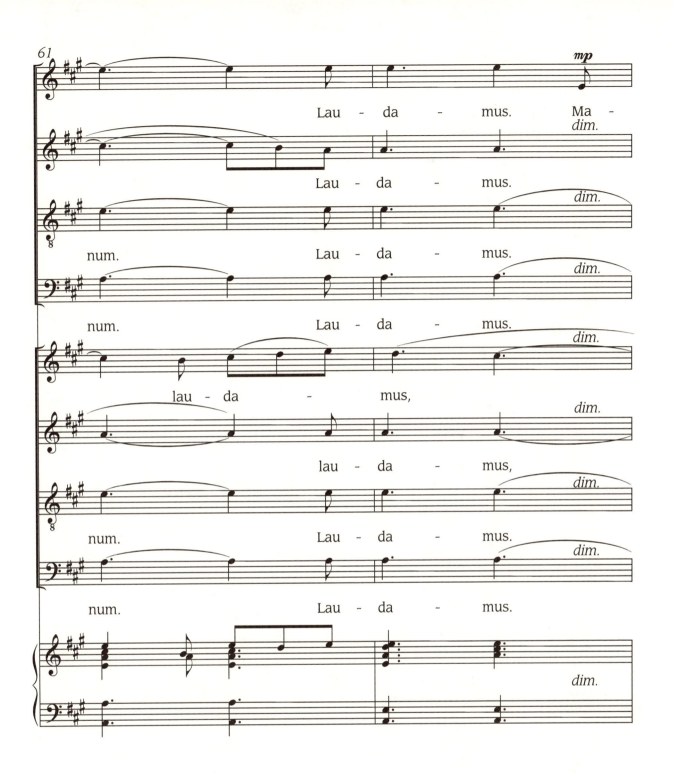

181

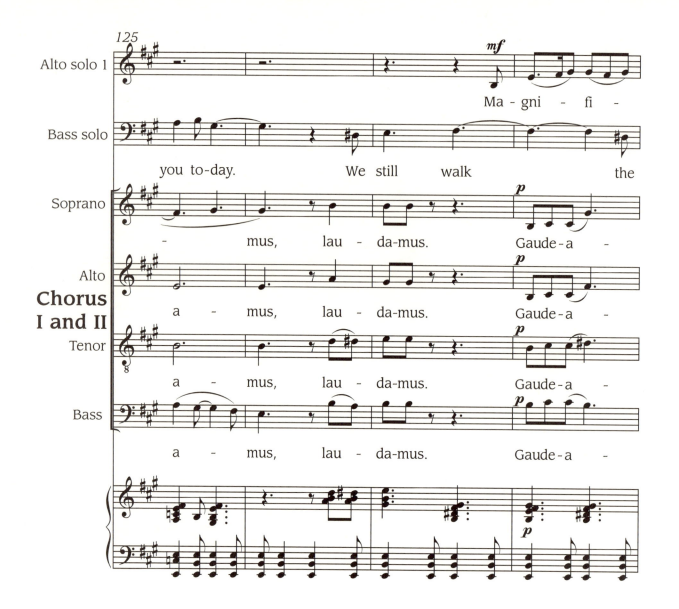

Song of Abraham
adapted from Hebrew blessings
words by Carolyn Brown Senier

*You gave us life
sustained us and
brought us to this day*

*You gave us life
sustained us and
brought us to this day*

*Baruch atah Adonai
Baruch atah Adonai
Eloheinu melech haolam
    shehechianu v'kiymanu
Baruch atah Adonai
    v'higianu lazman hazeh
Baruch atah Adonai
Eloheinu melech haolam*

*You have this one in the universe
    This one in the universe*

*You have this one in the universe
    This one in the universe*

*Baruch atah Adonai
Baruch atah Adonai
Eloheinu melech haolam
    shehechianu v'kiymanu
Baruch atah Adonai
    v'higianu lazman hazeh
Baruch atah Adonai
Eloheinu melech haolam*

*You gave us life
sustained us and
brought us to this day
(You gave us life and
brought us to this day)
(You gave us life
You have this one this one)
(You have this one)
(You gave us life)*

*(This one, you have this one
    in the universe)*

*Baruch atah Adonai
Eloheinu melech haolam shekachalo
baolamo
Baruch atah Adonai*

*Eloheinu melech haolam
(Baruch atah Adonai
Eloheinu melech haolam)
(Baruch atah Adonai
Eloheinu melech haolam)
(Baruch atah Adonai
Eloheinu melech haolam)
Baruch atah Adonai
Baruch atah Adonai
Eloheinu melech haolam
Shenatan meichochmato l'vasar vadam
Shenatan meichochmato l'vasar
vadam Adonai*

*Eloheinu melech haolam
You have given such knowledge and
wisdom to this one
Baruch atah Adonai
Eloheinu melech haolam
Baruch atah Adonai
Eloheinu melech haolam
(You gave us life sustained us and
brought us to this day)
(You have this one in the universe
this one in the universe)
Baruch atah Adonai
Eloheinu melech haolam
(You have this one in the universe)
(You gave us life sustained us and
brought us to this day)
Shekachalo baolamo
(This one in the universe)
Baruch atah Adonai
Eloheinu melech haolam
(Baruch atah Adonai
Eloheinu melech haolam)
(Baruch atah Adonai
Eloheinu melech haolam)
(Baruch atah Adonai Eloheinu
melech haolam)*

*You have this one in the universe
    (You have this one)
    You have this one*

    This song honors my friend Abe Barron, a gift to my life for twenty-seven years. He was a man of deep faith, of wisdom, and of love. After he died in the winter of 2003, his wife Gladys told me how important it was for Abe to let me know he loved me. His great heart enveloped so many of us, above all, Gladys, his children, his niece Amy, and his Irish family, including my husband, Richard and me. I know I have been loved by a special pilgrim in my life's journey. I wrote this music in his memory using the prayers he taught me, recalling his love of knowledge and learning and in gratitude for having such a one exist among us during his long, yet too short, life. The music seems to be in both the Phrygian and Hypodorian modes but also uses chromatic harmony in contrast to the mode and moves toward the major key of G. Counterpoint is an important musical component as the composition develops. The words "Baruch atah Adonai Eloheinu melech haolam" provide musical and spiritual foundations for all the counterpoints symbolic of Abe's life, the life sustained, as he would say, by the Eternal One.

Abraham Barron
1917-2003

בָּרוּךְ אַתָּה יְיָ אֱלֹהֵינוּ מֶלֶךְ הָעוֹלָם, שֶׁהֶחֱיָנוּ וְקִיְּמָנוּ וְהִגִּיעָנוּ לַזְּמַן הַזֶּה.

בָּרוּךְ אַתָּה יְיָ אֱלֹהֵינוּ מֶלֶךְ הָעוֹלָם, שֶׁנָּתַן מֵחָכְמָתוֹ לְבָשָׂר וָדָם.

בָּרוּךְ אַתָּה יְיָ אֱלֹהֵינוּ מֶלֶךְ הָעוֹלָם, שֶׁכָּכָה לוֹ בְּעוֹלָמוֹ.

Translation of Hebrew words
Baruch atah Adonai Eloheinu melech haolam shehechianu
v'kiymanu v'higianu lazman hazeh

Blessed are you, Adonai, our God, King of the universe, who has kept us alive, sustained us, and brought us to this day.

Baruch atah Adonai Eloheinu Melech haolam
shekachalo baolam

Blessed are you, Adonai, our God, King of the universe, who has this in his universe.

Baruch atah Adonai Eloheinu Melech haolam
shenatan meichochmato l'vasar vadam

Blessed are you, Adonai, our God, King of the universe, who who has given of his knowledge to flesh and blood.

Song of Abraham
in memory of Abraham Barron
for SATB Chorus and Piano

Words and Music by
Carolyn Brown Senier

Music © 2003 and © 2005 by Carolyn Brown Senier.
Copyright includes adapted words by Carolyn Brown Senier.

Additional copies are available from Haley's • P O Box 248 • Athol, MA 01331
800.215.8805   haley.antique@verizon.net

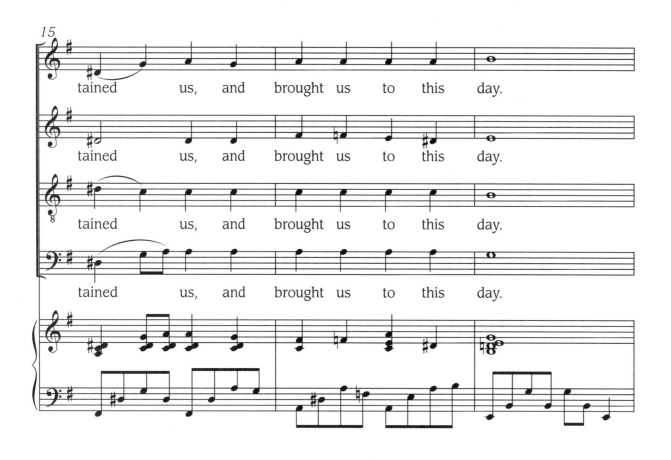

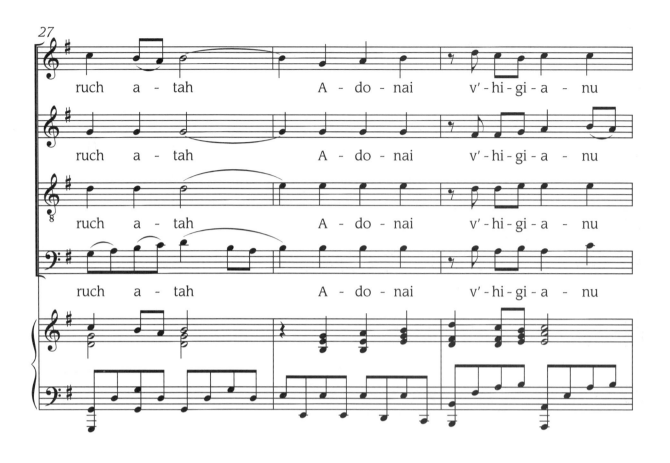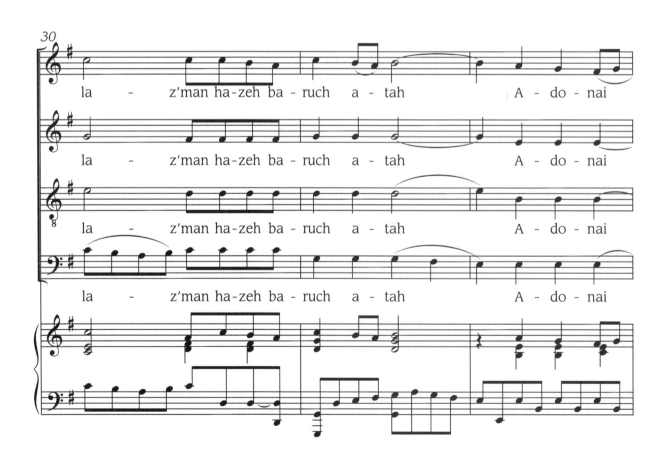

227

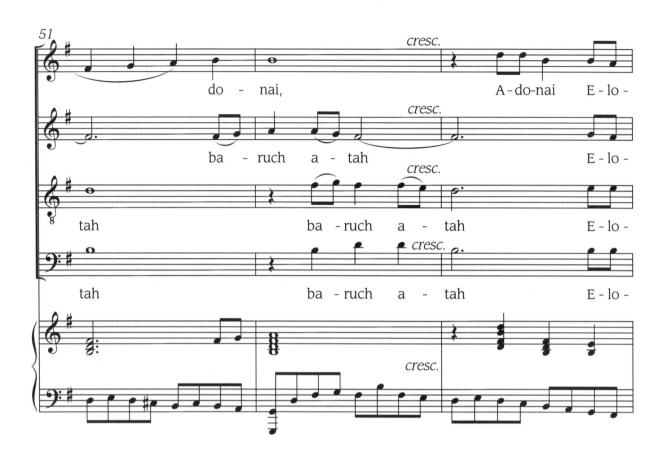

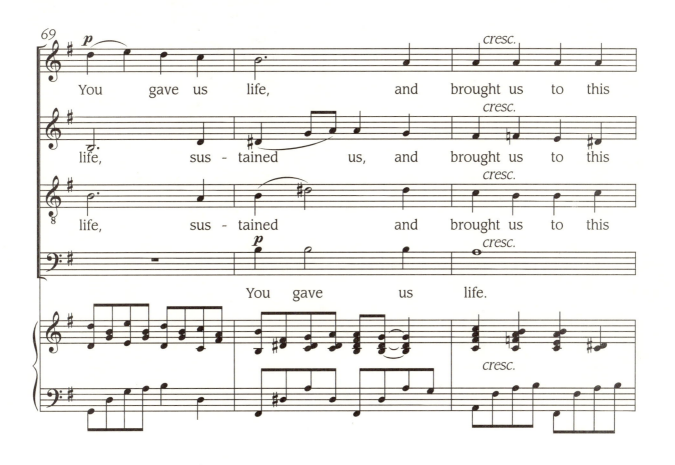

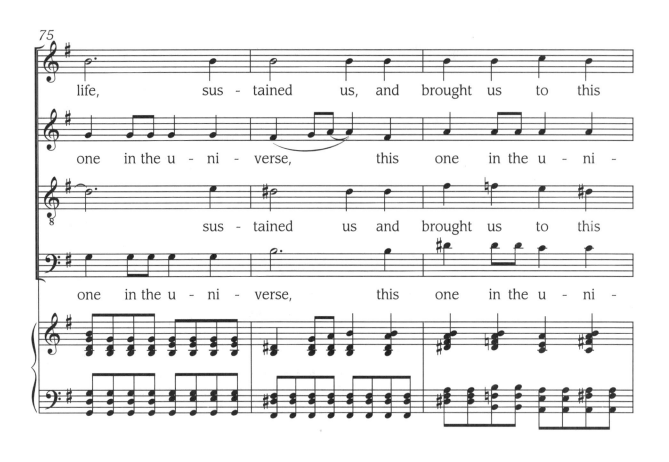
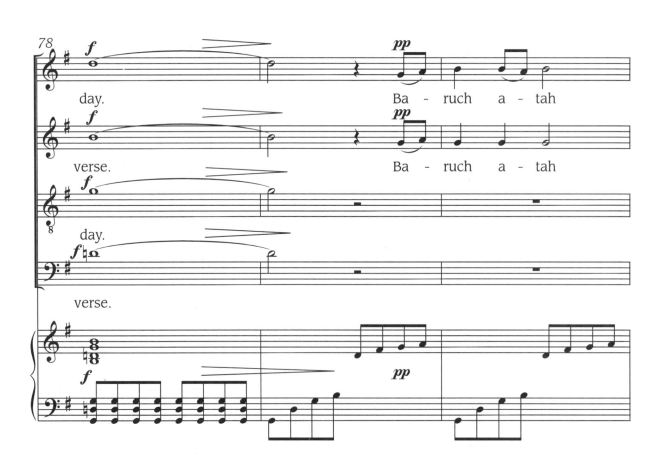

233

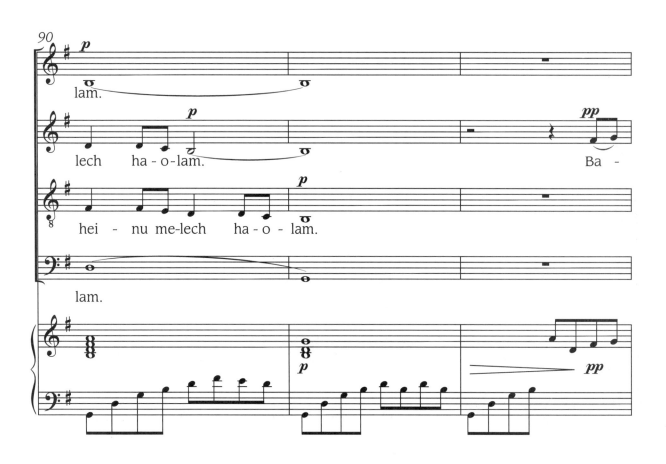

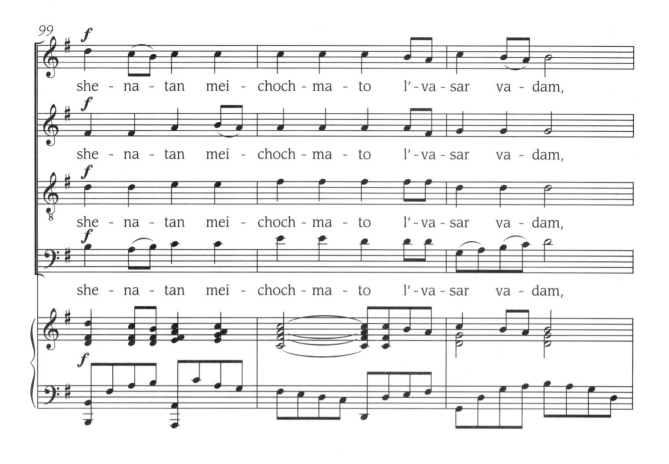
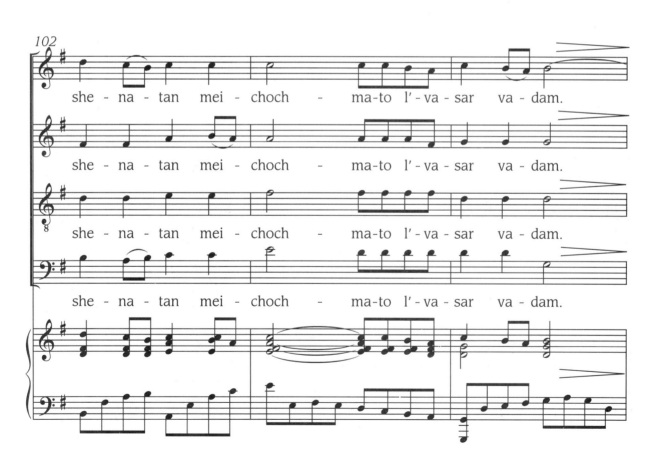

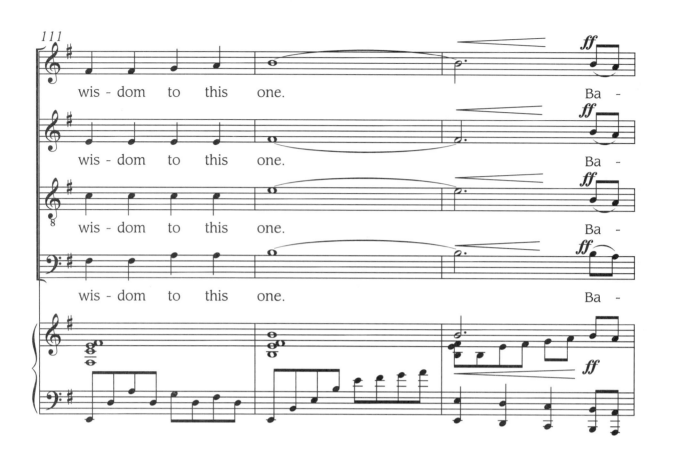
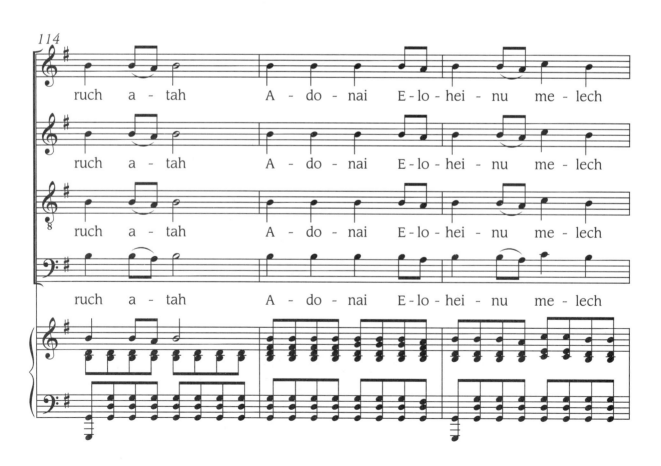

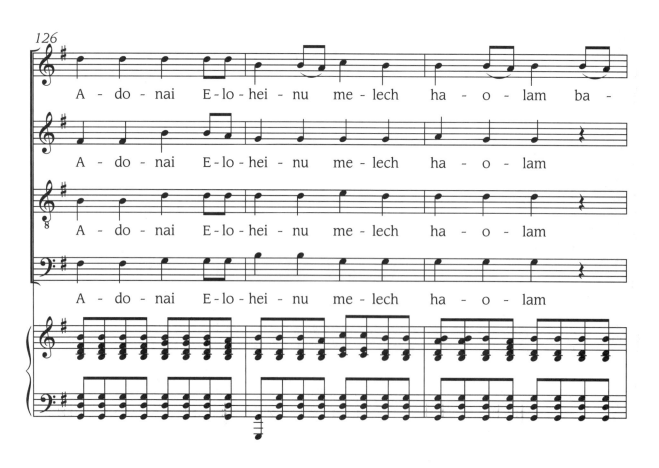

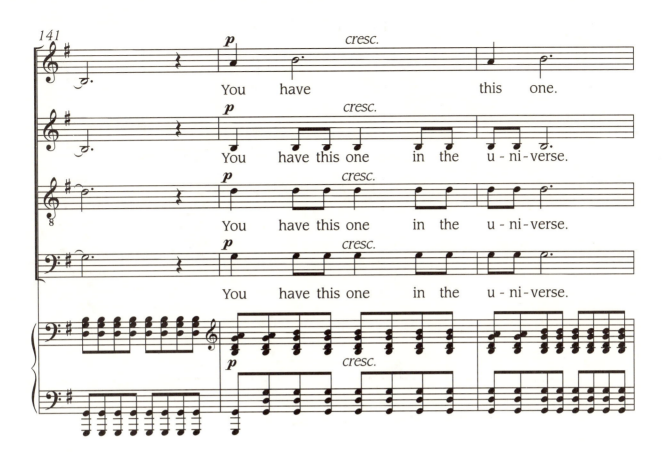

243

Thou Makest the Winds Thy Messengers
in three versions

adapted from Psalm 103 / 104
words in the final stanza by Carolyn Brown Senier

Thou makest the winds thy messengers
And thy ministers a flaming fire
Thou makest the clouds thy chariot
Thou walkest upon the wings of the wind
Thou commandest the springs to flow into the rivers
   which run among the hills
With thy word arose glorious sunlight

Glory to God, glory forever
Glory to God, glory forever

Thou makest the winds thy messengers
 (Glory to God, glory forever)
And thy ministers a flaming fire
 (Glory to God, glory forever)

Thou makest the stars thy holy light
In the dome of the heavens' sacred night
Thou makest the thund'ring waves so free
To cradle our voyage home to thee
Thou commandest the stones to tumble into rivers
   which break away from hills
And thy word awakens glorious sunlight

I remember high skies and racing clouds and a late winter afternoon. In that moment of contemplation at our motherhouse in Ridgefield, Connecticut, I felt I understood what the psalmist meant when he described the clouds becoming a chariot, the sky a highway for the races and the winds carrying them out of sight. That feeling is as clear as if I stood there now. I went to my desk and began setting this psalm to music.

At the beginning of the composition, the rhythm undulates slightly, almost a gentle breeze, and builds to the great winds, to the glory of the whole idea. All the musical themes come together, connecting the earth, the heavens, and the music, dissonance and harmony holding hands and mingling freely, until the final Amen, a common destination.

Thou Makest the Winds Thy Messengers

for SSAATBB Chorus, Congregation, and Organ, with Trumpets, ad lib.

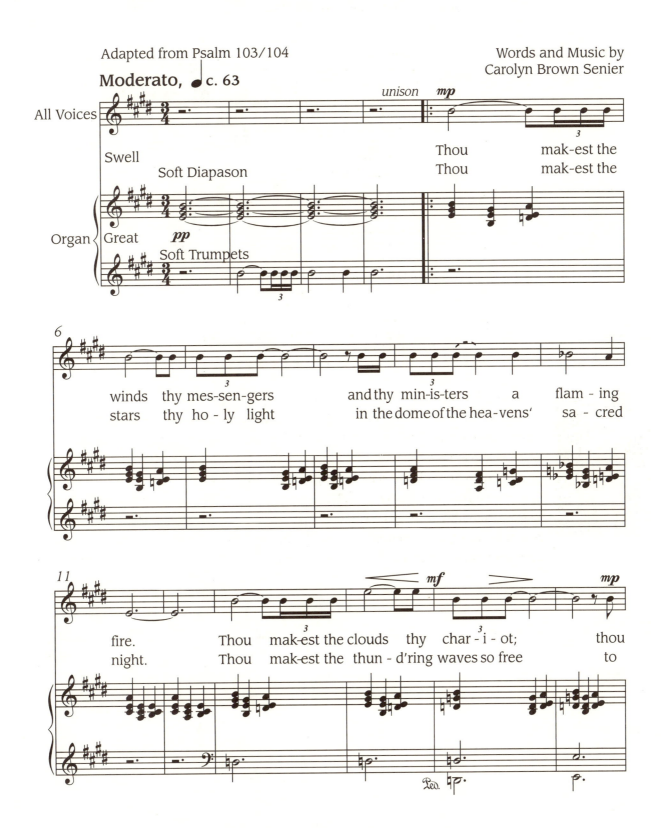

© 1965 by Carolyn Brown and © 2005 by Carolyn Brown Senier.
Copyright includes music and adapted words by Carolyn Brown Senier.
Additional copies are available from Haley's • P O Box 248 • Athol, MA 01331
800.215.8805   haley.antique@verizon.net

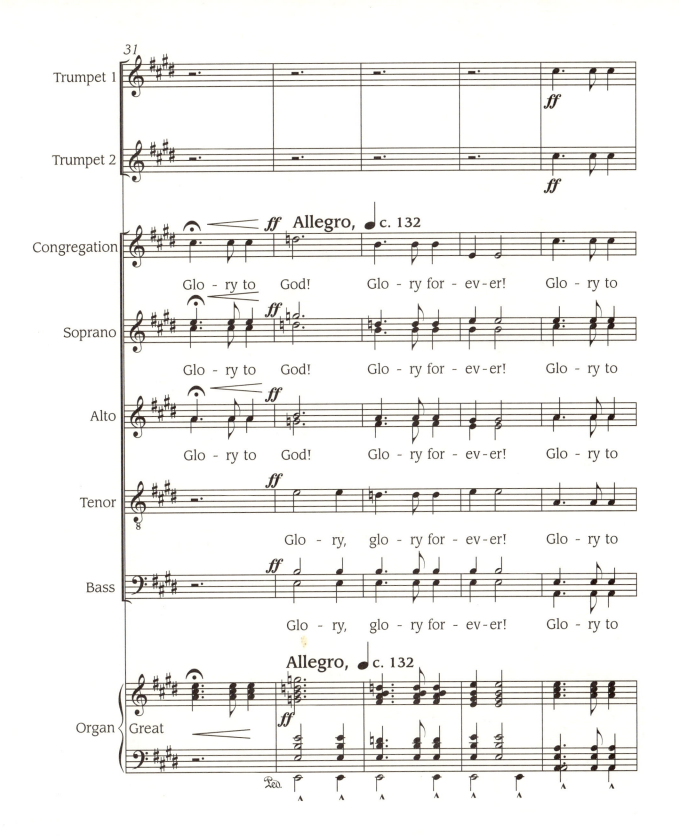

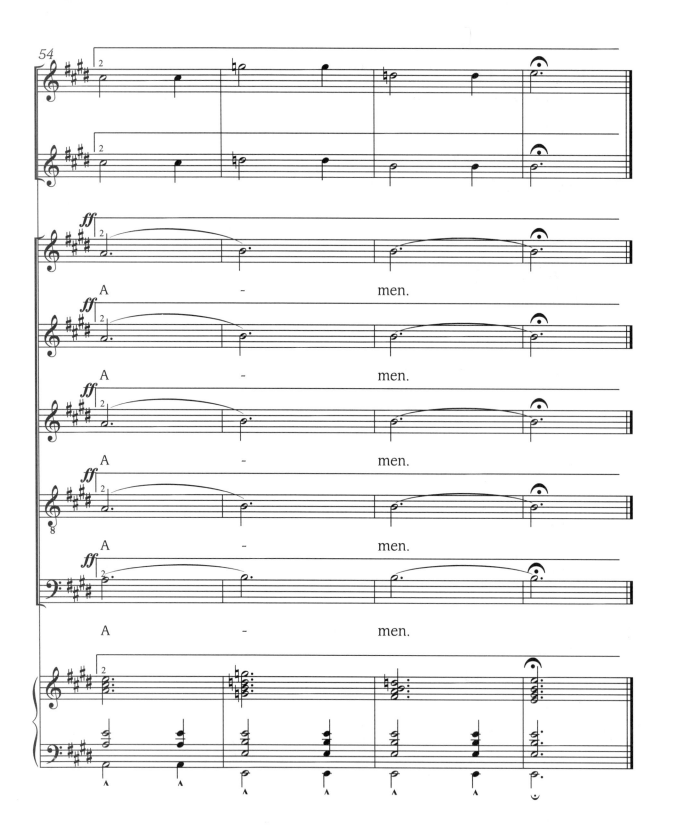

Thou Makest the Winds Thy Messengers

for Women's Voices, Congregation, and Organ with Trumpets, ad lib.

Adapted from Psalm 103/104

Words and Music by
Carolyn Brown Senier

© 1965 by Carolyn Brown and © 2005 by Carolyn Brown Senier.
Copyright includes music and adapted words by Carolyn Brown Senier.

Additional copies are available from Haley's • P O Box 248 • Athol, MA 01331
800.215.8805　　　　haley.antique@verizon.net

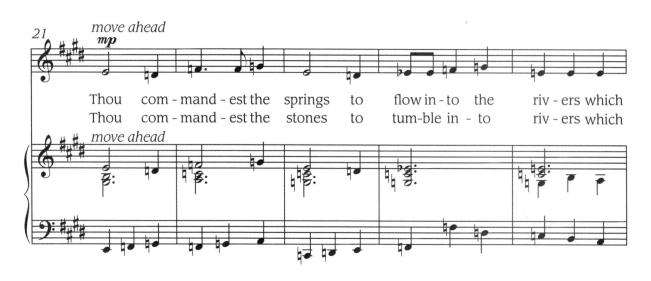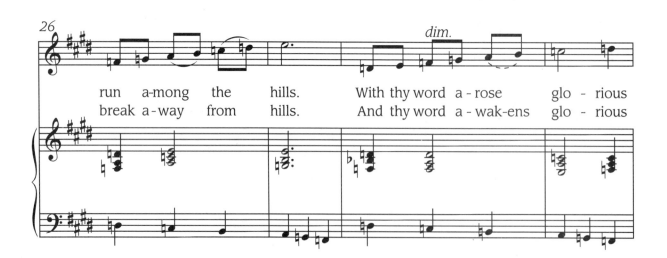

256

Thou Makest the Winds Thy Messengers

2 Trumpets in B♭

Words and Music by
Carolyn Brown Senier

© 1965 by Carolyn Brown and © 2005 by Carolyn Brown Senier.
Copyright includes music and adapted words by Carolyn Brown Senier.

Additional copies are available from Haley's • P O Box 248 • Athol, MA 01331
800.215.8805   haley.antique@verizon.net

You Know Me
adapted from Psalm 138 / 139

You are always there to guide me

You know me
You know me

O, Lord, you have probed me
And you know me
You know when I sit and when I stand
You understand my thoughts from afar
My journeys and my rest
   you scrutinize
With all my ways
You are familiar

O, Lord, you have probed me
And you know me
  (If I fly to the point of sunrise)
You know when I sit and when I stand
  (If fly westward across the sea)
  (You will always guide me)
  (You know me)

My journeys and my rest
You scrutinize
  (My journeys and my rest
  You are always there)
With all my ways you are familiar

If I climb to the heavens you are there
  (You are always there to guide me)
If I go to the depths of the sea
  (You are always there to guide me)
  (You know me
   You know me)
If I fly
If I climb
If I sing a song of love
  (You are there)

Even before a word is on my tongue
Behold, O Lord, you know the whole of it
You are always there

The whole of it
  (You know me)
The whole of it

    Psalm 138 / 139 had been living in me for a long time. I love its meaning and have been carrying around the melody for more than thirty years, intending someday to write a choral setting and finally doing it. The notion of being "known" completely is the compelling theme, having one's very thoughts be understood from afar, the journeys, the rests, the whole of it. It made me very happy when it was performed in January, 2003. The music moves from A minor to A major, weaving in and out, depending on the words. The chromatic counter themes are concise, making a point of being guided and known by some great Mysterious Reality.

You Know Me
for SATB Chorus and Piano

Adapted from Psalm 138/139

Words and Music by
Carolyn Brown Senier

Music © 1966 by Carolyn Brown and © 2002 and © 2005 by Carolyn Brown Senier.
Copyright includes adapted words by Carolyn Brown Senier.

Additional copies are available from Haley's • P O Box 248 • Athol, MA 01331
800.215.8805   haley.antique@verizon.net

Four Songs for a Woman of Galilee
Pageant Song

	Translation of Latin words
Ave Maria, gratia plena	Hail Mary, full of grace
Dominus tecum	The Lord is with thee
Benedicta tu in mulieribus	Blessed art thou amongst women
Et benedictus fructus ventris tui, Jesus	And blessed is the fruit of thy womb, Jesus.

(Prayer)
Sancta Maria mater Dei
(Ecce ancilla Domini)
Ora pro nobis peccatoribus
(Fiat mihi secundum verbum tuum)
Nunc et in hora mortis nostrae
Amen
  —Luke 1:28,38

Holy Mary, mother of God
(Behold the handmaid of the Lord)
Pray for us sinners
(Be it done unto me according to thy word)
Now and at the hour of our death
Amen

I began composing music when I entered the convent. My sixteen-year passage through religious life began with music, was sustained by music, and even now, music is still echoing in my life. The intangible, the notion of a Transcendent Being enveloping life, gave me something to think about and something to sing about. Hence, my journey into sacred music, into its study—beginning with early chant and polyphony.

The novitiate, in a modest three-story school building, was set in the middle of an apple orchard in Bourbonnais, Illinois. One side of it led to a very large cornfield, endlessly flat with corn enough for all of Illinois, or so it seemed. Nazarene College stood on the other side of the property, and oh! Did it ever have beautiful choral music. I listened to it longingly from an acoustically perfect orchard. Those beautiful sounds permeated our cloister. That was the place where music went to another level for me.

"Pageant Song" was my first attempt at composing music for the women's voices of the novitiate choir. I was still a postulant. The year was 1953, and in that year, I also wrote the "Ave Maria" section eventually sung at my sister Joan's wedding. Bill Lawlor, my father's friend, sang it in his grand bass / baritone voice. I can still hear his sound after all these years. The second part of the music, "Ecce ancilla Domini," was added a year later for a pageant celebrating the religious mystery of the Annunciation, in which an angel appears to Mary and asks her to be the mother of Jesus. The answer of Mary, "Ecce ancilla Domini," "Behold the handmaid of the Lord," and "Fiat mihi secundum verbum tuum," "Be it done unto me according to thy word," is meant to soar above the chorus and descend to a quiet, humble Amen.

Respice Stellam
words adapted from "Saint Bernard's Prayer" by Sister Mary Eileen Scott (Sister Saint Miriam of the Temple), CND

Respice Stellam
Voca Mariam
Should peril afright thee
Should doubt assail thee
Voca Mariam
Think upon her name

If she walks before thee
Thou shalt not wander
Thou shalt not be weary
Think upon her name

Neither the dark night
Nor the devouring waters
Shall encompass thee
Nor despair blind thee

Respice Stellam

Tho' the way be narrow
Above the torrent
Thou shalt reach the haven
Thou shalt reach the haven

Respice Stellam
Voca Mariam

Translation of Latin Words
Respice stellam
Voca Mariam
Look to the star
Call upon Mary

I composed "Respice Stellam," "Look to the Star," for a Marian feast day in the early 1960s while I was stationed in Staten Island, New York. I taught music there to elementary, junior high, and high school students as well to as the newly-professed sisters who were studying for their various degrees. Forty years later, I see a departure from the harmonies I had been using. I was trying to strengthen the words by adding more tonal dissonance for struggle and harmonic resolution to suggest feelings of safety and peace. I now think more adventurous harmonies began at that point in my musical development. Take, for instance, the words "Thou shalt reach the haven": the first time the phrase is used, it moves to dissonance on the word "haven" with a chord comprising B in the bass, C# in the tenor, E in the alto, F# in the second soprano, and B in the soprano. Then the repetition lingers on the word "reach," holding a G major and finally a D minor triad and resolving to a restful E major. This is how one can hold or paint words with sound. Although I originally wrote it for four equal unaccompanied voices, SSAA, I have since added men's voices and piano accompaniment for *The Mattawa Song Cycle*. In the middle section, I have kept the original score for women's voices for contrast, moving in and out of unison and harmony. I also employ this technique in the opening call of the music, an a cappella call, followed by five-voice harmony and piano accompaniment.

Hail, Mary (Supplication in Time of War or Sorrow)

Hail Mary, full of grace
The Lord is with thee
Blessed art thou amongst women
And blessed is the fruit of thy womb, Jesus.

Holy Mary, Vessel of Life
(traditional: Mother of God)
Pray for us sinners
Now and at the hour of our death
Amen
-Luke 1:28,38

This work came out of a period of great stress in the world and threats from all sides. At the time, I considered it my "Nuclear War Hail Mary." It is more a hymn of supplication than of praise. Its tone is serious. I used a passacaglia-like bass line to create a somber mood. The melody is chant-like and allows a lifting of the voice and heart in two places: "Blessed art thou among women . . ." and "Pray for us sinners . . ." Both of these musical lines refer to the people: thou and us and rise to the octave in both phrases, returning again to a simpler chant. While composed in a minor key, the composition nevertheless ends with an F major chord, a sound of hope.

Assumpta Est, Maria

Assumpta est, Maria
Assumpta est, Maria
In caelum

Gaudent angeli
Gaudent angeli
Gaudent angeli

Laudantes
Laudantes benedicunt Dominum

Maria virgo assumpta est

—from the first and second antiphons of "Second Vespers for August 15," *Liber Usualis,* published 1956 by the Society of Saint John the Evangelist, New York

Translation of Latin Words
Assumpta est Maria in caelum
Gaudent angeli
Laudantes benedicunt Dominum
Maria virgo assumpta est

Mary is assumed into heaven
The angels
Praise and bless the lord
The Virgin Mary is assumed into heaven

From 1953 to 1955, I was a postulant and novice in the Congregation de Notre Dame of Montreal founded by Marguerite Bourgeoys, the "Mother of Quebec." I was one of twenty-two young women, the first group to have novitiate training in the United States. We were sent to the congregation's training center in Bourbonnais, Illinois. I was asked to act as music director until an experienced one could be found. I was eighteen years old, and the other novices were eighteen, nineteen, and some in their twenties.

Our choir sang daily and at weekly liturgical services and occasionally gave small concerts. Eventually, Sister Claudette Chevrette (Sister Saint Andre Marie) came every week from neighboring Kankakee and taught the novices. These young aspirants to religious life were beautiful singers and harmonized freely. I wrote this piece specifically for their voices as well as for the celebration of the Feast of the Assumption of Mary on August 15. I rearranged it for SATB and the piano in the winter of 2003.

Pageant Song

(Annunciation)
for Two Soprano Soloists, SA Chorus and Piano

Music by
Carolyn Brown Senier

Music © 1953 by Carolyn Brown and © 2005 by Carolyn Brown Senier.

Additional copies are available from Haley's • P O Box 248 • Athol, MA 01331
800.215.8805　　　　haley.antique@verizon.net

Respice Stellam
(Look to the Star)
for SSATB Chorus and Piano

Words adapted from Saint Bernard
by Mary Eileen Scott CND

Music by
Carolyn Brown Senier

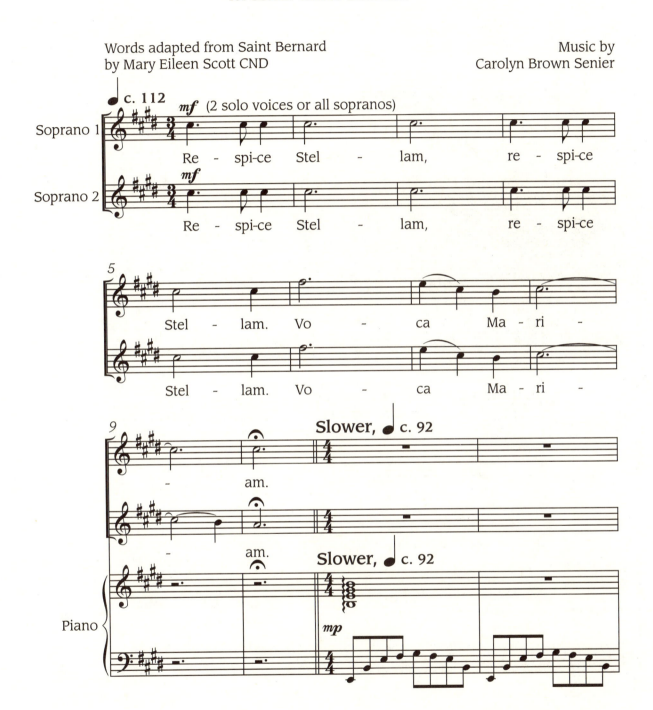

Music © 1962 by Carolyn Brown and © 2005 by Carolyn Brown Senier.
Words adapted from Saint Bernard © 1962 by Mary Eileen Scott, CND.

Additional copies are available from Haley's • P O Box 248 • Athol, MA 01331
800.215.8805   haley.antique@verizon.net

Hail Mary

Hymn of Supplication in Time of War and Sorrow
for Solo or Unison Chorus and Piano

Music © 1964 by Carolyn Brown and © 2005 by Carolyn Brown Senier.
Copyright includes adapted words by Carolyn Brown Senier.

Additional copies are available from Haley's • P O Box 248 • Athol, MA 01331
800.215.8805   haley.antique@verizon.net

Music © 1954 by Carolyn Brown and © 2005 by Carolyn Brown Senier
Additional copies are available from Haley's • P O Box 248 • Athol, MA 01331
800.215.8805   haley.antique@verizon.net

Love Songs
I'd Give You the Moon
Words by Dorothy Johnson

What can I give her
To show that I love her
To thank her for being with me?
I could buy diamonds
Shining like raindrops
Or pearls from the depths of the sea

I'd give you the moon
And the silver stars
If they were mine to give
But the most I can do
Is promise you
My love as long as I live

What can I give him
To show that I love him
To thank him for loving me?

Who can buy mem'ries
Wide as the rivers
That flow toward the deep blue sea

I'd give you the moon
And the silver stars
If they were mine to give
But the most I can do
Is promise you
My love as long as I live

The gifts that you've given
Are rarer than rubies
And finer than pearls from the sea
I count my blessings
For ever and ever
You gave your love
You gave your love to me.

I composed the melodies for the lyrics of Dorothy Johnson who, in collaboration with the composer Andy Lichtenberg (and previously, Steven Schoenberg), has produced and directed musicals for community theater projects at the 1794 Meetinghouse in New Salem, Massachusetts. The musicals have become a tradition and taking part in them has been a thoroughly enjoyable experience, one of which, with Dorothy's encouragement, led to a rekindling of my musical ideas and creative musical expression.

"I'd Give You the Moon" is a duet (with chorus) that was performed by my husband, Richard, and me in *Home Movies*, 1999.

Listen to Your Heart
Words by Dorothy Johnson

Why can't it be simple
The way it used to be
Why can't it be easy
Like counting one, two, three
We had such fun times
My good friends and me

Now ev'rything is changed
They're not the friends I know
Where did the good friends go

No one, but no one
Understands love
It is what it is
Scientists talk of biology
Or chemistry or psychology
But you see
There is no simple way
To define emotion
No simple way to explain devotion
We can only say what we know today

Listen to your heart
Echo: Ev'rything has changed
When your time is here
Echo: Not the friends I know
Your heart will always know
Echo: Nothing is the same
When your true love is here

Love can be a gift of precious stone
Something to borrow and not to own
It can last forever long after we are gone
Sometimes it appears like a wild red rose
Along a country road
You can see how it grows
Touched by April rain safe from winter snows

Listen to your heart
Echo: Ev'rything has changed
When your time is here
Echo: Not the friends I know
Your heart will always know
Echo: Nothing is the same
When your true love is here

"Listen to Your Heart" is a trio (with chorus) that my husband and I sang with young Dylan Flye in *Friends and Neighbors*, 2001.

Summer Days
words by Carolyn Brown Senier

Days are long and summer's here
My love is home this time of year
Summer stars have games to play
They move around from day to day
(Move around from day to day)
(From day to day)

Yet, one bright star has found its home
My love is here to see his own
Mist will rise above the lakes
But now love calls
(But now love calls)
(But now love calls)
(Now love calls)
My heart awakes

"Summer Days" is a song about the lake and the seasons and how they reflect a life. The mist speaks of colder weather. The water is still warm but the air is not. It will be winter soon. Nature and its meaning are often reflections of ourselves. The close harmony is vocally challenging.

When I Knew
words by Carolyn Brown Senier

When I Knew
  (When I knew)
When I knew
  (When I knew)
I loved you
Music raced beyond the room
to midnight skies
Then my love
  (Then my love)
When you touched my waiting heart
  (Touched my waiting heart, my waiting heart)
Galaxies of ancient stars danced in surprise
Ancient stars danced in surprise

Even the moon heard wonderful music
Magical strains in winter's night
Gentle old winds hummed our love song
And waltzed with the clouds in the light

When I knew
That loving you would always be
I could hardly carry
All the joy in me
Even now
When you hold your hand in mine
Midnight music
Races to the end of time

It seems only yesterday that Richard and I listened to the Chopin piano concerto, "Opus 21, #2," in 1972. Experiencing it together changed my life, because that is when I knew I had found someone who could share my future, an instinct that marriage would make love and the music possible. I wrote this song for him as a birthday present. The choral setting nods occasionally to Chopin's melodies, a tribute to memory, I hope, rather than a theft of tune.

I'd Give You the Moon

Words by
Dorothy Johnson

Music by
Carolyn Brown Senier

Music © 1999 and © 2005 by Carolyn Brown Senier.
Words © 1999 by Dorothy Johnson.

Additional copies are available from Haley's • P O Box 248 • Athol, MA 01331
800.215.8805   haley.antique@verizon.net

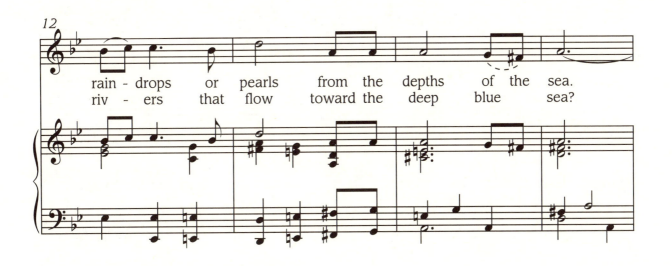

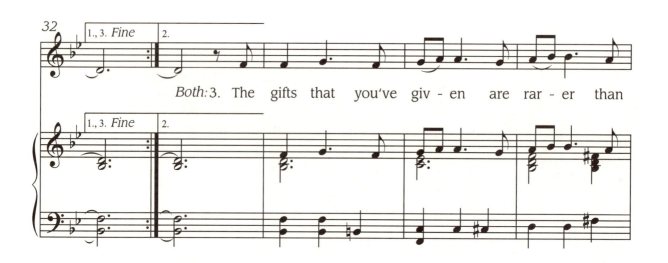

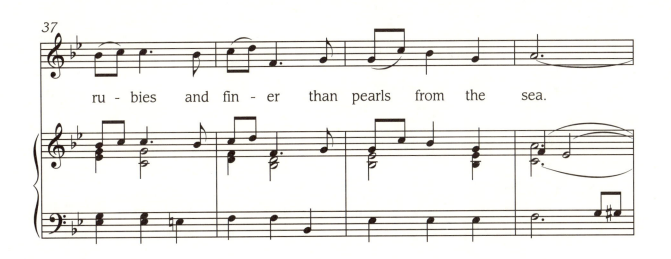

303

Listen to Your Heart

Words by
Dorothy Johnson

Music by
Carolyn Brown Senier

Music © 2001 and © 2005 by Carolyn Brown Senier. Words © 2001 and © 2005 by Dorothy Johnson.

Additional copies are available from Haley's • P O Box 248 • Athol, MA 01331
800.215.8805   haley.antique@verizon.net

309

Summer Days
for SATB Chorus and Piano

Words and Music by
Carolyn Brown Senier

Music © 2003 and © 2005 by Carolyn Brown Senier.
Copyright includes words by Carolyn Brown Senier.

Additional copies are available from Haley's • P O Box 248 • Athol, MA 01331
800.215.8805
haley.antique@verizon.net

When I Knew

for Richard

(with a nod to Frederic Chopin-Opus 21)
for SATB Chorus and Piano

Words and Music by
Carolyn Brown Senier

Music © 1996 and © 2005 by Carolyn Brown Senier.
Copyright includes words by Carolyn Brown Senier.

Additional copies are available from Haley's • P O Box 248 • Athol, MA 01331
800.215.8805   haley.antique@verizon.net

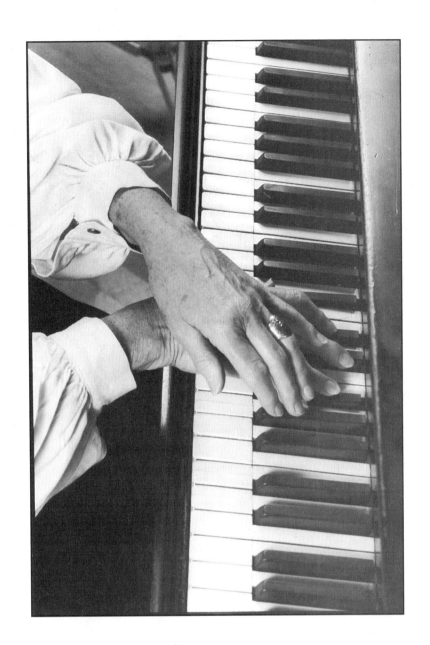

songs for congregational singing and for choir
preceded by annotations by Carolyn Brown Senier

Adoremus (1955) • SATB 332

Lamb of God (1966) • three equal voices 334

Celtic Prayer (2003) • unison 338

Creator Spirit, Come (1964) • unison 341

O, Praise the Lord, All Ye Nations (1964) • SATB 348

O, Praise Ye The Lord (1961) • SATB 351

The Ram (1965) • solo 355

Sing Joy to the Lord (1961) • SATB 358

Three Songs for Christmas 361
    Let the Heav'ns Be Glad (1964, 1967) • a cappella canon 362
    Lowly Shepherds (1956, 1967) • SATB 363
    Come Sing Alleluia (1960, 1967) • equal voices 364

Mass in Honor of Marguerite Bourgeoys (1964-1965) 366
    Lord Have Mercy • unison 368
    Glory to God • antiphonal: unison 369
    Creed • antiphonal: unison 374
    Holy, Holy, Holy • unison 386
    Blessed • unison 387
    Lamb of God • unison 388

Meditation Doxology (1966) • SATB 390

Adoremus

Adoremus in aeternam sanctissimum sacramentum
Adoremus in aeternam sanctissimum sacramentum
Adoremus in aeternam sanctissimum sacramentum

Translation of Latin Words
Adoremus in aeternam sanctissimum sacramentum
We adore the most holy sacrament forever

This is a hymn to be sung at the service of Benediction, when the Holy Eucharist is venerated.

Adoremus
Benediction Hymn

Music by
Carolyn Brown Senier

Music © 1955 by Carolyn Brown and © 2005 by Carolyn Brown Senier.
Additional copies are available from Haley's • P O Box 248 • Athol, MA 01331
800.215.8805 haley.antique@verizon.net

Lamb of God

*Lamb of God
Who taketh away
the sins of the world
Have mercy on us*

*Lamb of God
Who taketh away
the sins of the world
Have mercy on us*

*Lamb of God
Who taketh away
the sins of the world
Grant us peace*

An a cappella "Lamb of God" to be sung at Mass on a joyful feast day.

Lamb of God
for Three Equal Voices

Music © 1964 by Carolyn Brown and © 2005 by Carolyn Brown Senier.

Additional copies are available from Haley's • P O Box 248 • Athol, MA 01331
800.215.8805   haley.antique@verizon.net

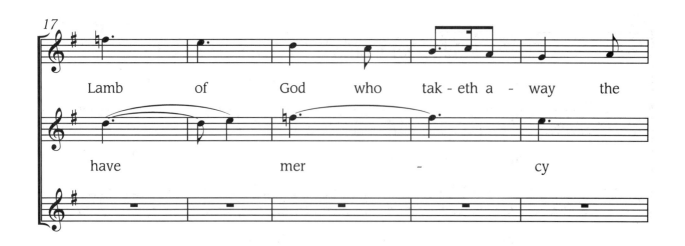
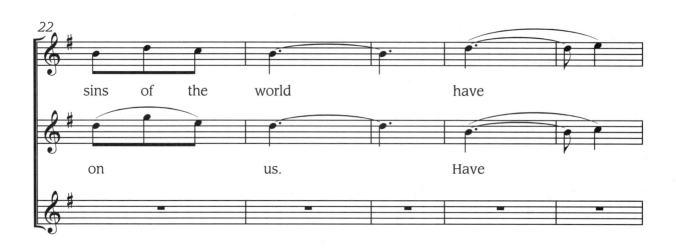
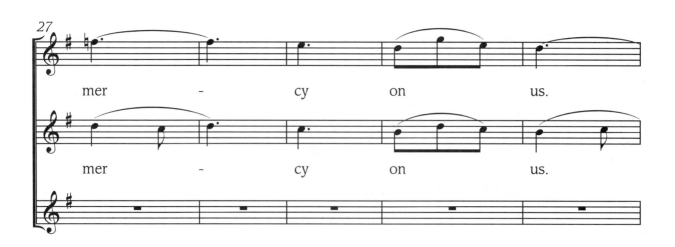

Celtic Prayer
adapted from the "Lorica" of Saint Patrick

We praise you, our Creator
We praise you, God of love
We praise your spirit
moving through our world

Be within us
Be about
On left hand
And on right
On left hand
And on right

We praise you, our Creator
We praise you, God of love
We praise your spirit
moving through our world

Be before us
Be around us
Be our journey's light
Be our journey's light

We praise you, our Creator
We praise you, God of love
We praise your spirit moving through our world
We praise your Holy Spirit in our world

The Irish in me shows up in this song. It is based on the "Lorica" of Saint Patrick and is written for unison singing. I wrote it in 2003. Occasionally, music begins in one tonality and ends in another. This piece begins in the key of D flat and ends in F major, yet it sounds modal with the use of open 5ths and octaves in the accompaniment.

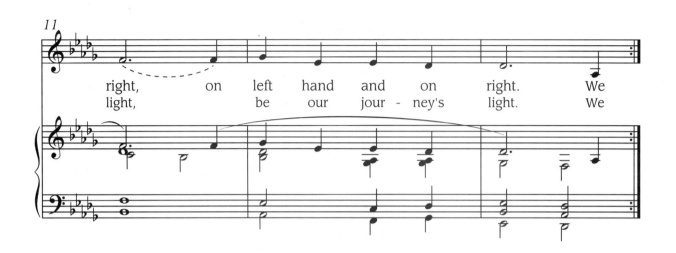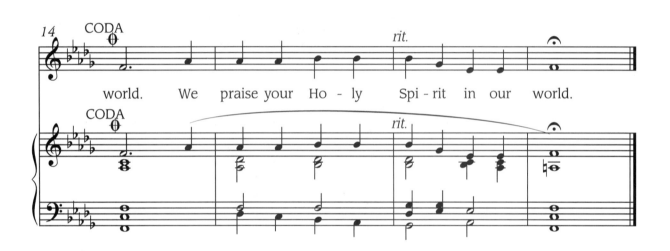

Creator, Spirit
freely adapted from "Veni Creator Spiritus"

Creator Spirit, come
And visit the souls that are yours
Fill with heavenly grace
The hearts that you created

You are called by the name of Paraclete
Gift of God Most High
Spring of Life, Fire, Love,
And the Soul's Anointing

Sacred gifts are yours to give
You are the blessing of a father's right hand
You, the clear Voice of all creation
Give our tongues the grace of speech
Kindle a light in our minds
Pour love into our hearts
And uphold with your unfailing strength
The frailty of our human nature
Drive our enemies far from us
And give us always the gift of peace
So that it may be with your grace ever guiding us
We may avoid all that is evil

Grant that through you we may know
The wonder of all love
And may we ever believe you to be
The Spirit of our living, loving God

Glory be to God our Creator
And to the Word of life and of love
And the Paraclete
Forever and ever
Amen

I read this translation of "Veni Creator Spiritus" while at a liturgical service in the Hartford, Connecticut, cathedral. There was no acknowledgement of the translator and I have tried without success to find out who it was. I took some liberties with the text in this setting.

The music should be sung as a strong chant, flowing yet rhythmically constant.

Creator Spirit, Come

for Unison Voices and Piano

Adapted from an anonymous translation

Music by
Carolyn Brown Senier

Music © 1964 by Carolyn Brown and © 2005 by Carolyn Brown Senier.
Copyright includes adapted words by Carolyn Brown Senier.

Additional copies are available from Haley's • P O Box 248 • Athol, MA 01331
800.215.8805   haley.antique@verizon.net

343

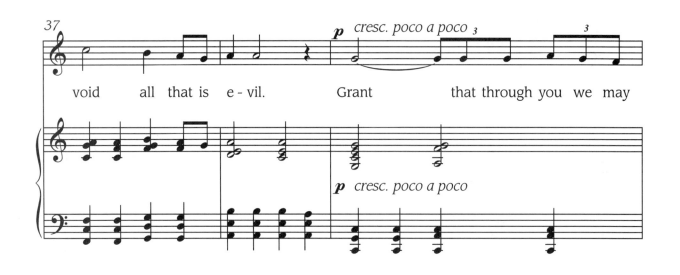
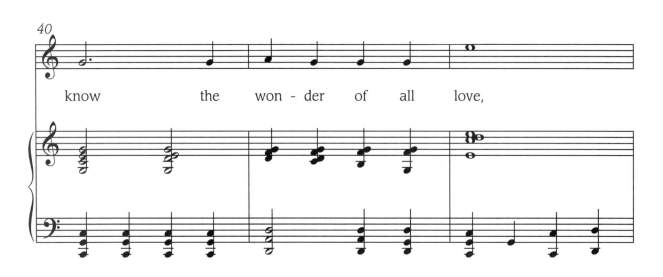

O, Praise the Lord, All Ye Nations

O, praise the Lord, all ye nations
Proclaim his glory, all ye peoples
O, praise the Lord, all ye nations
Proclaim his glory, all ye peoples

Because his mercy is confirmed upon us
And the fidelity of the Lord abides forever

O, praise the Lord, all ye nations
Proclaim his glory, all ye peoples
O, praise the Lord, all ye nations
Proclaim his glory, all ye peoples

Glory be to the Father
And to the Son
And to the Holy Spirit

As it was in the beginning
Is now
And ever shall be
World without end. Amen.

O, praise the Lord, all ye nations
Proclaim his glory, all ye peoples
O, praise the Lord, all ye nations
Proclaim his glory, all ye peoples
Amen

—*Psalm 116 / 117*

O, Praise the Lord, All Ye Nations

Entrance Hymn

Adapted from Psalm 116/117

Words and Music by
Carolyn Brown Senier

Music © 1964 by Carolyn Brown and © 2005 by Carolyn Brown Senier.

Additional copies are available from Haley's • P O Box 248 • Athol, MA 01331
800.215.8805   haley.antique@verizon.net

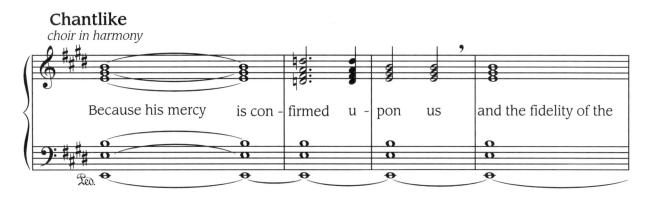
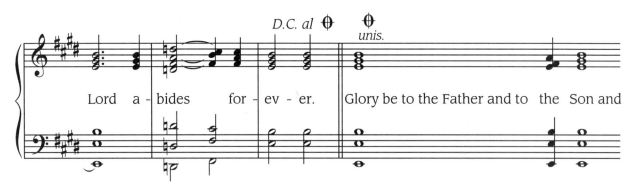
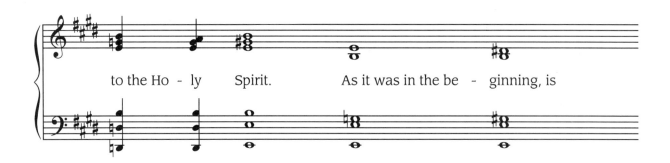

O, Praise Ye the Lord

Refrain:
O, praise ye the Lord
Praise God in his temple
Praise ye the Lord in the firmament of his pow'r

Praise the Lord
O, praise him for his might
Praise the Lord
For the greatness of his wonders

Refrain

Praise the Lord with the sound of the trumpet
Praise the Lord with the lute and the harp

Refrain

Praise the Lord with the timbrel and the dance
Praise the Lord with the instruments of strings

Refrain

Praise him upon the loud cymbals
Praise him upon the high-sounding cymbals
Let ev'rything that has breath, ev'ry thing that has breath
Praise the Lord

Refrain

Praise him upon the loud cymbals
Praise him upon the high-sounding cymbals
Let ev'rything that has breath, ev'ry thing that has breath
Praise the Lord

Refrain

—*Psalm 116 / 117*

Precise memory of events from forty years ago is neither easy nor always accurate. Certain ones stand out, like weddings and great feasts or terrible tragedies, such as President Kennedy's assassination. My father died in 1959, my sister Roselyn and young niece the year after. Cancer's heavy hand touched three generations in our family. I don't know how or why it happened, but many of my praise songs were composed during these sorrowful days, including "O, Praise Ye The Lord," which I set to paper one winter afternoon.

I was practicing the piano in the auditorium in Staten Island, and before I knew it, this psalm emerged. I remember singing it for the school custodian as he walked by. I wasn't very encouraged by his response. After all, it wasn't "I Want To Hold Your Hand" or some other Beatles' tune, but I kept working at it, and before long, my choirs sang it and liked it. I always marvel at their enthusiasm and joy when I hear it sung, because I had very little joy when I wrote it.

I remember driving by a Connecticut schoolyard years later and hearing two young children singing it as they went back and forth on a swing. It made me smile and reflect on how things carry on, sometimes because of us and sometimes in spite of us. The harmonies are quite traditional. I think tradition has made it popular: tradition of Old Testament thought and words and tradition of style and harmony, a combination that seems to be its strength.

Psalm 150, "O, Praise ye The Lord," was chosen by the Sisters of Christian Charity, based in Mendham, New Jersey. Their foundress, Pauline von Mallinckrodt, was to be

(continued on next page)

beatified by the Pope in 1982. I was honored to have my work chosen for inclusion at Mass in Saint Peter's Basilica commemorating her. My husband Richard and I decided to go to Rome to hear it. When we arrived at Saint Peter's, we encountered some two thousand pilgrims from Italy, Spain, and Germany who were connected with these nuns and who had been learning my music back home. I was introduced to the superior general of the order, Mother General Eisenhauer, who thanked me for having written the music and coming to the beatification. When they became aware of my arrival, the choir asked me to accompany them on the organ. But I had not played the organ for at least fifteen years, and never such an instrument. The organist, a Franciscan friar, graciously set the stops for me after Richard asked him in Italian and stood behind me as I set out to do my best.

Fortunately, on the previous night, a friend in Rome, Harry McNally, had asked me to play the piece on his piano. I thought to myself, "Thank God, at least I know how to play my own music." But I never expected to be playing it at Saint Peter's.

I remember being in a cold sweat. It was April, still chilly. I was covered with layers of sweaters and jackets as well as a woolen Irish cape. One by one I peeled them off, not missing a beat. First the purple cape fell to the basilica floor, then a beige jacket. With each verse, I was removing something so that I could breathe as well as command the keyboard. I didn't do very well on the pedals, being so out of practice. But my hands, at least, were limber, as I had been taking piano lessons at the Longy School in Cambridge with David Bacon, a much beloved teacher.

Later in the Mass, the friar repeated my psalm as an organ interlude. What sounds he produced! He was such a superior organist.

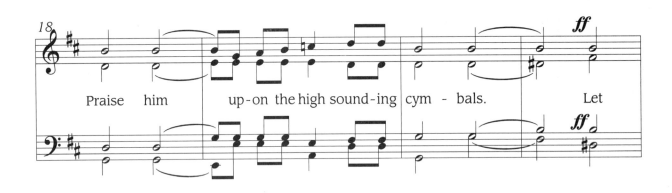
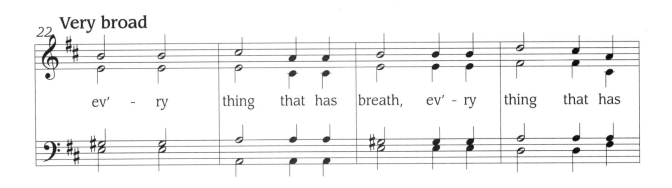
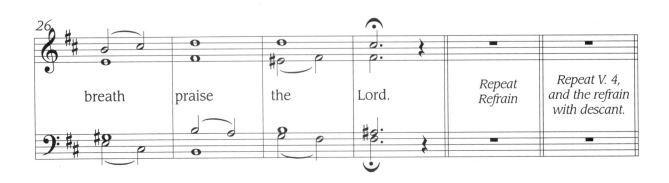

The Ram
*I searched
But there was no ram
in the bush
To give him
I searched
But there was no ram
in the bush
To give him
Then God said me . . .
God said me.*

Thomas Curran, a Jesuit priest, wrote this haiku poem:
"I searched, but there was no ram in the bush to give you, / Then you said me."

While browsing through the magazine *America*, a Jesuit publication, I found the small poem of seventeen syllables illustrating the biblical narrative in which Abraham is asked by God to sacrifice his son Isaac, for Abraham the most difficult surrender of all. I was touched by the verse, picked up my Giannini guitar, and set it to music. I have some beautiful memories connected to this piece. One was a connection to a program called Summer in the City, organized by Monsignor Robert J. Fox, a well-known parish priest in Spanish Harlem. We met in Ridgefield, Connecticut, where I was teaching. He had been invited to speak about social justice. Our religious superior asked me to bring the breakfast tray up from the kitchen to the guest dining room. We chatted, and much to my surprise, he asked me to be part of his summer program with people from all walks of life contributing their talents to enhance the lives of young people. I asked him, "What do you want me to do in your program?" and he said, "Just hang around and sing around and choose the music for daily liturgies." So I did. He sent me a car to have at my disposal. Off I went to New York where I "just hung around and sang around" and prepared group liturgical singing. Father Fox inspired us all with his message: "Invest yourself in the human condition in which you find yourself." During the offertory of the first liturgy, I found myself standing spontaneously, nodding to him, being acknowledged, and then singing "The Ram." There were hundreds of us in that field, and the only sounds were my voice and my guitar. Later that day, a perfect stranger came up and told me he had heard clear sound echoing through the woods adjoining our outdoor temple. He was moved by the music and its message, so he just kept walking towards it.

Another serendipitous moment was meeting the author of the poem. He was visiting our novitiate in Ridgefield, Connecticut, to give a retreat to the novices. He asked me to sing some of my music for him. I knew he was a poet, but I did not know he was the author of "The Ram." I didn't recall who had written it.

Jokingly, I said, "You probably wrote this" and then sang it for him, explaining that I had made a slight change in the wording for euphony's sake. When I finished, he told me he had written the words and said, "You may have it, my dear." He added, "Sometimes choice plus chance gives us a glimpse of eternity." I tried to find him forty years later, when I was doing research for this book. I learned from the Jesuits at America House in New York that he had died.

I used the word God instead of the word you because of the singability of the vowel in the 10-note melismatic portion of the melody. Hence, I returned to the traditional biblical image, and the poet was not unhappy with the change.

357

Sing Joy to the Lord
words adapted from Psalm 99 / 100 by Sister Martha Bowes (Sister Saint Martin of Lima), CND

Sing joy to the Lord
Serve God in your gladness
Give thanks to his name forever

How strong is his love
How merciful and faithful
Sing joy to the Lord forever

Bring to the Lord your bread and wine
Sing to the Lord your joyous praise

Sing joy to the Lord
Serve God in your gladness
Give thanks to his name forever

How strong is his love
How merciful and faithful
Sing joy to the Lord forever

Offer your gift to Christ the Lord
Offer yourself to be transformed

Sing joy to the Lord
Serve God in your gladness
Give thanks to his name
Amen

Sing Joy to the Lord

Offertory Hymn

Words by Martha Bowes, CND
Adapted from Psalm 99/100

Music by
Carolyn Brown Senier

♩ c. 100

Sing joy to the Lord, serve God in your glad-ness, give thanks to his name for-e-ver. How strong is his love, how mer-ci-ful and faith-ful. Sing joy to the Lord for-e- for-e-ver, for- for-e-

Music © 1961 by Carolyn Brown and © 2005 by Carolyn Brown Senier.
Additional copies are available from Haley's • P O Box 248 • Athol, MA 01331
800.215.8805   haley.antique@verizon.net

Three Christmas Carols

Written in utter simplicity, these carols are reflections on the birth of Jesus. I would like to give credit to a few old friends from those days for their contributions to my texts. Martha Bowes, CND, added parts of "Come Sing Alleluia." I can't recall exactly which words were hers, which mine, but I remember sitting with her in my music studio on Staten Island, searching for the word "tend" instead of "tell." There was a section in the song, somewhere around "the hills of Judah," where her thoughts and words were incorporated and formed "a cradle touched with light." My own words "the world's alleluias fill Bethlehem's caves tonight" were enriched by Martha's contribution.

Mary Ann Foley, CND, helped me find some rhymes in "Lowly Shepherds." I remember discussing the words of the second verse with her and the poetic license we would take with the use of the word "trod." We knew we were taking some liberties but we wanted the rhyme.

Let the Heav'ns Be Glad

Let the heav'ns be glad
and the earth rejoice before the Lord
Let the heav'ns be glad
and the earth rejoice before the Lord
For he comes
For he comes

—from the offertory antiphon,
midnight Mass of Christmas

This is a joyful round taken from the offertory of midnight Mass at Christmas to be sung while people carry gifts. Handbells or small bells might be added, and this carol could be sung on other occasions.

Lowly Shepherds
words by Carolyn Brown Senier

Lowly shepherds sought the Christ Child
Angels told them of his birth
To the cave that night they traveled
To give praise for all the earth
Alleluia, Alleluia
Lo! Their song is heard on high
Peace to those whose hearts adore him
Come! Make haste, the Lord is nigh

Angel voices still are ringing
Far beyond that starlit night
Filling us with hope and gladness
Who in faith now seek his light
Follow you the path of shepherds
Through the hills of Bethl'hem trod
And with hearts by love made humble
Come adore the Lamb of God

Written for unison or four-part chorale singing, this carol is a quiet contemplation in song noting the mystery of Jesus's birth and New Testament thought.

Come Sing Alleluia
words by Carolyn Brown Senier

The bells ring tenderly as shepherds tend their sheep
Angels' splendor falls upon us as we sleep
O Jesu, son of peace, a child to you may bring
A simple melody to lullabye his king

Come sing Alleluia
Come sing Alleluia
We bring Alleluia
This music to our king

The hills of Judah form a cradle touched with light
The world's alleluias fill Bethlehem's caves tonight

Childlike, shepherd-like, this emulates a folk song, sung in thirds with a Spanish flavor, a child's gift of sung alleluias on behalf of the world.

Let the Heav'ns Be Glad

Two and Three-part Canon
with Triangle ad lib.

Offertory for Midnight Mass of Christmas

Fast, joyful, like a trumpet call

Music by
Carolyn Brown Senier

Music © 1964 by Carolyn Brown and © 2005 by Carolyn Brown Senier.

Additional copies are available from Haley's • P O Box 248 • Athol, MA 01331
800.215.8805   haley.antique@verizon.net

Lowly Shepherds

Words and Music by
Carolyn Brown Senier

Music © 1956 by Carolyn Brown and © 2005 by Carolyn Brown Senier.
Copyright includes words by Carolyn Brown Senier.

Additional copies are available from Haley's • P O Box 248 • Athol, MA 01331
800.215.8805   haley.antique@verizon.net

Come, Sing Alleluia

for SA Chorus and Piano

Words and Music by
Carolyn Brown Senier

The bells ring tenderly as shepherds tend their sheep.

Angel splendor falls upon us as we sleep. O Jesu!

Son of Peace, a child to you may bring a simple melody to

Music © 1960 by Carolyn Brown and © 2005 by Carolyn Brown Senier.
Copyright includes words by Carolyn Brown Senier.

Additional copies are available from Haley's • P O Box 248 • Athol, MA 01331
800.215.8805   haley.antique@verizon.net

Mass in Honor of Marguerite Bourgeoys, Founder of the Congregation de Notre Dame de Montreal

Lord, Have Mercy

Lord, have mercy
Lord, have mercy
Lore, have mercy

Christ, have mercy
Christ, have mercy
Christ, have mercy

Lord, have mercy
Lord, have mercy
Lord, have mercy

Glory to God

Glory to God in the highest
And on earth, peace to those of good will
We praise you
We bless you
We worship you
We glorify you
We give you thanks for your great glory
Lord, God, heavenly King
God, the Father Almighty,
Lord, Jesus Christ, the only begotten Son
Lord, God, Lamb of God,
Son of the Father
You who take away the sins of the world
Have mercy on us
You who take away the sins of the world
Receive our prayer
You who sit at the right hand of the Father
Have mercy on us
For you alone are holy
You alone are Lord
You alone, O Jesus Christ,
Are most high
With the Holy Spirit
In the glory of God the Father
Amen

Creed

I believe in one God
The Father almighty
Maker of heaven and earth
And of all things visible and invisible
And I believe in one Lord, Jesus Christ
The only begotten Son of God
Born of the Father before all ages
God of God, Light of Light, True God of True God
Begotten not made
Of one substance with the Father
Through whom all things are made
Who for us and for our salvation
Came down from heaven
And he became flesh by the Holy Spirit
Of the Virgin Mary
And was made man
He was even crucified for us
Suffered under Pontius Pilate
And was buried
And on the third day
He rose again (according to the scriptures)
He ascended into heaven
And sits at the right hand of the Father
He will come again in glory
To judge the living and the dead
And of his kingdom there will be no end
And I believe in the Holy Spirit,
the Lord and Giver of life,
who proceeds from the Father and the Son,
who together with the Father and the Son is
   adored and glorified and
who spoke through the prophets
And one holy, catholic, apolostolic church
I confess one baptism for the forgiveness of sins
And I await the resurrection of the dead
And the life of the world to come
Amen
Amen

Holy, Holy, Holy
*Holy, holy, holy
Lord, God of hosts
Heaven and earth
are filled with your glory
Hosanna in the highest*

Blessed
*Blessed is he who comes
in the name of the Lord
Hosanna in the highest*

Lamb of God
*Lamb of God
Who takes away
the sins of the world
Have mercy on us*

*Lamb of God
Who takes away
the sins of the world
Have mercy on us*

*Lamb of God
Who takes away
the sins of the world
Grant us peace*

Over the sixteen years of my life as a sister in the Congregation of Notre Dame I wrote many settings of parts of the Mass, sometimes a Kyrie (in Greek in the traditional Latin Mass), sometimes a Sanctus, sometimes a complete Latin Mass. This setting was chosen for this book, because of the simplicity of its unison singing, its overall balance, and its use of the vernacular.

Mass
in Honor of Marguerite Bourgeoys
for Soprano, Alto, and Piano
Lord Have Mercy

Music by
Carolyn Brown Senier

Music © 1964-65 by Carolyn Brown and © 2005 by Carolyn Brown Senier.

Additional copies are available from Haley's • P O Box 248 • Athol, MA 01331
800.215.8805   haley.antique@verizon.net

Mass
in Honor of Marguerite Bourgeoys
Glory to God

Music by
Carolyn Brown Senier

Music © 1964-65 by Carolyn Brown and © 2005 by Carolyn Brown Senier.
Additional copies are available from Haley's • P O Box 248 • Athol, MA 01331
800.215.8805   haley.antique@verizon.net

Mass
in Honor of Marguerite Bourgeoys
Creed

Music by
Carolyn Brown Senier

Music © 1964-65 by Carolyn Brown and © 2005 by Carolyn Brown Senier.

Mass
in Honor of Marguerite Bourgeoys
Holy, Holy, Holy

Music by
Carolyn Brown Senier

Music © 1964-65 by Carolyn Brown and © 2005 by Carolyn Brown Senier.
Additional copies are available from Haley's • P O Box 248 • Athol, MA 01331
800.215.8805   haley.antique@verizon.net

Mass
in Honor of Marguerite Bourgeoys
Blessed

Music by
Carolyn Brown Senier

Music © 1964-65 by Carolyn Brown and © 2005 by Carolyn Brown Senier.
Additional copies are available from Haley's • P O Box 248 • Athol, MA 01331
800.215.8805
haley.antique@verizon.net

Mass
in Honor of Marguerite Bourgeoys
Lamb of God

Music by Carolyn Brown Senier

Music © 1964-65 by Carolyn Brown and © 2005 by Carolyn Brown Senier.
Additional copies are available from Haley's • P O Box 248 • Athol, MA 01331
800.215.8805   haley.antique@verizon.net

Meditation Alleluia

Alleluia, alleluia, alleluia, alleluia, alleluia

Alleulia, alleluia
(Alleluia)

Alleluia, alleluia, alleluia

Praise, O Creator
Praise, O Great God
Praise to your Holy Spirit

Alleluia, alleluia, alleluia, alleluia

Alleluia, alleluia, alleluia, alleluia, alleluia, alleluia, alleluia

Praise, O Creator
(Alleluia)
Praise, O Great God
(Alleluia)
Praise to your Holy Spirit
(Alleluia, Alleluia)

Amen
(Alleluia)

Traditional words
Praise to the Father
Praise to the Son
Praise to the Holy Spirit

The praise in this piece is born in stillness. This music is designed for use as a meditation hymn within the liturgy. The song embraces all the contemplation and prayer of the congregation, which precedes it and gives it voice. The alleluias respond as random aspirations within the gathering. It is an organ prayer, in which the human voice is used as a musical instrument, to accompany and give fullness to the organ. The voice functions, as it were, like the foundation stop on the organ, but it is a stop with words: "alleluia" and "praise." If there is no mixed chorus, the doxology could be sung in unison: the congregation's melody is written in the score. The melodies are repeated over rhythmic changes in each verse, starting quietly and ending in full voice. I had the melody quite early at Ridgefield, Connecticut, in the 1960s, but I never completely wrote it down until I retired to Lake Mattawa. Sister Reine LaFontaine (Sister Saint Reine Marie) always asked me for this music. With a choir of ten sisters from the Congregation de Notre Dame, I finally gave it to her at her funeral in 2002.

Meditation Doxology

for SATB Chorus and Organ
with Congregation and Soprano Descant

Words and Music by
Carolyn Brown Senier

Music © 1966 by Carolyn Brown and © 2005 by Carolyn Brown Senier.
Copyright includes adapted words by Carolyn Brown Senier.

Additional copies are available from Haley's • P O Box 248 • Athol, MA 01331
800.215.8805   haley.antique@verizon.net

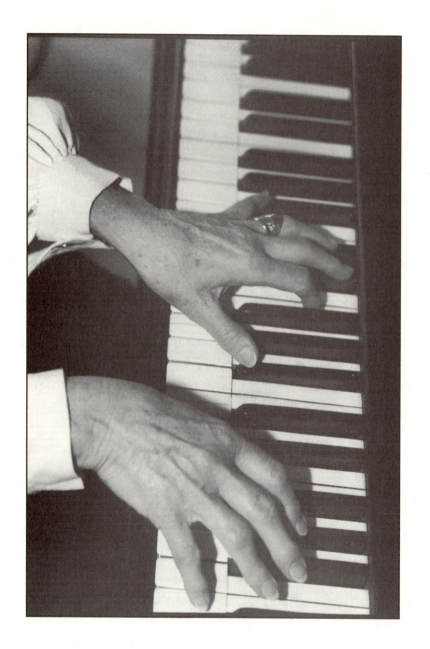

acknowledging all who have been part of the journey
good fortune has been my traveling companion

by Carolyn Brown Senier

Time became music again after we retired and moved to Lake Mattawa.

Time and quiet allow the music to fill me and overflow like the unfrozen spring after a long winter along the northeast side of our cottage. *The Mattawa Song Cycle* emerged from this gentle and beautiful setting that is our home.

Good fortune has been my traveling companion since I was born. My family knows this, my friends know this, and I want to acknowledge with joy all of you who have been part of the journey, who cared for the music and for me. You are truly the wind and the water moving and cradling me across the cove:

- my father, Edward Godfrey Brown, who loved to develop his students' hands for the piano, who worried about my hands when I would catch baseballs without a glove, who talked to me about the parable of the talents when I was not aware of such things, and who knew more than anyone how I needed music for my life
- my mother, Rosalene Carolan Brown, mother of nine, who brought me into the world last but gave me a great beginning. The music of the family party was in full swing by the time I arrived, and the harmonies and rhythms were secured. She always picked out the most beautiful melodies in every work, whether it was the "Flower Song" in the opera *Carmen* or a tune she wanted me to play over again on the piano

They both gave us a home life of music. Providing a home filled with music meant listening to the radio, *The Telephone Hour,* Saturday operas, and to Eddie Moriarty, pianist, who taught me to play "The Brook"; Bill Lawlor, bass baritone, who sang Sunday evening after Sunday evening in our living room while my father accompanied him and he sang the words "No rose in all the world" for my mother.

The first time this occurred, I was very young, and we—Bobby-Donny-Dicky-Carolyn—huddled on the top stairs listening in amazement as the singing began.

Home meant countless gatherings of musicians, of banjos, guitars, bass fiddles, wind instruments, drums. It meant quartets and choirs and playing piano duets with Dad and piano duets with Don. It meant growing up with Bach, Mozart, Beethoven, Haydn, Chopin; with Richard Rodgers and Vladimir Horowitz and Claudia Muzio and with a family character, Jeanette Cody, singing a rollicking song called "Bluebird." My sister Kaye brought her husband's family of musicians—mother, father, brother, uncle—all playing some sort of instrument: clarinet, piano, other wind instruments, even an ocarina (we called it a sweet potato). It was always fun to hear an old German favorite they sang—something about going over to Schmidt's house. When Ed McElligott joined our family, we gained a professional drummer, and the rhythm only got better.

Home meant listening, always listening. Listening to Verdi's *Requiem* with Bob, listening to Ed provide tremolo for melodies while chording harmonies on his banjo, to Joan playing "The Moonlight Sonata," to Don's performance of "The Warsaw Concerto." It meant listening and watching Roselyn teach me those I IV V chords in "Silent Night."

In the early days, Martin Cunningham let me sing in the church choir in Saint Francis Xavier Parish, "Uncle Louie" Boisvert gave me the experience of performing on the radio every week either singing, playing the piano, or doing creative sound effects. His program was called *Young Stars on Parade.* Sister Saint Reine Marie taught me to play the organ and grounded me in great choral music at Waterbury Catholic High School. Father Peter Cuny hired me to be his organist, and I stumbled into being a choral director when I was fifteen. The musical journey had just begun.

I entered the Congregation de Notre Dame at eighteen and became a sister. I met Sister Frances McManus, novice mistress, the superior who saw to it that I would continue my music education. She hired Mary Rita Partlow, a piano teacher from DePaul University who came fifty miles by train each week from Chicago to Bourbonnais, Illinois, to teach me. Sister Frances and those in charge of our education within the community sent me to various music schools: New York College of Music, Hunter College, Manhattanville College of the Sacred Heart, Boston University. During those sixteen years, I studied music, taught music, and became involved in liturgical music in a special way.

In the mid 1960s, while I was stationed at the novitiate in Ridgefield, Connecticut, this involvement became greater, but I was not alone in the endeavor. In particular, Sister Kathleen Deignan, Sister Mary Ann Foley, Sister Carmelia Cassano, Sister Barbara Arnesen, and in general the sisters of the Congregation de Notre Dame were all there singing their hearts out during the many programs we organized . . . and keeping me organized in those days was nearly a fulltime job for some of them.

And now, Sister Kathleen Deignan, composer, singer, writer, teacher, still part of my life, part of this book, is sharing insights in the foreword of our history going back beyond thirty-nine years of harmony.

The teachers at New York College of Music, particularly Ugo DiDeo and Vladimir Padua, were outstanding. The first taught harmony, the second, piano.

At Hunter College, Dr. Anders Emil taught choral music with fierce energy and understanding. Mildred Waldman coached me at the piano in the music of Chopin and Mendelssohn.

Summers at Manhattanville during the sessions of Pius X School of Liturgical Music were the best. Never did I live and breathe and exist in music in such a way. Every day, all day. I took it in as if I could never get enough of it. Mother Josephine Morgan was in charge of the program. She was full of talent and humor and goodness. She brought excellent teachers from other music schools as well for the summer sessions. She brought us Theodore Marier, Ralph Hunter, Dom Baron, and Dom Gajard, monks from Solemses, France. She also brought voice teachers, music history teachers, instrumentalists, concerts. What marvelous music there was contained in each. We studied and studied and concertized and went home exhausted and full and happy.

At Boston University Dr. Jack Lemons, Dr. Robert Choate, and Leon Tumarkin urged me on to a master's degree in music. Through this network, I was hired to teach music in Newton, Massachusetts. Samuel Turner and Dr. Olive Eldridge became my principals and trusted me with their music programs.

Sam Turner, Florence Clark, and the Turner family became our friends. We gathered many evenings in the early days with song, and they lovingly carried me into the experience of gospel music. Flo's "Down Here, Lord," "Early One Morning," and "Lullabye to a Black Man Child" are musical gems I hold dear.

And I met Richard, "tall tree, right arm, warm friend," who added layers of music, of harmony and counterpoint to the manuscript of my life. He also arrived in this world in the middle of a large musical family. He taught me all the songs I had missed out on since I was eighteen: "You Are Too Beautiful," "Long Before I Knew You" . . . Together we found Mahler's "Resurrection" and Puccini's *Turandot* and Verdi's *Nabucco*. In more than thirty years of a loving marriage, music has been at its heart.

Together we see the music continue in our families. Nieces and nephews abound in the legacy, and their children are more proficient in their instruments than any of us in earlier generations, composing, obtaining music scholarships, playing with orchestras at an early age, having their own bands.

Richard and I became business owners of Celtic Weavers in 1976. We had to squeeze music into our day. During this time, I began again to study piano at the Longy School of Music in Cambridge, where David Bacon, a beloved teacher, kept me at my development and technique. He taught in a way that often encompassed and compared literature and poetry with certain phrases in the composition under study.

And now here we are at the lake, living in a sweet cottage with a beautiful, large music room built by Tony Palmieri. Lake Mattawa is situated in north central Massachusetts, seventy miles west of Boston. The woods here are full of remarkable artistic, talented individuals. It is a privilege to live among them. We found the 1794 Meetinghouse thanks to Doris Abramson and Dorothy Johnson and soon became involved in the musical life there. Dorothy got me started again as a composer. I set her words for "I'd Give You the Moon" to music for her show *Home Movies:* the song is contained in this volume.

Marcia Gagliardi of Haley's Publishing in Athol and of the Meetinghouse was the catalyst for this project. She is a woman of vision, of courage and kindness and is truly sensitive to the world around her. Her uncanny intelligence lights up her work—and work she does.

Gathered around us for this whole enterprise are many. Ted Horman was more than generous with his time and talent. He patiently and always with good humor decoded my manuscripts and handwriting to produce printed music. Jeremy van Buskirk carefully digitized the manuscript for the Mass. Susan Aery also deciphered notes and computerized music manuscripts. She has an eye and an ear for the sound. Years before this book, we were discovering these sounds together.

Mary-Ann DeVita Palmieri wrote the biographical profile during a joyous year of questions and answers together. She has a rare ability of being an openhearted listener, bringing joy and honesty into any room she enters. Miryam Ehrlich Williamson edited copy with professionalism and diligence, and, often working with his wife Edna Haven, Rand Haven indexed *The Mattawa Song Cycle*, for him not a task but a discovery of our joint lives and relationships.

Sister Florence Bertrand works at the CND archives in Montreal where she found Cecilia Labrecque's name for me. Donald E. Denniston of the Boston University library staff located my master's thesis. Hope Chirino of Warner Brothers in Florida expedited the copyright reassignment for several of my compositions from Warner Brothers back to me.

My nieces Kathleen Brown-Carrano and Claire Lamontagne found family photos from the earlier era. The pictures can't help but widen our smiles and stir the chuckles in us.

Cantor Bruce Malin of Cape Cod Synagogue gave generous advice to "Song of Abraham," providing help with the transliteration, accented syllables, and written Hebrew text. I am also particularly grateful to Miryam Williamson for adding her knowledge of Hebrew and to Rabbi David Bauer for vetting the Hebrew text.

Richard Chase carefully recorded music for the CD and, with his wife Lynn, designed the album cover. Gretchen Saathoff, always a superb accompanist with fine musicianship provided articulate input for the harmonies of the piano scores.

The Lake Mattawa Singers and musicians of the Mark Morris Dance Company in New York thrilled me with their insightful and sensitive interpretations of my music under the direction of Geoffrey Hudson.

The Board of Directors of the 1794 Meetinghouse, Inc., in New Salem has consistently and enthusiastically encouraged me in developing and presenting my music, as have all the singers in Quabbin Valley Pro Musica. Hattie Nestel has generously encouraged and promoted my music behind the scenes.

Because of the generous support of the International Music and Art Foundation of Vaduz, Liechtenstein; the Composer Assistance Program of the American Music Center in New York City; the Western Massachusetts Community Foundation; and many individual and business donors, the realization of my music in this way has been possible.

Nicholas Thaw, executive director of the 1794 Meetinghouse, trusted in us, supported us with enthusiasm and care. He has a special talent for making things possible, gently shepherding our project, and he seems to love us as well as enjoy his work here. His arms have that stretching quality that allows him to embrace the whole community. They match his heart.

And then there is Geoff, salt of the earth. Geoffrey Hudson, born into music. Not only is he gifted but he is a gift to our community, to the 1794 Meetinghouse, to Quabbin Valley Pro Musica, to me. He is a brilliant composer, conductor, cellist, orchestrator, and musician. Those of us privileged to make music with him breathe in the atmosphere of his knowledge and deep love of music. He has given me confidence in my return to composing. He showed a sensitive ability to edit and listen while realizing, among other things, how I needed coaching for those tenor and bass voice ranges. His care concerning the manuscripts has been exceptional, making certain that the music looks the way it is supposed to sound. He has brought my music to life in concert performances. More than that, he brings great music to life in us, always looking for the musical line, for balance and beauty amidst the rhythms, melodies, and harmonies. Yes, Geoff is a gift to our community, and in my life and my heart, he is a grace. May his own signature, his beautiful music, fill the world's concert halls.

All of you, my Richard, my family, my friends, the spirit of goodness in all life—thank you for being part of my life, for breathing goodness from your own. Truly this is at once the rarest and most abundant of echoes in my songs.

supporters of the mattawa song cycle

More than $250.00

Dorothy Johnson and Doris Abramson, New Salem, Massachusetts

Jan and Jack Borden, Athol, Massachusetts

Composer Assistance Program, American Music Center, New York, New York

Marcia Gagliardi, Athol, Massachusetts

Edna and Rand Haven, Athol, Massachusetts

Dorothy E. Hayden, Athol, Massachusetts

Highland Press, Athol, Massachusetts

International Music and Arts Foundation, Vaduz, Liechtenstein

Mary-Ann and Tony Palmieri, New Salem, Massachusetts

Stan's Liquor Mart, Athol, Massachusetts

Western Massachusetts Community Foundation

Dorothy and Bucky Williams, New Salem, Massachusetts

www.susanwilsonphoto.com

To $250.00

Peter Gagliardi, Athol, Massachusetts

Hattie Nestel, Athol, Massachusetts

Susannah Whipps, Athol, Massachusetts

To $165.00

Gladys Barron, Centerville, Massachusetts

Katharine Bentley, Pennsauken, New Jersey

Lee Howe and Mel Wagner, Orange, Massachusetts

To $125.00

Breezeway Farm Consulting, Inc., New Salem, Massachusetts

Shirley and Peter Hebert, Athol, Massachusetts

*But how great my surprise
when at the day's end
I emptied my bag on the floor
to find a least little gram
of gold among the poor heap. . . .
There came a sound
in the dead of night. . . .
The night was still dark
when the drum sounded . . .
Open the doors, let the conch-shells be sounded!*

from *Gitanjali*
Rabindranath Tagore, 1913

music in progress: Carolyn at work on manuscripts

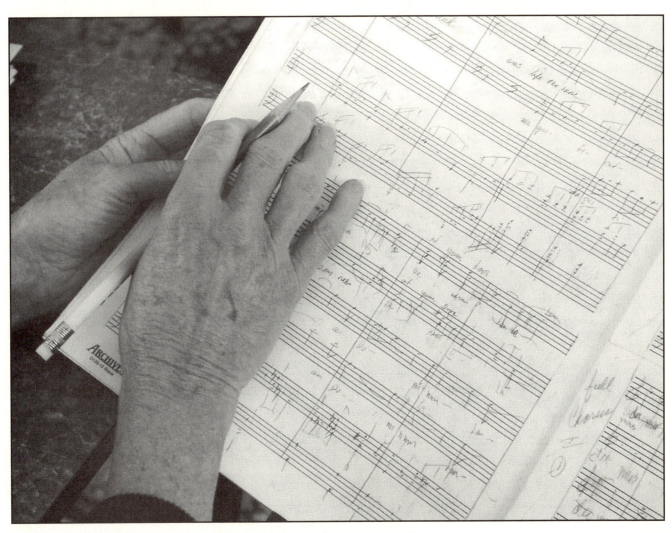

Carolyn at work on the evolving manuscript for "In Praise of Names," c. 2004

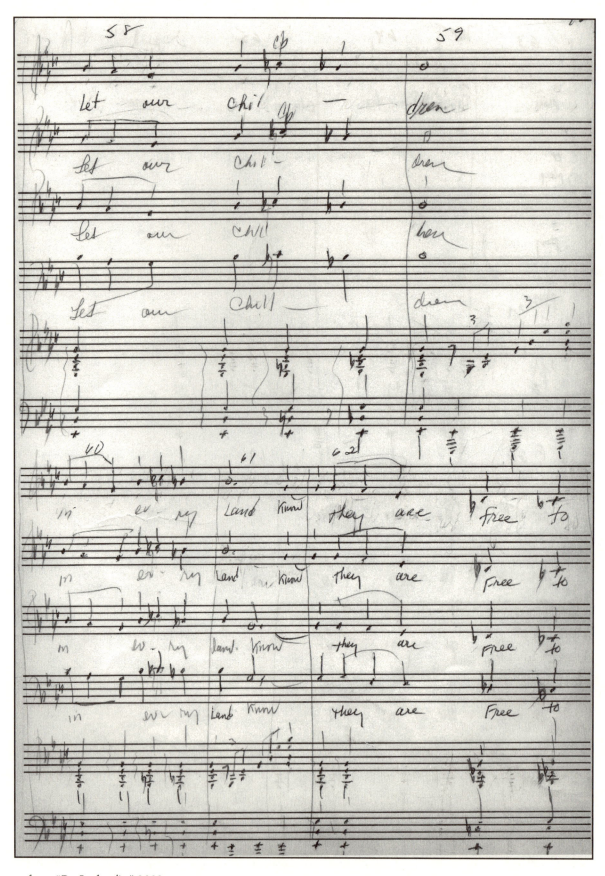

from "De Profundis," 2002

from "Pageant Song," 1954

from "Song of Abraham," 2003

from "I'd Give You the Moon," 1999

The light of . . . music illumines the world.
The life breath of . . . music runs from sky to sky.
The holy stream of . . . music
breaks through all stony obstacles
and rushes on.

from *Gitanjali*
Rabindranath Tagore, 1913

Carolyn's family gathered for a Christmas celebration, center photo, in 1949. More recently, in other photos, they have gathered to celebrate special occasions and each other.

a Brown family primer by Carolyn Brown Senier

Enumerating my relatives is a daunting task. Sheer numbers don't begin to express what makes us a clan. Not wanting to change a hair, a turn of phrase, or the way someone walks, giving just the right embellishment or none at all, I will mark a brief Brown family register centering on my sisters and brothers.

Katherine married Emil Mark. They have five children, thirteen grandchildren (twelve living, one deceased), and four great grandchildren.

Patricia died as a child.

Roselyn married Joseph Shea. They had no children. She died in 1960.

Joan married Edward McElligott. They have five children and nine grandchildren. She died in 1998.

Edward married Barbara O'Brien. They have eight children, seventeen grandchildren, and five great grandchildren.

Donald married Jeannette Lamontagne. They have two children and three grandchildren. He died in 2004.

Richard married Lorraine Swanson. They have five children (four living, one deceased) and two grandchildren.

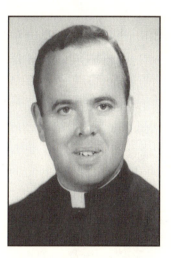

Robert has been a brother with the order of the Holy Cross for more than fifty years.

I married Richard Senier. We have no children.

When I think about listing aunts and uncles and cousins, I am confronted with the near impossible. I am reminded of the song "When I Was A Lad . . ." from *The Pirates of Penzance* by Gilbert and Sullivan: "We are his sisters and his cousins and his aunts."

There are many to enjoy. I remember my father's comment as we gathered around his bed at the end of his life: "I started out with only a father, but look what I have now—a dynasty."

Carolyn's 1973 Boston University master's thesis

music as an integral part of contemporary liturgical celebrations

Written to fulfill requirements for the Boston University master of music degree, Carolyn's thesis constitutes a treasure of insight into her musical thinking. It was written at a crucial juncture in the history of American sacred and Roman Catholic liturgical music. It also contains information about vibrant and progressive reformist ideas grounded in Roman Catholicism, other religious traditions, and secular disciplines.

In the early twenty-first century, the condition of music in the American Roman Catholic church has been much studied. Books on the subject include *Why Catholics Can't Sing, The Culture of Catholicism and the Triumph of Bad Taste* by Thomas Day; *From Sacred Song to Ritual Music, Twentieth Century Understandings of Roman Catholic Worship Music* by Jan Michael Joncas and *Knocking on Heaven's Door, American Religion in the Age of Counterculture* by Mark Oppenheimer. Uniformly, researcher-critics appear to agree that post-Vatican II American Catholic music often offers little fulfillment of promise that invigorated the late 1960s days when Carolyn served the Bridgeport diocesan liturgical commission.

In weighing Carolyn's 1973 words against descriptions of twenty-first century American Catholic music, one may wish the philosophies she advanced had prevailed. She describes music as metaphysical, an entré to transcendent worship. Her understanding is anchored in comprehensive understanding of chant. She is conversant with European and American musical traditions. Inspired by theological spirit, Carolyn's thesis envisions profound possibility for the future of Catholic liturgy and music. Unfortunately, it is not the future that was to be.

In Carolyn's *Mattawa Song Cycle*, one experiences sound and word demonstrating that appealing melody, complex harmony, vernacular language, and sincere intention can transcend the mundane. This is the future that could have been.

The thesis is entirely reprinted below. Carolyn agrees that masculine universal pronouns date the writing and that, if she were writing it today, she would have been attentive to a more gender neutral approach. That said, we have honored her wish that the thesis be presented here as she wrote it in 1973. Formatting has been altered to conform to the style of this book.

CHAPTER I
THE PROBLEM AND DEFINITIONS OF TERMS USED

Liturgical celebrations are an enigma. There exists severe tension among worshippers, a tension caused by their belief in God and by their need for expressing this belief.[1] The expression, like the belief, must be contemporary and relevant to the believer. When institutions set up criteria for expression, however, formalism soon replaces freedom of spirit and in a very short time the believers are diverted from belief in God to belief in the institution and the form.

This study does not seek to probe the age-old question of belief and unbelief. It deals with the experiences of believers and their struggles to achieve meaningful religious expression. Given the existence of ritual and celebration, the question of what is good for the believer, here and now, is as important today as it was a century or two ago, or as long as man has felt the need for worship.

In a tradition-minded church change takes place very slowly and stability is defined by adherence to the tradition. This is why liturgical music and texts which once expressed a faith experience that was very real and vital have lost much of their significance for modern man. One thinks immediately of the body of chant found in the manuscripts of the Middle Ages. Dom Gajard, late authority on Gregorian Chant, describes a twelfth century Agnes Dei as one which develops two kinds of prayer attitude, one very humble, the other a great cry for mercy.[2] While the music in itself is beautiful and calls to mind the faith of the past, a modern person must be conversant with Latin phrases if he is to realize (make real) the music symbols of neum notation. Yet, as recently as ten years ago, this form of liturgical music was prescribed for those persons preparing for service in Catholic parishes.

But not every music is a proper vehicle for religious expression. It takes courage to discard certain contemporary or past compositions as not being suited to liturgy when they have often arisen out of genuine religious feeling. The problem, then, for the church musician is how to keep pace with man's contemporary need without giving him methods of expression which are bound to fail him. It is a human problem, but a sense of tradition and history can be of great help.

I. THE PROBLEM

Statement of the Problem. The purposes of this study were

(1) to explore the meaning of celebration and to investigate the theological basis of Christian celebration;
(2) to examine the sociological and psychological factors which affect liturgy;
(3) to discuss the role of ritual in liturgical communities; and
(4) to present compositions which exemplify principles contained in the quest.

Importance of the Study. The musician within the church community is becoming increasingly confused. The document of Vatican Council II which deals with sacred music reiterates that religious singing by the people is to be fostered with skill. Though an apparently simple utterance it contains manifold challenges for the musician. He is called upon not only to create music suitable to the needs of the community but also to create a climate which will foster greater liturgical understanding.

Movement away from traditional structures of a "frozen liturgy" becomes either a threat to "status quo" security or a challenge to creativity. It seems imperative for today's church musician to rediscover within himself the basic reason for his position as minister of music for a particular worshipping community. The discovery will affect not only him but his music and those who will be touched by its power.

II. DEFINITION OF TERM USED

Ministerial Function. This is the only term used in the study which needs explication. It has a twofold direction. The first is concerned with the function of music as it is directly related to the liturgical action taking place. The second takes into consideration the particular assembly participating in the liturgy. Music cannot fulfill its ministerial function in liturgy if either aspect is neglected. Music which fulfills the ministerial function in worship attains this delicate balance between liturgical and communal demands.

III. SOURCES OF DATA

The sources of data in this study consist of writings in the fields of sociology and psychology which provided firm bases for the investigation of liturgy in today's society. Liturgical books and studies were critically examined, particular emphasis being given to the documents of Vatican II and writings subsequent to the issuance of these documents. Music literature related to liturgy was studied. Discussion with members of liturgical commissions and with liturgical musicians of various faiths provided valuable and practical assistance to the development of this study.

IV. ORGANIZATION OF THE STUDY

The study pivots around the concept of celebration. Celebration is viewed as part of life in Chapter II and as a part of theology in Chapter III. Chapter IV discusses man as a social being whose deepest religious expression is not divorced from his psychological existence but intimately bound up with it. In Chapter V the natural repeated expression of man's needs is seen as ritual. Chapter VI carries the previous themes into the basic understanding of liturgical music as an integral part of man's celebration. Chapter VII contains a personal contribution of musical compositions as a response to the creative opportunities liturgy affords church musicians. Chapter VIII contains a summary and conclusion and recommendations for further study.

CHAPTER II
CELEBRATION

Celebration is part of the human situation. Man needs to celebrate life. As he advances in technology and science and expands his vision of the universe and the world he lives in, a corresponding advance within the boundaries of his personal and communal values and vision is needed for balance and fulfillment. He does not glory in what is outside of himself without giving glory to what he is within, *i.e.,* if men were not gifted with tremendous ambitions and drives technology would not exist. There would be few technological triumphs in communication, in science, in industry unless man used the powers within his being to arrive at them. The danger lies in celebrating the "things" of man rather than the "fact" of man in relation to things. This is what celebrations means. It is man taking time to attend to what he is and who he is in his present state.

The nature of celebration is threefold. It is rooted in the past, expressed in the present and contains explosive power for the future. Humanity is enriched with energy that began its pulsations long ago, energy which has been building up and pulling man away from the boundaries of his closed world. This energy, released at the beginning of time, reaches us and lives in us now at this point in history. The paradox is that the more fully this energy is used, the more powerful it becomes for future generations.[3] It is not exhausted by use, rather it is developed and nurtured to greater power by use.

Events of history are recreated by looking back and seeing how events of the past have made a contribution to the "now" of man. Events of history both personal and communal are re-created by taking hold of oneself, one's life experiences. Man has the unique ability to incorporate into his own life the joys of other people and the experiences of previous generations.[4]

There are many levels of life experience which are causes for celebration. Some are more significant than others and therefore more festive in expression. There are personal experiences, patriotic experiences, even international experiences which man takes time to acknowledge in a special way. Some of these might be birthdays, days of national independence or moon landings. Cox writes that

> . . . our capacity to relate ourselves to time requires more than merely intellectual competence. Well-tabulated chronicles and sober planning alone do not keep us alive to time. We recall the past not only by recording it but by reliving it, by making present again its fears and delectations.[5]

The action of celebration is now and contemplation is part of this action. Heschel states that to celebrate means "to contemplate the singularity of the moment and to enhance the singularity of the self. What was shall not be again."[6] Although part of our mystery is revealed in such contemplation, our full dimension as a people continually unfolds in the present. Each individual is related to this totality and contributes to its growth. This relatedness underscores our responsibility toward each other. Individuals are important to one another. Our stature as individuals is significant (*i.e.,* "it has sign value") to others.

Celebration is full of such significance, of "sign value," and through celebration the meaning of the sign unfolds and becomes more present to men right now. An example of this would be the occasion of Mother's Day, a festival common to Americans. When families take time to attend to the "mother" qualities of their parent they gain a fuller realization of all that she is within herself and for others. In celebrating their mothers, they simultaneously acknowledge her being and become inspired by her being. Therefore, celebration helps man to give his attention to the transcendent meaning of his actions and to concentrate on the sublime or solemn aspects of living, in order to rise above the confines of consumption.[7]

Inspiration is the ground of a more significant life. A more significant life is the future orientation of our major celebrations.

In order for man to be inspired he must have attained insight into himself and his purpose in life. Celebrations, by renewing this purpose helps man to grow and to create his environment. The future is in the hands of man. Jung writes that

> . . . anyone who has insight into his own action, and has thus found access to the unconscious, involuntarily exercises an influence on his environment.[8]

Only the man who can celebrate can fully participate in life. Hugo Rahner points out that a fully developed man is one who celebrates.[9]

Essentially celebration is communal. Since each man is a product of group membership the feeling of community, of belonging-ness, is essential to normal living.[10] Read emphasizes the necessity for community when he says, "We establish love by communication, and over against the unconscious group soul, we must create a conscious group soul, a community of integrated and interrelated personalities."[11] This belonging-ness helps man to establish right relationships necessary to human development and achievement. Bonner says that

> . . . it may very well be a truth which history might some day demonstrate, that the peace and freedom about which men dream will be realized when they universally share goals and obligations with one another.[12]

Each person brings to the celebration of our collective history the life that has developed within him which is now becoming new history. Balance between the individual and the community must be earnestly sought if celebration is to be a ceremony in which each finds something of his own to share with others

The need for community is grasped and expressed by many modern writers. Brameld maintains that

> . . . the single strongest need among human beings, whatever their race, creed, or nationality, is to find a common ground—a common ground on which to stand not against one another, but with one another.[13]

Thomas Hopkins expresses the concept of community in terms of group process which he defines as

> . . . the way people work together to release an emergent quality, called psychological climate...or cooperative unity, through which each discovers and develops his inner capacities, realizes better the nature of his self, releases more of his past experiences and learns how to create this emergent quality in all life situations.[14]

In this way creative ability, previously unknown, is released into society, is released into a group whose past has made it one and whose present celebration gives it the impetus to become yet more one.

Summary

Ordinary living becomes more significant when man takes time to celebrate. The effect of celebration is both inward, refreshing and renewing the whole man, and outward, continuing the faith-centered dynamism of human society.

Celebration is as integral to the evolutionary process as bodily functions, population migrations, or interplanetary travel.

CHAPTER III
CHRISTIAN CELEBRATION: SOME THEOLOGICAL ASPECTS

Some people believe in God. Seeing their lives in relation to a supreme being outside of themselves we can justly call them religious. According to Cox, a religious person

> . . . is one who grasps his own life within a larger historical and cosmic setting. He sees himself as part of a greater whole, a longer story in which he plays a part.[15]

This study is not primarily concerned with the names of God, nor with the various theophanies of the world's history. Man has chosen through the centuries to describe his relationship to God. World religions have continued to carry their themes forward in diverse manners. There can be unity in diversity, especially when certain aspects of familiar themes are stressed. While Christians have been the object of the pundit's scorn for their divisions, it is possible to praise them for their retention of much of their Founder's spirit. The continuity of belief is strengthened by expression, by celebration, and these are conditioned by a variety of influences, among which are environment and order.

The Christian is a person who has a faith vision set upon the man called Jesus, a faith vision which adds a dimension to his own life. He experiences "living and moving and having his being"[16] in the God to whom he is related. Being "in God" transforms human "beingness." Teilhard de Chardin writes that "in the new humanity which is begotten today the Word prolongs the unending act of his own birth."[17] Man is fulfilled, filled so full of what is beyond himself that he must cry out in ecstasy, echoing the restless cry of Saint Augustine. Thus a new and more dramatic form of celebration is called for. It is called liturgy. Liturgist John Giuliani, exploring the nature of Christian liturgy, has said that at heart

> . . . liturgical life is rooted in the mystery of Incarnation. For it is the Christ, the God-Man, who leads us in prayer. We must be taken into the movement of Christ. We must make contact with the mystery of his passage through death to resurrection. Although this took place in history, it must in some way be made present to us in the church so that we can share in it.[18]

By symbolic re-presentation of the saving work which Christ enacted in the historical past, the liturgy makes that saving work present. The liturgy re-actualizes the Paschal mystery now so that men can join themselves to it. What happened in Christ, the head, is meant to happen to us, the members, namely that "divine love makes itself felt in the world in the human love of the Incarnate Son of God."[19]

The outpouring of love is the future-directed aspect of liturgy. Liturgy, however, does retain the present and past aspects of all celebration. The "Spirit" rests not only on our past achievements, on our future goal, but on our efforts on our way. To say, "I am the Way . . . ,"[20] implies movement toward something. As members of the Body of Christ, Christians regularly come together and then disband into the world creating the cosmic temple. Those who are building the temples are involved in the work of unifying, sanctifying, proclaiming and witnessing.

The liturgy builds up those who are united into a holy temple of the Lord, into a dwelling place for God and the Spirit to the mature measure of the fullness of Christ, and at the same time marvelously strengthens their power to proclaim Christ.[21]

As the Father expresses his love for mankind through the flesh of his Son, so through that same flesh of Jesus man's response draws him toward the Father, into the inner life of God. And the inner life of God is communal. "I and my Father are one."[22]

The revelation of God's life as communal has deep significance for the Christian community. Christian community is human community charged with the life of the man-God. Christ's Passover is open to every man so that each one might experience his own personal sonship to the Father in union with the one community of sonship.

In recent theological writings and theory focus has

come to be centered on communal aspects of liturgical celebration. This new emphasis was a natural reaction against the predominantly individualistic orientation which had dominated liturgical theology and piety for centuries. But it is essential that reaction not cause liturgy and particularly liturgists to lose a sense of balance in this area.

Jung points out a danger in "seeking for that certainty which will keep me, as an individual, from dissolving in the crowd.[23] He believes that

> . . . real and fundamental change in the individual can come only from the personal encounter between man and man, but not from communities or Christian baptisms, en masse, which do not touch the inner man.[24]

He finds support for this thesis in some basic tenets of Christian belief which he thinks should not be forgotten. He writes that

> . . . unlike other religions, Christianity holds at its core a symbol which has for its content the individual way of life of a man, the Son of Man, and that it even regards this individuation process as the incarnation and development of the self requires a significance whose full implications have hardly begun to be appreciated.[25]

In his subsequent criticism of Christian community, however, he fails to take into account its deeper significance. He says:

> When the Church tries to give shape to the amorphous mass by uniting individuals into a community of believers with the help of suggestion and tries to hold such an organization together, it is not only performing a great service, but it also secures for the individual, the inestimable boon of a meaningful life form. These, however, are gifts which as a rule confirm certain tendencies and do not change them. As experience unfortunately shows, the inner man remains unchanged however much community he has. His environment cannot give him as a gift that which he can win for himself only with effort and great suffering.[26]

It is true that the community understood simply as a socio-political assembly of persons has no power in itself to change or transform. But the man of Christian faith-vision understands the essence of authentic Christian community because he has celebrated it in the liturgy. He finds its transforming power in what Jung has called those implications that have not fully been appreciated in its core symbol: the person of Jesus Christ.[27]

Summary

Liturgical experience is concerned with people and how they feel about each other and about God. It is communal but the community shares a faith-vision that transcends mundane purposes. Goals, means, terrestrial and celestial concerns, are all under the umbrella of a hardly definable faith experience. The faith which impels the Christian to liturgy and to celebration is a mystery every bit as strange and wonderful as the mystery of his own existence.

CHAPTER IV
SOCIOLOGICAL AND PSYCHOLOGICAL FACTORS WHICH AFFECT CELEBRATION: THEIR IMPLICATIONS FOR THE MINISTER OF MUSIC

The recent rise in the formation of diocesan liturgical commissions by church leaders offers real opportunity for more genuine and truly representative liturgies. Many parishes experience the painful discovery that the training and liturgical orientation of their choir directors and organists is inadequate for their own needs in a changing society and a changing church.

As an outgrowth of modern ecumenical process communication has become all important. Examination of confessional differences has led to the discovery of similarities which defy dogmatism and institutional coercion. The great cry of "Freedom" which echoes through the world today, admittedly most vocal in the freer countries, is often accompanied by liturgies and celebrations, profane and religious.

But freedom has responsibilities and Christians who desire a voice in their communities, a movement away from either absolutism or anarchy, are finding that it is not easy to secure liturgists who are both properly equipped and concerned with relevant church ministry. The task of ordering community celebrations, therefore, is no longer left to the fiat of a despotic choir director or pastor in an increasing number of parishes. There is a struggle for the sharing of responsibility and of direction by people whose feet are firmly planted on earth and whose desire is to see their real world reflected in their celebrations. This does not necessarily mean that the minister is out of date, but rather, he must be aware that the first duty of ministry is to minister and that closely allied to it is the continual search for the signs and symbols, the very pulse of life. For the minister of music this can be a joyous search since the poetry and music of life greet the sensitive person at every turn. The church musician is no less part of the real world if he chooses to be, no less in need of communal sharing, no less in need of communal input.

Stephen C. Rose submits a description of the church in terms of three basic resources, *i.e.*, the work of abandonment, of teaching, and of chaplaincy.[28] Within the latter description he includes the musician whose ministry is bound up with the liturgical life of the church. The ever increasing importance and standing of the liturgist makes it imperative for him to grow in understanding of basic sociological aspects of liturgy. *His artistry, then which is needed within the framework of community more than ever, will be firmly rooted in true liturgical needs.*

The document of Vatican II which deals with sacred music states that "religious singing by the people is to be skillfully fostered."[29] This statement, though apparently simple, contains many challenges for the musician. He is expected now to assume greater musical responsibility toward the whole community which far exceeds the responsibility of maintaining a church choir. The musician is required not only to create music suitable to the needs of the community, but also to create a climate which will foster greater musical and liturgical understanding and meaningful involvement. The structure of liturgical celebration is gradually being shaped by the needs of the worshipping community, thus necessitating diversity of forms for liturgy. Such diversity increases the scope of a musician's ministry.

The fact that communication is at the heart of all ministry has great significance if music is to be more than just something "tagged on" to a ceremony. *Liturgical music is meant to be an expression that can be understood by the community and one which the community can make its own.* This is a sociological and psychological orientation for the occupation with artistic values. This orientation is a challenge to his creative abilities rather than a threat and compromise to "good art."

The Need for Community and its Implications for Liturgy

The subject of community and communication within society is of growing importance for sociologists, psychologists and liturgists. Tournier writes about the lack of communication and its effect in society. His reflections point out the need for communication, as when he states, "Most of our contemporaries, dragooned and drowned in our mass society, caught in the vortex of speed, find themselves isolated in unbelievable spiritual solitude."[30]

These insights concerning social and psychological needs are not merely empty words. Read strongly states that

> . . . we must love one another or die. We establish love by communication and over against the unconscious group soul (referred to by Jung) we must create a conscious group soul, a community of integrated and interrelated personalities. The means towards this end are always active.[31]

To insure the deepest meaning within the liturgical activity is the constant striving of liturgical ministers. Liturgists are gradually turning to sociologists for direction in their ministry. To listen to sociologists is part of ministry.

Canon Francois Houtart, Director of the Center of Socio-Religious Research at Louvain University, and General Secretary for the International Federation of Institutes for Social and Socio-Religious Research, presented a paper at an international colloquium held at Louvain in June, 1967. The nature and scope merit consideration with this research, his topic being *Sociological Aspects of the Liturgy*.[32] He said that in every social body such as the church there are three functions of importance, *i.e.*, communication, socialization, and creating a sense of belonging. They relate to foundations of every society in which men are joined through reciprocal relationships in pursuit of a given goal. Communication is at the very center of all human relations.

He observes two reasons for this avenue of inquiry into the role of liturgy which pertain to this study: first, the present transformation of society and culture throughout mankind which places the church in a new situation; second, the conviction that liturgy can play a very important role in these matters. The church must depend more and more upon its own resources to carry out its function in a society and culture which by reason of their growing autonomy no longer guarantee automatic service to the church.

He justifies his assertion briefly by reviewing aspects of the transformation of mankind as a whole and of the institution which is the church. The twofold transformation concerns men and nature and social relationships among men.

The church, by reason of its human and social character, participates in the profound changes in the world and mankind.

From a sociological point of view, every institution results from the combination of a set of values with an organization intended to serve them. Within its own institution Vatican II has set up a powerful machinery for change and with a giant stride reversed the weight of "value concern" from "ecclesial value" in its own right to service of the gospel. Contemporary sociology of institutions calls such decision "critical decision," *i.e.*, relating to the definitions of the church itself and of its objectives.

The inward objectives of the church, which are those of its pastoral function, can find expression through two orientations. On the one hand, there is the purpose of helping each Christian to assimilate evangelical values, norms and attitudes. On the other hand, there is the goal of establishing a community, a people. These are precisely the two functions of socialization.

The major importance given by Vatican II to the Catholic's participation and his personal responsibility shows that it is really a matter of internalizing Christian values. Membership in the church is defined less in juridical terms than by the effective participation in the life of the community.

Vatican II has placed the emphasis on values, and this will have a much more explosive effect on organization than a simple organizational reform. However, for those for whom the sense of belonging to the church was based on external social control, security is lessened or even lost.

It is probable that the role of the liturgy in the church as a body will continue to increase, at the very moment when a profane, pluralistic and mobile society is offering fewer opportunities for the automatic transmission of religious values and norms, and fewer stable forms of belonging that assure cohesion to the religious group. Ecclesial society must therefore increase its role in those areas through specific action.

The liturgy can play a major part in the evolution if it becomes more accessible (a channel of communication), *more closely linked with the happenings of life* (a transmission of values and norms of Christian behavior), *and more diversified* (offering multiple forms to manifest the fact of belonging to the church of Jesus Christ).

This brings us to the basic study of communication. Communication is at the very heart of social life. It structures and constitutes every kind of community. All communication presupposes rites, ceremonies, vocabularies, conventions, signs, symbols, gestures, and words that make up their backbone.

Communication is accomplished in a variety of ways. Signs and symbols are used when there is no need to go beyond language. But there is a non-intentional or non-explicit communication. Even before a person or group establishes the desired communication with another person or group, the image projected by the person or group is already a form, a communication which will influence explicit communication.

Besides consideration of the mechanics of communication such as the transmitter, receiver, signal, or support for communication and feedback, Houtart emphasizes its cultural and social context. In all communication there must be a minimum zone of common culture if the signal emitted by the transmitter is to be understood by the receiver. The common zone varies according to the kinds of communication. There is a kind of universal human language that everyone understands. But in the measure that the sign emitted becomes more conventional or symbolic the necessity of this common zone increases. This is true of all religious communication whether verbal or symbolic. Whether we want to teach, inspire to action, arouse the expression of an emotion, or to provide a sign of transcendent reality, there must be a common cultural zone for effective communication.

The church is essentially communicative. It communicates more than a body of information or teaching. It communicates a life, Jesus Christ. While the maximal communication can be perceived only through faith, the sociologists and psychologists can say in what measure the sign of life is perceived and under what conditions. For example, if one has studied the question he can tell in what measure and under what conditions a given symbol is efficacious as a support to communication.

In today's society the liturgy assumes a place of importance because religious communication is also becoming a specific activity that is not measured by the culture as a whole. It is therefore necessary that the social and psychological content of liturgical action be more compact. Liturgical action is no longer simply a cultural act of a pre-existing community. It is becoming increasingly one of the means by which a given community of Christians is constituted. This has been always true theologically but not socially and psychologically.[33]

Church musicians must come to grips with these sociological facts if their music is to attain its true ministerial function, if they are to be liturgically relevant within their specialized ministry.

On the threshold of real liturgical renewal the liturgist cannot go back in time to look for art music that was suitable for the culture of the past. The treasury of music which is preserved by the tradition of the church was directly linked with the kind of liturgical experience that is no longer relevant. Although the aesthetic value of this music still exists, much of it has no direct integral application to present day liturgy.[34] The creative musician has his role to play now as never before in the Catholic church. Liturgy is now open to receive the innumerable styles of musics with which this generation of believers has become familiar.

The style of music for a particular service also has definite relationship to the size of the community of worshippers. Houtart distinguishes three types of groups in relation to the size of the liturgical participation: *the small group*, defined on the basis of the opportunity it affords all members to have interpersonal contacts (from fifteen to twenty persons); *the assembly* which includes a larger number of persons whom we can already characterize as a public because interpersonal relations are expressed only by collective reactions or symbolic gestures; *the throng* which involves the presence of a public that cannot be held in a place normally used by an assembly, *i.e.,* a place of worship such as Yankee Stadium.

Sociologists question liturgists concerning the possibility of inventing forms appropriate for each of these types. As of now, a single liturgical form exists which is adapted with varying degrees of success to the diverse kinds of groups or publics.[35]

Small groups are able to offer peculiar advantages for certain types of liturgical experiment. Experiments on liturgy are delicate matters dealing with persons on a level of profound instincts, profound beliefs, profound needs, profound behavioral patterns. Small groups are less likely to violate persons by misunderstanding them and engaging in careless or thoughtless actions in experimentations.

Small groups lend themselves particularly to experiments in connection with the celebration of the word and discussion on the word, or in ways of manifesting solidarity in the communion rite, or in a more intensive and spontaneous kind of petitionary prayer. Hovda said

> . . . while the experiments of small groups may be of great value to our future experimenting with larger groups, we cannot assume that what works, what is effective in the small group celebration is going to be equally successful in the other kind.[36]

Individuals who participate in the assembly may not want to be integrated into small-group relationships. There is obviously no objection to the assembly's giving various small groups the opportunity to come together or to form under its aegis, but the two realities must not be confused.[37]

Liturgy plays a role in religious socialization that can become more significant in the future. The first aspect of socialization has been closely related to communication. The second aspect is linked to belonging; belonging with the people of God everywhere in the world and within a particular group of people.

Belonging to the church is determined less and less by geographic, cultural or judicial solidarity.

Belonging involves a psychological reality. An attitude is created in a person who reacts favorably to an object (in this case, the church). This attitude originates by way of conversion or education, but it can increase or decrease.

But belonging has also a social aspect; it is the group to which one belongs. Membership in the church is normally accomplished through the mediation of very specific groups. According to Carrier, four conditions are required if the church is to play its part as an authentic object of religious belonging. There must be a minimum of interaction and hence of participation in the activity of the group, acceptance of its values and norms, a certain identification with the group, and finally, acceptance of the member by the group.

Present day participation in ecclesial activity has changed. Pre-technical society was characterized by membership in several basic groups which carried out all the functions the individual normally expected of society. Group membership revolved around the large family, the village or the neighborhood. Religious functions followed this social model.

In secular society, individuals belong to many monovalent groups which carry out a clearly defined function relating to gainful employment, leisure, the family, and so on. In the area of religion, likewise, monovalent groups have multiplied. Hence groups and movements directed to the deepening of religious life, mutual assistance and support have arisen.

Belonging to the church is therefore diversified, not only by reason of the various types of groupings or activities in which individuals take part and that have specialized objects, but also by reason of the multiple opportunities that exist within the activities. Liturgy is an example of this. The bond between the parish as geographically defined and the Eucharistic assembly is becoming more flexible by reason of urban mobility, tourism, secondary residences, and the extension of the Saturday evening mass.

This twofold phenomenon of distance with respect to the natural group and of diversities in modes of belonging gives reason for thinking that the liturgy is going to play an important role in the matter of religious belonging. *The psychological aspect of belonging will be fostered if the liturgical act becomes integrated into the culture of the individual, both because the words, gestures, and symbols are meaningful to him, and because he has been initiated into what is specific in religious communication.*

Belonging has a social significance which presupposes a conscious role and hence a responsible participation in a group. Obviously there are many forms of responsible participation. The liturgy does not have a monopoly on it. However, we may wonder as to the real depth of participation on the part of a great many people in the liturgy in its present form. In this connection we cannot forget that in urban areas only a minority belonging to every distinct social group really participates in weekly worship (the percentage is from ten to thirty percent in the cities of Western Europe or of Latin America, and from thirty to sixty percent in the cities of North America). Is not the liturgical assembly as now constituted in many places so completely imprisoned in a given cultural pattern that the group of practicing Catholics acts as a kind of negative reference? There are those who refuse to be identified with this socio-cultural group, and consequently, to participate in the activities, even of a religious nature, that give expression to its culture. And even for those who go to the Sunday assemblies the opportunities for participation remain limited. Once again the question arises: are there not other forms that might be more suitable which could be geared to the small group?[38]

The challenge for the musician is rooted in the same sociological facts as liturgy itself. There is an increasing philosophical and educational interest in the function of music in a changing society, as a form of human communication and as a real human need.[39] The recent symposiums at Tanglewood and at Manhattanville College, New York, give contemporary evidence of this. Educators all over the country are striving to incorporate music more and more within an ever more scientifically oriented curriculum. The existence of a technological society accents the need for beauty, that intangible reality with which music becomes so bound. Contemporary society calls for the establishment of "common ground" on which its members can meet. But as Brameld maintains

> . . . this common ground cannot be cultivated merely by technological advancement. It can be cultivated also, and far more tellingly, through the symbols of mythical communion . . . symbols that proclaims the universality of human strivings and human hopes in ways that music or drama or other creations of the aesthetic man are able to proclaim them.[40]

Summary

Religious belonging and communication are deeply grounded in sociological and psychological reality, a fact finally reaching theologians and liturgists. Symbols of liturgical expression are alive to meaning only insofar as they are created within a sociological and psychological framework. Liturgical celebration can be a unique means of expressing the partial truths of several sciences, acknowledging the perfect truth of the transcendent God from an always changing but always dependent world.

CHAPTER V
RITUAL

An action which is the natural expression of man's physical, psychological or spiritual need becomes ritual when repeated for a reason beyond the act itself. It is repeated because the past even with which it is associated is now recognized as significant. Ritual actions retain meaning to the extent that their symbols are clear and the past action commemorated still has significance in the presence. Symbols are the stuff of which ritual is made. "Symbols are important means of reference and communication. But symbols also function as a means of formulating experience."[41]

Ritual is a vehicle of man's celebration of himself; it captures and contains history in the Judaeo-Christian tradition. In earlier traditions the rites celebrate the mysteries of nature. Within celebration rituals link us to a world of memories, gestures, values and hopes that we share with a larger community.[42] Annual or occasional ceremonies provide the principal focus of living. When one looks at traditional societies like Bali, for example, he finds that celebration is inseparable from ritual. Activities which are highly stylized are repeated from celebration to celebration, from procession to procession, from year to year. Such activities are essential parts of the whole. However, Cox writes that

> . . . we should see it not as a content to which people must comply, but as a structure within which they can pulsate and pirouette in unprescribed ways.[43]

Because ritual is repeated action it tends to become commonplace and static, unrelated to the present moment of the celebration. As Gardner notes, "nothing is more readily observable in the life of organizations than the triumph of form over spirit."[44] By means of its symbols ritual focuses our attention on an event of the past to make that event new in order that we might be made new. Thus ritual must be translated into the "now idiom," for what is happening is not a reliving but a new birth. If the event becomes new then the ritual must be open enough to accept newness, must encourage us to be free in our response to the event which touches us. There must be room for "spontaneous ritual."

Too often our celebrative potential remains dormant. Archaic ritual frequently hinders the spirit of modern man, and what was once intended to free our expression becomes now a hindrance. However, there must be a continuity in ritual as well as spontaneity. A person who, on a plea of preserving spontaneity, refuses to submit to any religious discipline, will find his piety becoming extinguished. Just as we were not able to grasp life apart from the automatic living phenomena of the body and the mind, so we are unable to conceive of spiritual life detached from all concrete and regular expression.[45] Gardner warns us to guard

> . . . against the notion that continuity is a negligible if not reprehensible factor in human history. It is a vitally important ingredient in the life of individuals, organizations, and societies. Particularly important to a society's continuity are its long-term purposes and values . . . By being relatively durable, they enable a society to absorb change without losing its distinctive character and style.[46]

Further, ritual in any era is conditioned by the society of the celebrants. In fact, ritual is not only largely determined by environment but contributes to the very identity of man. Tournier observes

> . . . it is impossible to understand a Frenchman, a Finn, a Greek or an American without putting him in the context of the scenery of his life, the history of his people, the background of his family, his job, his *festivals*, and his *customs*.[47] (italics are the author's)

But today's society is accused of "losing the power of celebration."[48] Cox puts forth an even stronger indictment of our present ability to celebrate:

> Whatever forms of festivity and fantasy remain to us are shrunken and insulated. Our celebrations do not relate us, as they once did, to the parade of cosmic history or to the great stories of man's spiritual quest. Our fantasies tend to be cautious, eccentric, and secretive. When they do occasionally soar, they are appreciated only by an elite. Our feasting is sporadic or obsessive, our fantasies predictable and politically impotent. Neither provides the inspiration for genuine social transformation.[49]

Heschel suggests that "a renewal of our strength will depend on our ability to reopen forgotten resources."[50] There is such a thing as creative tension. It is important to build creatively from the tension between celebration's spontaneity and ritual's routine. Christianity has here a mission to remind man that he has cause for rejoicing and then to offer him the means to sing his joy. It is better to fulfill this mission that the second Vatican Council called for renewal, a return to the roots of Christianity. "In this assembly, under the guidance of the Holy Spirit, we wish to inquire how we ought to renew ourselves, so that we may be found increasingly faithful to the gospel of Christ.[51] At this time there is particular need for liturgy to be intense. This is always true because of the intensity of the reality to be communicated, the reality of God Himself. "Our faith needs to be aroused, supported and guided; it must be given a favorable atmosphere to which our whole being contributes for its development."[52] In the present circumstances, however, in its attempt to reach the whole man, liturgy must compete with other communications media, such as movies, television and recordings. No longer has the church the prerogative of being the center of pageantry for its people as it was until the last two decades. Further in the past the church ceased to be the stimulus and vehicle for the music of the world's great composers. It is the creative opportunities which liturgy affords composers which the remainder of this paper will explore.

Summary

Man needs ritual for a meaningful liturgical life. Ritual is conditioned by various types of societies and makes its own contributions to them. Of the arts with which ritual binds itself so intimately, music has a place of prominence.

The need for openness is seen once again if ritual is to be truly responsive to the needs of contemporary society. Stripped of much of the unnecessary trappings of an earlier, more mundane ecclesial concept, the church has a grand opportunity for returning to the spirit of the Gospel, by doing that which she can and ought to do better—than any other body—worship and celebrate.

CHAPTER VI
LITURGICAL MUSIC

Song has from earliest times had an association with public worship. This is true of all cultures, whether pagan or religious. Indian songs, for example, can be traced to the pre-Buddhist epoch (about 600 B.C., and earlier), in which the music consisted "mostly of the cantillation of the holy books of the *Veda*."[53]

Through the course of history this response of creatures to their Creator or Supreme Being through Song has been reiterated. The Roman Catholic liturgy which originally fostered much public proclamation through song, passed through hundreds of years of historical change and developments. By the nineteenth century there was a serious decline in the grand tradition of religious musical composition. Public unity was absent from public worship. Hovda quotes this observation from *The Christian Failure*, by Ignace Lepp:

> It looks as if the five hundred odd people who assemble at Mass meet there purely by chance, and the more I see of this the more I realize the gulf between the present-day parish and the Christian communities of the first centuries.[54]

We became a people of traditions, some of which often hindered the purpose of a liturgical life. Total involvement of the congregation through public participation became improbable if not impossible. The general attitude toward liturgy was not associated with the lives and community worship of God's people. Rather, it was associated with the notions of private isolation in prayer. An hour or two of the week was set aside during which the faithful, however sincere, spent some quiet moments in prayer at Mass. These moments were, in many cases, times of isolation from the brethren kneeling in the same pew. Private, not public prayer was the type most frequently fostered at Mass.[55]

Singing was relegated for the most part to the choir. A competent choir performed "difficult and beautiful music" while the congregation remained critics or spectators. Often, even the competent choir was lacking and so was beautiful music. The essential note of prayerful interior response through song seemed far removed in many cases from the music at Mass. Congregational singing was rare. When the people did sing, the type of hymn was apt to be the sweet nineteenth century second rate music whose texts would now repel us.[56]

This long period of silent worship excluded the possibilities of a public proclamation and a public response through song to faith experience. A possible exception would be the Betsingmessen of the German Catholic area

(Bavaria, Austria, and especially the Rhineland).[57] The Betsingmessen literally means the Pray Sing Mass. But the Catholic population as a whole rarely sang good hymns. This was the condition that prompted Pope Pius XI to say, "It is in truth altogether necessary that the faithful should not behave like strangers or mute spectators."[58]

In the past, Pope Saint Pius X issued general directives on Sacred Music. In his *Motu Proprio* he wrote:

1. Sacred music, being a complementary part of the solemn liturgy, participates in the general scope of the liturgy, which is the glory of God and the sanctification and edification of the faithful. It contributes to the decorum and the splendor of the ecclesiastical ceremonies, and since its principal office is to clothe with suitable melody the liturgical text proposed for the understanding of the faithful, its proper aim is to add greater efficacy to the text, in order that through it the faithful may be more easily moved to devotion and better disposed for the reception of the fruits of grace belonging to the celebration of the most holy mysteries.
2. Sacred music should consequently possess, in the highest degree, the qualities proper to the liturgy, and in particular sanctity and goodness of form.[59]

The *New Ordo Missae* of 1970 gives these musical priorities for parochial usage:

I. ACCLAMATIONS: should be sung even at masses where little else is sung
   a) The Alleluia - introduces the Gospel; all stand to sing it.
   b) The Sanctus - unison; choir and congregation
   c) Memorial Acclamation- all four should be used; communal expression of belief.
   d) Great Amen - communal approval of the Eucharistic Prayer; unison; choir and people.
   e) Great Doxology to Lord's Prayer - should be tied into the Lord's prayer musical setting when possible.

II. PROCESSIONAL SONGS: vital to our sense of community,
   a) Entrance Song - options:
      1) Introit antiphon with psalm; or
      2) Simple Gradual replacement; or
      3) Appropriate hymn or refrain with verses
   b) Communion Song - same options as above.

III. RESPONSORIAL PSALM: after first Reading in the Liturgy of the Word
   a) can be recited, as is the present custom, with lector and people.
   b) could be sung: simple setting of the refrain, intoned first by a cantor, and then repeated by all, and after each of the verses sung by the cantor.
   c) seasonal responses that can be used, facilitating the congregation's learning the response; used on several succeeding Sundays.

IV. ORDINARY CHANTS
   a) Lord, Have Mercy - can be sung in its simple six-fold state; or used in the Penitential Rite III: cantor, people, choir.
   b) Gloria - can be alternated between people and choir and / or cantor. On special occasions choir alone.
   c) Lord's Prayer - should be a straight-forward simple setting. Workable version is II in the Sacramentary.
   d) Agnus Dei - accompanies the fractio (breaking of the bread). It is a litany in structure and the people can respond, "Have mercy on us," to the invocation, "Lamb of God . . . world." It can be sung many times; the last time conclude with, "Grant us peace."

V. SUPPLEMENTARY SONGS
   a) Offertory - when the proper text is not sung it is not recited. An appropriate hymn could be sung; the choir could sing a motet; instrumental piece. The action is very short in duration.
   b) Thanksgiving Psalm or Hymn - if silence is not observed after the communion rite, a hymn or psalm could be sung by all or by choir, or by soloist.

CONCLUSIONS

From the preceding priorities certain patterns of song emerge. The following could be considered a "standard" pattern for most congregations:
   a) Entrance Song
   b) Alleluia
   c) Sanctus
   d) Memorial
   e) Great Amen
   f) Communion Song

Other parts will be added according to season, solemnity of the feast, and musical resources. Choirs could certainly sing before Mass, at the offertory, communion, recessional as well as lead and enhance the singing of the congregation: descants harmonies, antiphonal arrangements. There are many options, and these should be employed. Variety is a key factor in light of the new rubrics. But this kind of variety in the liturgy presumes competence, both musical and liturgical. Tokenism or token liturgy will get token response from the community.

There must be planning, deliberation, serious dialogue between all parties in setting up the Sunday Liturgy, *e.g.*, pastor, assistant pastors, parish musician (organist, choir director, leader of song), members of liturgical committee of the parish council, etc. In such deliberations three judgments must come to bear on the choice of music for the Eucharistic celebration:

1. Musical judgment - is the music aesthetically and technically good? This is the musician's area of competence. It is primary and basic. Once this has been determined then there must be liturgical judgment.
2. Liturgical judgment - the nature of the liturgy itself will help to determine what kind of music is called for, what parts are preferred for singing, and who should sing what.
3. Pastoral judgment - indispensable for good liturgy. The music could be fine, liturgically correct but unable to be sung. The background of the people must be considered.

Certain textual requirements must be observed if the music is to render the liturgy relevant. There are four classes of texts:

1. The Word - Gospel, other readings, Creed
2. Acclamations - listed above

3. Psalms and hymns - responsory between the readings; entrance, communion and concluding songs; Offertory and Gloria.
4. Prayers - Sacerdotal (collect, over gifts, Postcommunion), Eucharistic (with sung words of Institution), People's (litanies; Kyrie, Agnus Dei / Responses, throughout.) If the texts are to be rendered musically correct great care must be taken in the selection of those whose services are employed in the liturgy: the lector, the cantor, the choir, the celebrant.

> There is no place in the liturgy for displays of virtuosity for its own sake. However, an individual singer can effectively lead the people and inspire them with his ability to proclaim God's word, *e.g.*, psalm verses of the responsory, antiphonal song, etc. Where there is no choir, the cantor is its replacement.[60]

While this list of musical priorities provides a practical outline for parish musicians, the manner of incorporating them within liturgical services may and should change with each style of celebration.

Liturgical worship is centered in the Eucharist, that moment in Christ when his Body, the Church, ritually enacts her own identity and is confirmed through ritual by his power. Because the Mass is so central to the communal life of the Church constant efforts are being made to revitalize this for the people at worship. The crucial position of the Incarnation in an understanding of the Church demands that the worshipping Christian respond in body as well as in soul.

Such body-soul response is becoming more evident in certain parts of the country. Some creative leaders are incorporating legislative norms with celebration's spontaneity. The New *Ordo Missae*, A document concerning General Instruction and New Order of the Mass, promulgated by Pope Paul VI, April 3, 1969, Issued by the Sacred Congregation of Rites. A colorful and unusual liturgy was experienced by a group of 2500 children in Louisville in April, 1968. On the arena floor, in addition to four movie screens, were an altar, piles of cardboard boxes with magazine covers pasted on them (made to resemble large building blocks), 140 chairs for children who had special functions in the celebration, and about forty colorful banners of many sizes which were carried in from several directions. The Somersets Band ("Rock and Roll on Purpose") provided music and singing-accompaniment with good musicianship and enthusiasm.

Some students dressed in clown suits. Others held gas-filled balloons and released them during one of the acclamations. The presiding celebrant, wearing a broad orange stole, proclaimed the theme of the celebration: "I'm Glad I'm Alive." The children responded throughout the celebration with joyous clapping of hands and their priests led them in prayer.

The first of two readings, a psalm of creation and a section of Ecclesiasticus, were accompanied by the interpretive dance of two children. The second reading was pantomimed by two others. The singing and the stomping and clapping were often deafening, particularly at the Alleluias, but they were also very inspiring.

Students had baked bread in their own classrooms and this was carried to the altar where it was placed on the blocks. The central prayer was a "Thank You, God" litany which contained some very creative and often thrilling Alleluia responses. At the singing of the Lord's Prayer all joined hands.[61]

The following unedited letters give an idea of the liturgical experience of the children:

> When I walked into the place called Convention Center there seemed a whole new life in there, the children, the band, and all that went with it seemed to burst out joy to God. This films seemed to be different in a new age. With the colorful balloons bursting I forgot if this was really true or not. When I walked out I forgot my troubles and the world seemed new to me.
>
> I think the main reason was to be happy and thankful together. To be happy for our hands, feet fingers, and voices we clapped, stamped, snapped, and sang. If an older person was there they would not have thought it very religious. I think it was, because we were giving thanks to God, our Father . . . .
>
> I had the time of my life. I seem to have let my joy go, let it fly away. I let everybody know that I was at the celebration. I let my glorious cry to the hearts of people and God. I let my yell, my cry and the clapping, singing be heard to everyone and God heard it, I know it, because God let me live in a life of joy.
>
> . . . the music helped us to share our happiness, friendship and fun . . .

Liturgy can also employ the musical idiom of jazz. During the 1968 Liturgical Conference at Washington, D.C., the music of Edward V. Bonnemere at a Eucharistic celebration welded a congregation of 5,000 people into a very alive, very vocal unity. Bonnemere is a jazz musician and director of music at the Church of St. Thomas the Apostle, Harlem. The theme of the Conference was "Revolution: Christian Responses."

The celebration began with talented artists from the Erika Thimey Dance Theatre, Washington, D.C., who danced toward the altar and onto the platform. A jazz combo struck the downbeat for the procession.

> Be strong
> Do not be afraid
> Our God will come
> Will come to save us
> Be strong
> Do not be afraid
> Our God will come
> Will come to save us

rang through the congregation. Between the repetitions of this antiphon the choir continued to sing,

> Tell those who are frightened
> Be strong
> Tell those who are frightened
> Do not be afraid . . .

Bonnemere's instrumental Offertory followed the readings, prayers and greetings of peace. The congregation then sang the anamnesis in jazz idiom.

Dying you destroyed our death
Rising you restored our life
We will sing of you
Till you are seen by all the world.

At the end of this prayer there was a tumultuous crescendo of "Amen."

During the communion service another jazz congregation-choir arrangement was sung. The Thimey dancers rhythmically circled the altar, whereupon the congregation joined hands as the recessional grew in volume and the voices of the people sang,

Salt of the Earth
Light of the world
Leaven in the dough and mustard seed.

Lengthy applause burst from the congregation, testimony to the vitality of the music, the dance, and the celebration.[63]

The liturgical musician cannot be part of the worshipping community unless he knows what it is to worship and to worship in union with others. He must be open to the Spirit before he becomes open to the spirit of the group.

Genuine liturgical music shares the threefold orientation of the celebration which it serves: it reflects the faith which the composer has lived; it stimulates faith in those who participate in its execution; it is itself prayer, praise of the One in whom we believe. For the Christian who cannot even say, "Father," unless the Spirit move him (Romans, 8:14), all genuine praise is the surging of the Spirit. For the sound of the voice of God is too great for human words to contain and therefore at times it must be expressed in song. The man who praises, whether in silence or in song, actively yields to the Spirit of God, which moves throughout creation. He is able to understand the poet whose song is but a plaintive little strain, mingling with the great music of the world.[64]

But further, the song must say, in a way the people can make their own, what is deepest in themselves, their attitude before God. In order for a group to make a piece of music its own it is not necessary that it be written with that group in mind. Sometimes the musician must wait for the group to be able to enter into a work, to be comfortable with it, vocally and theologically. Members of a group can become so much in tune with one another's feelings about music and about faith that the choice of music is not imposed by the liturgist but arises freely from the unity of the group. Shared song is a real human experience; it therefore has potential as a deeply religious experience.

Another liturgical experience in which music played an integral and enriching role was a Eucharistic celebration which was felt to be a "Mass on the World," recalling and sharing the reflections of Teilhard de Chardin in Hymn of the Universe. For it was a prayer to

. . . make the whole earth my altar and
on it . . . offer you all the labours and
sufferings of the world . . . it is to your
body in this its fullest extension—that is,
to the world become through your power
and my faith the glorious living crucible
in which everything melts away in order
to be born anew; it is to this I dedicate
myself with all the resources which
your creative magnetism has brought
forth in me . . .[65]

Seven young women who had lived together for some years in a religious order were joined by a priest whom they knew well and with whom they had often worshipped. Among their shared experience was a familiarity with liturgical music, including some of their own compositions, so that having sung together happily and often it was possible for them to sing spontaneously. The members of the group had been trained and had practice in preparing music for liturgy. They had, too, a relationship with one another which was built upon acceptance and each person felt free to contribute as the moment and the atmosphere permitted, whether by song, silence, or prayer. They spent the weekend together at a cottage near a lake. Early one afternoon the priest gave form to his meditation on the face of Christ by carving it in sand, an icon-like sculpture about seven feet long. By late afternoon the others joined him around the sand-carving which became an altar for the Eucharist. They felt as if the whole earth were the support for the altar, symbolizing the fact that their worship was a conscious attempt to join in the praise offered by all of creation. The liturgy followed the outlines of the traditional Roman Mass but there was room for meditation and creative response.

Despite the freedom and spontaneity it was distinctly apt for a liturgy begun at the water's edge to include a musical reference to that dramatic account in Matthew where Jesus calls Peter to walk on water. "Lord, If It's Really You" drew added meaning for the assembly and if there was a touch of humor in the application it was not without justification.

Readings from Paul's letter to the Romans and John's description of the Last Supper were followed by reflection and song. Paul had spoken on the movement of the world toward Christ. Jesus urged his disciples to bear fruit to the world. Communion time was silent except for the running of the water and when the liturgy concluded, after some two and a half hours, the group turned to see God's sun beginning to set. Spontaneously they sang the four part "Christ as Light" of Russell Woolen. Their action showed what their worship had meant to them. It is possible to have such experiences when there is a musical as well as liturgical community.

Summary

Diversity of style need not be at odds with the spirit of unity among God's people. The ability to be open to new ritual and new music, to be ever searching for fresh insights and new attitudes toward liturgy is a sign of life and excitement in our liturgies.

Sameness is not always the sign of unity. It can spring from the lack of faith as well as from the lack of hope. If the problem of change has been the perennial task of the philosopher it requires the attention of the church musician as well, who can and ought to assist the community of believers in expressing this seeming contradiction.

CHAPTER VII
ORIGINAL COMPOSITIONS CREATED FOR
LITURGICAL CELEBRATIONS

The basic endeavor of this paper has been to discover the function of contemporary liturgical music and to act creatively, if limitedly, in response to the discovery. The musical compositions which are contained in the following pages have been used by specific church groups in a variety of liturgical celebrations. They seemed to meet the needs of these worshipping communities as the words and music became prayer. It is because of this experiential knowledge, *i.e.*, of having re-created this music with groups of people at liturgical functions that the compositions are offered as musical, artistic, and liturgical contributions.

Each of the compositions is an expression of praise and an attempt to free the words of glory so that they spring, have life. They illustrate in a particular way the basic philosophy of this study.

1. "Psalm 103, Thou Makest the Winds Thy Messengers" (see page 244-257)
2. "O, Praise Ye, the Lord" (see pages 351-354)
3. "Praise the Lord, All Ye Nations" (see pages 348-350)
4. "For He Comes" (see pages 361-365)
   "Let the Heav'ns Be Glad" (see page 362)
   "Come, Sing Alleluia" (see page 364)
   "Lowly Shepherds" (see page 363)
5. "Hail, Mary" (see pages 291-293)
6. "Gloria" (see pages 369-373)
7. "Praise to the Father"

CHAPTER VIII SUMMARY, CONCLUSIONS, AND RECOMMENDATIONS

The purposes of this study were
1) to explore the meaning of celebration and to investigate the theological aspects of Christian celebration;
2) to examine the sociological and psychological factors which affect liturgy;
3) to discuss the role of ritual in liturgical communities;
4) to present compositions which exemplify principles contained in the study.

The study was concerned primarily with an investigation of the ministerial function of music in the contemporary liturgy of the Church. Since the structure of liturgical celebrations is shaped by the needs of the worshipping community, church leaders are recognizing the necessity for adapting the form of public worship to contemporary life. Hence, these factors necessitated broad understanding of sociology and psychology as well as deep understanding of liturgy and liturgical music.

I. SUMMARY

Celebration. The study was concerned with the concept of celebration as a part of life and as a part of Christianity. Viewed against the background of technology and scientific expansion there appears a contrasting need within man to celebrate what he is, that which is his nature. Man alive, alive to his past, alive in his presence and also alive to his future, is celebrant.

Christian Celebration. Viewed as a part of Christian theology celebration was called liturgy. The Christian concept of community is revealed as central to all liturgical activity.

Sociological and Psychological Factors. Research has revealed that liturgy has been a powerfully celebrative experience for some people. It was considered as a necessity that liturgy not be separated from the rest of man's environment. Social and psychological content of liturgical experience have become important to liturgists. They realize that liturgical action is more than a cultural act of a pre-existing community. It is becoming one of the means of developing religious communication and constituting Christian community.

Rituals. Rituals of new origins and meaning and clarity are being developed to give scope to diversity of spirit as well as to unity of spirit among men. Rituals lose their effectiveness when they become strict structures whose only ability is to restrain men and not to leave them free for meaningful worship. This does not negate the importance of continuity in ritualistic expression. However, it cries out against tradition for its own sake alone.

Liturgical Music. A full liturgical experience needs music, music which integrates and binds man's rituals with man's meaning. A study of cultures from earliest history reveals this fact. Research into Roman Catholic history shows that music was always an important part of liturgy. It also reveals that there is serious lack of meaning for modern man in many areas of the church's life, particularly in liturgical functions. Liturgists are trying to renew meaning and liturgical musicians are being urged to contribute their talents to such renewal. The music of liturgy is undergoing drastic change. The *New Ordo Missae* of the Vatican emphasizes anew the musical priorities for parochial usage. The manner of incorporating these priorities was illustrated by several liturgical descriptions.

Liturgical Compositions. The final chapter contains original musical compositions which were written as an outgrowth of this study. They attempt to illustrate its basic philosophy which views music as an integral part of liturgy.

II. CONCLUSIONS

Based on the ideas compiled during the study these conclusions are suggested:

1. That there is a serious need in church communities for relevant liturgical experience.
2. That an ever increasing number of experts in the field of psychology and sociology support this need.
3. That liturgical revitalization could powerfully affect our society by nurturing Christian relevancy as well as by fostering a sense of purpose in life.
4. That church musicians, because of the very nature of their art, which is to touch the spirit of man, and because their art is integral to liturgical celebrations, have a consequential role in our society.
5. That liturgy which is open to newness encourages and challenges the creative abilities of man.

III. RECOMMENDATIONS FOR FURTHER STUDY

Based on the investigation and research involved in this study, the following recommendations are made:

1. That further studies delve into the existence and style of what is known as underground liturgies. Roman strictures in the last decade were largely ignored by some worshipping communities.
2. That an investigation of Maslow's concepts of peak experience and self actualization be applied to liturgical experience.
3. That dance in American society be investigated and made applicable to American liturgical experience.
4. That research which concerns balancing the demands of liturgy and art in musical expression be explored.
5. That a multi-media approach to liturgical style be studied and evaluated.

Endnotes:
[1] Rudolf Otto, *The Idea of the Holy* (London: 1929, revised edition)
[2] The Benedictines of Solesmes, *The Liber Usualis* (Tournai, Belgium: Desclee & Cie, 1966, p. 25
[3] Frank D. Ashburn, *Peabody of Groton* (Cambridge: The Riverside Press, Inc.,

1967), p. 71

4. Harvey Cox, *The Feast of Fools* (Cambridge, Massachusetts: Harvard University Press, 1969), p. 7
5. *Ibid.*, p. 13
6. Abraham Joshua Heschel, *Who Is Man* (Stanford, California: Stanford University Press, 1965), p. 115
7. *Ibid.*, pp. 116-117
8. C.G. Jung, *The Undiscovered Self* (New York: A Mentor Book: New American Library, 1964), pp. 120-121
9. Hugo Rahner, *Man at Play* (London: Burns & Gates, 1965), p.28
10. Hubert Bonner, *Group Dynamics* (New York: The Ronald Press Company, 1959), p. 303
11. Herbert Read, *The Grass Roots of Art* (Cleveland: The World Publishing Company, 1964), p. 101
12. Bonner, *op. cit.*, p. 303
13. Brameld, "World Civilization: The Galvanizing Purpose of Public Education," *Phi Delta Kappan*, November, 1962, p. 61
14. Thomas Hopkins, "What is Group Process?" in *Perspectives on the Group Process*, C. Gratton Kemp (Boston: Houghton Mifflin Co., 1964), p. 24
15. Harvey Cox, *The Feast of Fools* (Cambridge, Mass: Harvard University Press, 1969), p. 44
16. Pierre Teilhard de Chardin, *Hymn of the Universe* (New York: Harper & Row, 1969), p. 24
17. John, 14:21
18. John Giuliani, "Theology of Music," address given at Bridgeport, Connecticut, during diocesan liturgical conference, 1967, permission to quote secured.
19. *Ibid.*
20. John, 14:6
21. *The Constitution on the Sacred Liturgy of the Second Vatican Council* and *The Motu Proprio of Pope Paul VI*, Study Club Edition (New Jersey: Paulist Press, 1964), p. 138
22. John, 10:30
23. Carl G. Jung, *The Undiscovered Self* (New York: A Mentor Book: New American Library, 1964), p. 100
24. *Ibid.*, pp. 40-41
25. *Ibid.*, pp. 59-60
26. *Ibid.*, p. 70
27. *Ibid.*, p. 60
28. Stephen C. Rose, *The Grass Roots Church* (New York: Abingdon Press, 1966), p. 9
29. Walter M. Abbott, ed, *The Documents of Vatican II* (New York: Guild Press, 1966), p. 172
30. Paul Tournier, *The Meaning of Persons* (New York: Harper & Row, Publishers, 1957), p. 42
31. Herbert Read, *The Grass Roots of Art* (Cleveland: The World Publishing Company, 1964), p. 101
32. Francois Houtart, "Sociological Aspects of the Liturgy," *Worship*, Volume 42, Number 6 (June-July, 1968), pp. 342-350
33. Houtart, *op. cit.*
34. Rembert Weakland, O.S.B., "Music and Liturgy in Evolution," *Liturgical Arts*, Vol. 35, Number 3 (May, 1967), p. 1.
35. Houtart, *op. cit.*, p. 353
36. Robert Hovda, "The Underground Church," *Liturgy*, Volume 13, Number 5, (May, 1968)
37. Houtart, *op. cit.*, p. 353
38. *Ibid.*, pp. 363-364
39. Abraham A. Schwadron, *An Interpretation of Philosophy for Contemporary Music Education*. (unpublished doctoral dissertation, Boston University) 1962, p. 221
40. Theodore Brameld, "World Civilization: The Galvanizing Purpose of Public Education," *Phi Delta Kappan*, (November, 1962), p. 61
41. Susan K. Langer, *Problems of Art*, (New York: Chas. Scribner, 1957), Chapter 9, "The Art Symbol and the Symbol in Art," pp. 124-139
42. Harvey Cox, *The Feast of Fools* (Cambridge, Mass.: Harvard University Press, 1969), p. 110
43. John W. Gardner, *Self Renewal* (New York: Harper & Row Publishers, 1964), p. 131
44. no note
45. Paul Tournier, *The Meaning of Persons* (New York: Harper & Row, Publishers, 1957), p. 116
46. Gardner, *op. cit.*, pp. 6-7
47. Tournier, *op. cit.*, p. 21
48. Abraham Joshua Heschel, *Who is Man* (Stanford, California: Stanford University Press, 1965), p. 117
49. Cox, *op. cit.*, p. 4
50. Heschel, *op. cit.*, p. 118
51. Walter M. Abbott (ed), *The Documents of Vatican II* (New York: Guild Press, 1966), p. 172
52. Pie-Raymond Regamey, *Religious Art in the Twentieth Century* (New York: Herder, 1963), p. 18
53. Homer Ulrich & Paul A. Pisk, *A History of Music and Musical Style* (New York: Harcourt, Brace & World, Inc., 1965), p. 5
54. Robert W. Hovda (ed), *Sunday Morning Crisis* (Baltimore: Helicon, 1963), p.º5
55. Theodore Klauser, *A Brief History of Liturgy* (Minnesota: The Liturgical Press, 1953), p. 27
56. Ernest Wright, *The Old Testament and Theology* (New York: Harper & Row, Publishers, 1969), p. 20
57. U. Gotteslob, *Gebet und Gesangbuch* (Diocese of Innsbruck: F. Enuch, Publisher)
58. John Harmon, The Parish, When is it Alive? When Should it Die? Address given at Baltimore during the National Liturgical Conference, June, 1965
59. *The Constitution on Sacred Liturgy of the Second Vatican Council and the Motu Proprio of Pope Paul VI*, Study Club Edition (New Jersey: Paulist Press, 1964), p. 69
60. "Liturgy," *Journal of Liturgical Conference*, Vol. 13, No. 5 May 1968, p. 2
61. *Ibid.*, Vol. 13, No. 6, June 1968, p. 5
62. *Ibid.*, Vol. 13, No. 7, (September, 1968), p. 4
63. Rabindranath Tagore, "Gitanjali" (Macmillan and Co., 1962), p. 11
64. Pierre Teilhard de Chardin, *Hymn of the Universe* (New York: Harper & Row, 1965), p. 19, p. 37.

BIBLIOGRAPHY
1. Collected Documents

Abbott, Walter M. (ed) *The Documents of Vatican II.* New York: Guild Press, 1966.

Paul VI, *General Instruction and the New Order of the Mass*, 1969.

2. Books

Ashburn, Frank D. *Peabody of Groton.* Cambridge: The Riverside Press, Inc., 1967.

Benedictines of Solesmes (ed) *The Liber Usualis.* Tournai, Belgium: Desclee & Cie, 1956.

Berenson, Bernard. *Aesthetics and History.* Garden City: Doubleday and Co., Inc., 1954.

Bonner, Hubert. *Group Dynamics.* New York: The Ronald Press Company, 1959.

Bosanquet, Bernard. *A History of Esthetic.* Cleveland: The World Publishing Company, 1957.

____. *Three Lectures on Esthetic.* London: Macmillan and Company, 1923.

Brameld, Theodore. *Philosophies of Education in Cultural Perspective.* New York: Holt, Rinehart and Winston, 1955. Toward a Reconstructed Philosophy of Education. The Dryden Press, 1956.

Cassirer, Ernst. *An Essay on Man.* New Haven: Yale University Press, 1944.

The Constitution on the Sacred Liturgy of the Second Vatican Council and the Motu Proprio of Pope Paul VI. Study-Club Edition. New Jersey: Paulist Press, 1964.

Cox, Harvey, *The Feast of Fools.* Cambridge, Massachusetts, Harvard University Press, 1969.

Croce, Benedetto, *Esthetic.* (translated by Douglas) New York: The Noonday Press, 1909.

Deiss, Lucien. *Spirit and Song of the New Liturgy.* Cincinnati, Ohio: World Library of Sacred Music, 1970.

Dewey, John. *Art as Experience.* New York: P. Putnam's Sons, 1934.

Gardner, John. *Self-Renewal.* New York: Harper and Row, Publishers, 1964.

Gavin, Carney et al. *The Word.* Readings in Theology compiled at the Canisianum, Innsbruck. New York: P. J. Kenedy & Sons, 1964.

Ghiselin, Brewster (ed). *The Creative Process.* New York, The New American Library, 1955.

Gotshalk, D. W. *Art and the Social Order.* New York: Dover Publications, 1947.

Greeley, Andrew M. *The Church and the Suburbs.* Glen Rock: Deus Books, 1963.

Heschel, Abraham Joshua. *Who is Man?* Stanford, California: California: Stanford University Press, 1965.

Hauser, Arnold. *The Social History of Art.* Vol. 4 New York, Vintage, 1958.

Hopkins,, Thomas. "What is Group Process?". Kemp, Gratton. *Perspectives on the Group Process.* Boston: Houghton Mifflin Co., 1964.

Hovda, Robert W. (ed). *Sunday Morning Crisis.* Baltimore: Helicon, 1963.

Jung, C. G. *The Undiscovered Self.* New York: The New American Library, 1964.

Klauser, Theodore. *A Brief History of Liturgy.* Minnesota: The Liturgical Press, 1953.

Langer, Susanne K. *Feeling and Form.* New York: Charles Scribner's Sons, 1953.

____. *Philosophy in a New Key.* New York: Penguin Books, Inc., 1942.

____. *Problems of Art.* New York: Charles Scribner, 1957

Maritain, Jacques. *The Responsibility of the Artist.* New York: Charles Scribner's Sons, 1960.

Maslow, Abraham H. *Religions, Values, and Peak-Experiences.* Columbus, Ohio: Ohio State University Press, 1964.

Mills, C. Wright. *The Sociological Imagination.* New York: Oxford University Press, 1959.

Meyer, Leonard B. *Emotion and Meaning in Music.* Chicago: University of Chicago Press, 1956.

Mueller, John. *The American Symphony Orchestra.* Bloomington: Indiana University Press, 1951.

Otto, Rudolf. *The Idea of The Holy.* London: 1923, rev. ed, 1929.

Rahner, Hugo. *Man at Play.* London: Burns and Oates, 1965

Read, Herbert. *The Grass Roots of Art.* Cleveland: The World Publishing Co., 1964.

_____. *The Redemption of the Robot.* New York: A Trident Press Book, 1966.

Regamey, Pie-Raymond. *Religious Art in the Twentieth Century.* New York: Herder and Herder, 1963.

Rose, Stephen C. *The Grass Roots Church.* New York: Abingdon Press, 1966.

Santayana, George. *Reason in Art.* New York: Collier Books 1962.

_____ *The Sense of Beauty.* New York: Charles Scribner's Sons, 1896.

Tagore, Rabindranath. *Stray Birds.* London: Macmillan and Co., 1962.

Teilhard de Chardin, Pierre. *Hymn of the Universe.* New York: Harper & Row, Publishers, 1969.

Tournier, Paul. *The Meaning of Persons.* New York: Harper & Row Publishers, 1957.

Ulrich and Pisk. *A History of Music and Musical Style.* New York: Harcourt, Brace and World, Inc., 1963.

Weiss, Paul. *Religion and Art.* Milwaukee: Marquette University Press, 1963.

Williams, Raymond. *Culture and Society: 1780-1950.* Garden City: Anchor Books, Doubleday and Company, Inc., 1960.

Wright, Ernest. *The Old Testament and Theology.* New York: Harper & Row, Publishers, 1969.

3. Periodicals

Ashwortch, H. "De Cena Domini" (English Trans.) *Notitiae* (Sacra Congregatio pro Culto Divino). Vol. 53, April, 1970.

Benn, Oleta A. "Esthetics for the Music Educator: The Maturation of the Esthetic Sense." *Journal of Research in Music Education*, IV, Fall, 1956.

Betz, Johannes. "Sacrifice and Thanksgiving." *Theology Digest,* Vol. XVII, No. 1, Spring, 1969.

Boe, John. "Church Music and Aggiornamento: An Anglican View." *Chicago Studies,* Vol. 5, No. 2, Summer, 1966.

Brameld, Theodore. "World Civilization: The Galvanizing Purpose of Public Education." *Phi Delta Kappan,* November, 1962.

Connare, Most Rev. William G., D. D. "Exploring the Musical 'Dimensions of the New Order of Mass." *Sacred Music,* Vol. 97, No. 1, Spring, 1970.

Harrison, G.B. "Englishing the Liturgy." *America,* Vol. 122, No. 18, May 6, 1970.

Hitchcock, H. "Here Lies Community: R.I.P." *America,* Vol. 122 No. 21, May 30, 1970.

Houtart, Francois. "Sociological Aspects of the Liturgy." *Worship,* Vol. 42, No. 6, 1968.

Hovda, Robert. "The Underground Church." *Liturgy,* Vol. 13, Number 5, May 1968.

_____. "The Prayer of General Intercession." *Worship,* Vol. 44, ' No. 8, 1970.

Huqhes H. Stuart. "Mass Culture and Social Criticism" *Daedalus,* Boston: American Academy of Arts and Sciences, Spring, 1960.

Kaplan, Max. "Art in a Changing America." *Report for Music in American Life Commission VIII.* Washington: Music 'Educators National Conference, 1958.

_____. "Music, Community and Social Change." *Music Educators Journal*, 43: 64-67, Sept., 1956.

Keifer. Ralph. "Noise in Our Solemn Assemblies." *Worship,* Vol. 45, No. 1, 1971.

____. "Squalor on Sunday." *Worship,* Vol. 44, No. 5, 1970.

Kennedy, Eugene. "Here Lies Community: Deo Gratias:" *America,* Vol. 123, No. 4, August 22, 1970.

Leonhard, Charles. "Research: Philosophy and Esthetics." *Journal of Research in Music Education,* III, Spring, 1955.

Mannheim, R. L. and Cummins, A. "Musical Traits of Racial Groups." *Sociology and Social Research*, 45: 56-65, October, 1960.

McManus, Frederick R. "New Order of Mass." *American Ecclesiastical Review.* Part I, Vol. CLXI, No. 3, September, 1969;

Part II, Vol. CLXI, No. 6, December 1969;

Part III, Vol. CLXII, No. 1, January 1970;

Part IV, Vol. CLXII, No. 3, March, 1970.

McNaspy, C. J. "Liturgical Music Today." *America,* Vol. 123, No. 15, Nov. 14, 1970.

Meyer, Leonard B. "Some Remarks on Value and Greatness in Music," *Journal of Aesthetics and Art Criticism,* XVII, June, 1959.

Prezio Francis, OFM. "Religious Folk Music." *American Ecclesiastical Review*, Vol. CLXIII, No. 2, Aug. 1970.

Reimer Bennett. "Leonard Meyer's Theory of Value and Greatness.: *Journal of Research in Music Education,* X, Fall, 1962, 87-99.

Riedel, Johannes. "Folk, Rock and Black Music." *Worship,* Vol. 44, No. 9, 1970.

Schoen, Max. "Psychological Problems in Musical Art," *Journal of Research in Music Education*, 3:33, Spring, 1955.

Schuller, Gunther. "Music is Not Enough!" *Listen,* December, 1963.

Siedlecki, E.J. "Liturgical Reform: Diagnosis and Prognosis." *Chicago Studies,* Vol. 6, No. 3, Fall, 1967.

Tillard, J. K. R. "Christians United in 'the desire for the Eucharist'." *Theology Digest,* Vol. 6, Mo. 3, Fall, 1967.

Torrance E. Paul. "Creativity." *What Research Says,* Series D. C.: American Educational Research Association, National Education Association, April, 1963.

Ward M. "New Liturgy, Give it a Chance" *America,* No. 122, Mo. 21, May 30, 1970.

Wojcik, R. J. "New Design of Liturgical Music." *Chicago Studies,* Vol. 6, No. 2, Summer, 1967.

Weakland, Rembert. O.S.B. "Music and Liturgy in Evolution." *Liturgical Arts,* Vol. 35, No. 3, May, 1967.

4. Unpublished Materials

Fowler, Charles B. "A Reconstructionist Philosophy of Music Education." Unpublished doctoral dissertation, Boston University, 1964.

Giuliani, John. "Theology of Music." Address given at Bridgeport, Connecticut, during Diocesan Liturgical Conference, 1967.

Joaquim, Manuel. "A Rationale for Aesthetic Education." Implications for Teacher Preparation Programs in the Humanities for Elementary and Secondary Schools. Unpublished doctoral dissertation, Boston University, 1968.

Schwadron, Abraham A. "An Interpretation of Philosophy and Esthetics for Contemporary Music Education." Unpublished doctoral dissertation, Boston University

index

A

Abraham (the prophet) 355
Abraham. See "Song of Abraham"
Abramson, Doris vi, 120, 122, 403, 405
"Adoremus" (Brown Senier 1955, 2005) xii, 331, 332-333
Advent xvi, 51
Aery, Susan vi, 403
Aggiornamento xvi
Agnus Dei 37
Alabama
    Selma 57
Albritton, William "Britt" 132, 133
Allen, Dr. H. Freeman 73, 74
Allen organ 49, 52
Alvear Palace. See Argentina: Buenos Aires
Ambrosian chant 48
Ambrosians 23
America magazine 355
America House. See New York: New York City
American 12, 34, 46, 51. See also Italian American
American market 95
American Music Center. See New York: New York City
Andy Capp. See Capp, Andy
Andy Gump. See Gump, Andy
Annunciation 37, 273. See also "Pageant Song"
Arcade. See Rhode Island: Providence
Archdiocese of Bridgeport. See Connecticut: Bridgeport
Archdiocese of New York 41
Argentina
    Buenos Aires 99
        Alvear Palace 99
Armandale Pier. See Scotland
Armstrong, Neil 60
Arnesen, Barbara (formerly Sister Barbara Arnesen) vi, xi, 43, 47
Arnold Arboretum. See Massachusetts: Boston
arthritis. See rheumatoid arthritis
"Assumpta Est Maria" (Brown Senier, 1954, 2005) xi, 137, 275, 294-297
Atlantic Ocean 41, 70
Athol. See Massachusetts
Attorney, United States. See Chiara, Margaret Mary
Aunt Nell. See Downey, Ellen "Nell" Finley Daly
Aunt Nellie. See Downey, Ellen "Nell" Finley Daly
Auntie Mame 99
Australia 94, 99, 118
"Ave Maria." See "Pageant Song"

B

Bach, Johann Sebastian 41, 401
Bacon, David 111, 352, 403
Baez, Joan 57
Bahama Islands (Bahamas) 71, 72
    Nassau 72, 73
Bahama Star. See SS Bahama Star
Bahamas. See Bahama Islands
Baltimore. See Maryland
Baltimore Catechism xix
Baron, Dom 48, 402
barracuda 72
Barron, Abraham (Abe) 80, 93, 99, 106, 107, 126, 127, 218, 219, 220
Barron, Gladys vi, xi, 80, 99, 108, 218, 405
Bauer, Rabbi David Dunn 403
Beatles 45, 351
Beethoven, Ludwig van 39, 401
Behnke, Matthew 128, 132, 133
Benedictine monastery. See France: Solesmes
Benedictus 37
Bentley, Katharine 405
Bergeron, Adam 132, 133
Bermuda 32
Bernstein, Leonard 45
Bertrand, Sister Florence 403
Bessette, Leo 115
Bethlehem 361
Bigge, Mary 82
Bill ("poor Bill") 8
Bishop Walter Curtis. See Curtis, Bridgeport Bishop Walter
"Blessed" (Brown Senier 1964-1965, 2005) xii, 331, 367, 387
Bloomingdale's 111
"Bluebird" 401
Bobby-Donny-Dicky-Carolyn 7, 8, 9, 14, 401
Boisvert, Louis ("Uncle Louis") 7, 23, 25, 402
Borden, Jack 120, 405
Borden, Jan 120, 405
Boston. See Massachusetts
Boston Bay Shoreline cruise. See Massachusetts: Boston
Boston Globe 75
Boston Public Gardens. See Massachusetts: Boston
Boston Public School teacher 90. See also Morris, Patricia
Boston Sunday Post 77
Boston Symphony. See Massachusetts: Boston
Boston University. See Massachusetts: Boston
Boston University Magazine. See Massachusetts: Boston: Boston University
Bostonian Hotel. See Massachusetts: Boston
Boudreau, Lynn 132, 133, 140
Bourbonnais. See Illinois
Bourgeoys, Mother Marguerite 33, 49, 51, 275. See also Canada: Montreal: Place Marguerite Bourgeoys
Bourse Building. See Pennsylvania: Philadelphia
Bowes, Sister Martha (Sister Saint Martin of Lima) 358, 359, 361
Brahms, Johannes 54, 56
Breezeway Farm Consulting, Inc. 405
Breithaupt, Georgia 20, 23, 24, 26
Bridgeport, Diocese of. See Connecticut: Bridgeport
Bridgeport. See Connecticut
Bridgeport Liturgical Commission. See Connecticut: Bridgeport
Bridgeport Post. See Connecticut: Bridgeport
British Isles 99, 118. See also England; Ireland; Great Britain; Northern Ireland; Scotland
Brodeur, Barbara 24
Brönte, Charlotte 118
Brookline. See Massachusetts
Brothers of the Holy Cross 14, 31, 406
Brown. See Browns
Brown, Barbara O'Brien 14, 406
Brown, Carolyn. See Brown Senier, Carolyn
Brown, Christopher (Carolyn's nephew) 98
Brown, Donald (Don; Donny) vi, xi, 1, 4, 6, 7, 8, 14, 27, 54, 61, 94, 163, 199, 401, 406, 415
Brown, Edward (Ed) 7, 12, 14, 16, 27, 109, 163, 198, 401, 406, 415
Brown, Edward Godfrey (Eddie; Mr. Edward G. Brown; Carolyn's father) xv, 10, 11, 13, 14, 16, 17, 23, 38, 42, 49, 401, 415
Brown, Edward Godfrey (letter written by) 38
Brown, Edward Godfrey (photo) 44
Brown, Gloria 109
Brown, Jeannette Lamontagne 14, 406, 415
Brown, Joan. See McElligott, Joan Brown
Brown, Katherine. See Mark, Katherine Brown
Brown, Lorraine Swanson 14, 55, 406, 415
Brown, Mark (Carolyn's nephew) 98
Brown, Mrs. See Brown, Rosalene Carolan
Brown, Patricia (Tricia) 14, 163, 200, 406, 414
Brown, Patrick 10
Brown, Richard (Dick; Dicky) xi, 1, 4, 6, 8, 9, 14, 27, 32, 55, 108, 163, 198, 406, 415
Brown, Robert (Bob; Bobby) 1, 4, 6, 8, 11, 14, 19, 27, 31, 57, 163, 198, 401, 406, 415
Rosalene Carolan (Mrs. Brown; Carolyn's mother) 8, 10, 11, 13, 14, 16, 17, 18, 21, 36, 42, 55, 59, 74, 75, 83, 85, 94, 95, 108, 115, 401
Brown, Roselyn. See Shea, Roselyn Brown
Brown-Carrano, Kathleen vi, xi, 110, 111, 403
Brown Senier, Carolyn (Mrs. Senier; formerly Sister Carolyn Brown; formerly Sister Saint Roselyn of Jesus, CND) cover, ii, v-vi, viii, x, xi, xii, xviii-xxvi, 1, 3-27, 29-65, 68-111, 113-127, 128-132, 135-137, 139-141, 163, 164, 218, 220, 244, 245, 259, 276, 281, 291, 299, 300, 304, 312, 317, 333, 335, 339, 342, 349, 353, 356, 359, 361-364, 368, 369, 374, 386-388, 398, 401, 408, 415, 416
Brown Senier, Carolyn, works of:
    The Mattawa Song Cycle (2005) cover, i, v, xi, xviii, xxi, 127, 163, 274, 132, 401, 403, 405
    "Adoremus" (1955, 2005) xii, 331, 332-333
    "Celtic Prayer" (2003, 2005) x, xii, 331, 338-340
    "Creator Spirit, Come" (1964, 2005) xii, 331, 341-347
    "De Profundis" (2002, 2005) xi, 123, 126, 127, 129, 131, 137, 140-162, 408
    Four Songs for a Woman of Galilee 137, 273
        "Pageant Song" (1953, 2005) ii, iii, xii, 37, 137, 273, 276-280, 409
        "Respice Stellam" (1962, 2005) xii, 137, 273, 274, 281-290
        "Hail, Mary (Supplication in Time of War or Sorrow)" (1964, 2005) xii, 137, 274, 291-293
        "Assumpta Est Maria" (1954, 2005) xii, 137, 275, 294-*297*
    "In Praise of Names" (2005) xi, xvii, 127, 137, 163-217, 407

"Lamb of God" (1964, 2005) xii, 331, 334-337
Love Songs xii, 137, 298, 300-303
"I'd Give You the Moon" (1999, 2005: lyrics by Dorothy Johnson) xii, 121, 126, 137, 298, 300-303, 411
"Listen to Your Heart" (2001, 2005: lyrics by Dorothy Johnson) xii, 137, 298, 304-311
"Summer Days" (2003, 2005) xii, 127, 137, 299, 312-316
"When I Knew" (1996, 2005) xii, 127, 137, 299, 317-328
Mass in Honor of Marguerite Bourgeoys, Founder of the Congregation of Notre Dame (1964-1965, 2005) xii, 139, 331, 366-389
"Lord, Have Mercy" (1964-1965, 2005) xii, 331, 366, 368
"Glory to God" (1964-1965, 2005) xii, 51, 331, 366, 369-373
"Creed" (1964-1965, 2005) xii, 331, 366, 374-385
"Holy, Holy, Holy" (1964-1965, 2005) xii, 331, 367, 386
"Blessed" (1964-1965, 2005) xii, 331, 367, 387
"Lamb of God" (1964-1965, 2005) xii, 331, 367, 388-389
"Meditation Doxology" (1966, 2005) xii, 331, 390-399
"O, Praise the Lord, All Ye Nations" (1964, 2005) xii, 331, 348-350
"O, Praise Ye the Lord" (1961, 2005) vi, xii, xvi, 47, 91, 110, 331, 353, 354
"The Ram" (1965, 2005) xii, 331, 355-357
"Sing Joy to the Lord" (1961, 2005) xii, 137, 358-360
"Song of Abraham" (2003, 2005) xi, 126-128, 218-243, 331, 403, 410
Three Christmas Carols xii, 331, 361
"Let the Heav'ns Be Glad" (1964, 2005) xii, 331, 361, 362
"Lowly Shepherds" (1956, 2005) xii, 331, 361, 363
"Come, Sing Alleluia" (1960, 2005) xii, 331, 361, 364-365
"Thou Makest the Winds Thy Messengers" (196554, 2005 in three versions) vi, xi, 47, 137, 244-257
"You Know Me" (1966, 2002, 2005) xi, 137, 258-272, 331
Browns xii, 8, 11, 12, 13, 16, 17, 18, 26, 406
Bronxville. *See New York*
Buenos Aires. *See Argentina*
Buskirk, Jeremy van. *See van Buskirk, Jeremy*
Butler, Arlan 119

C

California
  Los Angeles 71
Cambridge. *See Massachusetts*
Canada 33, 39, 118
  LaValle University 39
  Montreal 33, 34, 403
    Our Lady of Bon Secours Chapel 33
    Place Marguerite Bourgeoys 33. *See also Bourgeoys, Mother Marguerite*
  Quebec City (Quebec) 98
Canadian(s) 33, 88
Canary Islands. *See Spain*
Cape Cod. *See Massachusetts*

Cape Cod Synagogue. *See Massachusetts: Cape Cod*
Capella, Marie 20, 24
Capp, Andy 78
Carbonara, Dr. and Mrs. 57
Cardinal Spellman scholarship 50
Carmen 401
Carnegie Hall. *See New York: New York City*
Carolan, Dede 21
Carolan, Maryann 6, 8, 9
Carolan, Rosalene. *See Brown, Rosalene Carolan*
Carousel 25
Carrano. *See Brown-Carrano*
Carrano, Matthew 110
Carroll, James 40
Carroll, Mother Catherine 55
Catholic. *See Roman Catholic*
Catholic Church. *See Roman Catholic Church*
Catholic High. *See Connecticut: Waterbury: Waterbury Catholic High*
Catholic Youth Organization(s) 22, 24, 52
catsup. *See ketchup*
Celtic contingent 97
"Celtic Prayer" (Brown Senier 2003, 2005) xii, 331, 338-340
Celtic soul xv
Celtic Weavers. *See Massachusetts: Boston: Faneuil Hall Marketplace*
Centerville. *See Massachusetts*
Central America 118
Central Park South. *See New York: New York City*
CFO 94
Chaisson, Richard 116
Chansonneures 25
Charles River Publishers. *See Massachusetts: Boston*
Charlie Brown 64
Charron, Gail (Sister Gail Charron) 45
Chase, Lynn 404
Chase, Richard 132, 133, 404
Chevrette, Sister Claudette (Sister Saint Andre Marie) 36, 275
Chiara, Margaret Mary (United States Attorney for the Western District of Michigan) vi, xi, 56
Chicago. *See Illinois*
Chilton, Elizabeth 132, 133
Chipping Campden. *See England: Cotswolds*
Chirino, Hope 403
Choate, Dr. Robert 64, 402
Chopin, Frédéric François 39, 69, 95, 118, 299, 401, 402
Christian xvi
Christianity 65
Christmas xvi, 17, 20, 23, 40, 47, 49, 78, 80, 85, 100, 107, 108, 126, 361
Christmas Eve. *See Christmas*
Christmastide. *See Christmas*
City College of New York. *See New York: New York City: Manhattan: East Sixty-eighth Street*
Civic Center. *See Connecticut: Hartford*
civil rights movement 46
Clair de Lune 23, 124
Clark, Florence vi, xi, 110, 118, 119, 402
Clay, Sarah 132, 133
CND. *See Congregation of Notre Dame*
Cody, Jeanette 18, 401
Columbia. *See Maryland*
Columbia (University). *See New York: New York City*
"Come, Sing Alleluia" (Brown Senier, 1960, 2005) xii, 331, 361, 364-365

commercial law 44
Common Reader. *See Massachusetts: New Salem: New Salem Common: Common Reader Bookshop*
Common Reader Bookshop. *See Massachusetts: New-Salem: New Salem Common*
Community Foundation of Western Massachusetts vi
Company of Mary 49, 52
Composer Assistance Program. *See New York: New York City: American Music Center*
Concerts for Young People 45
Confraternity of Christian Doctrine (New England Confraternity of Christian Doctrine) 51, 53
Congregation of Notre Dame (Congregation of Notre Dame de Montreal; CND; Notre Dame; Sisters of the Congregation of Notre Dame of Montreal) xv, xvi, xvii, 20, 31, 32, 33, 34, 35, 36, 37, 39, 40, 41, 42, 45, 47, 49, 50, 51, 52, 54, 55, 56, 57, 58, 60, 61, 75, 76, 92, 127, 273, 275, 281, 358, 359, 361, 367, 402, 403
Congregation of Sisters of Christian Charity (Sisters of Christian Charity) 91, 351
Congregationalist 106
Connecticut xvi, xix, 1, 5, 6, 7, 12, 24, 30, 32, 35, 41, 42, 49, 50, 51, 52, 54, 55, 58, 87, 110, 111, 244, 341, 351, 355, 402
  Bridgeport xix, 30, 41, 50, 51, 52, 55, 65
    Archdiocese of Bridgeport 50
    Bridgeport Liturgical Commission xx, 52, 61
    Bridgeport Post 52, 53
    Diocese of Bridgeport xix, 51
    Sacred Heart University 52
    University of Bridgeport, Connecticut 30, 52
  Cheshire
    Waverly Inn 10
  Hartford (Hfd.) 38, 88, 89, 341
    Civic Center 88
  Meriden 9
  Merritt Parkway 75
  Middletown 38
  Milford 38
  New Haven 38, 41
    Yale Bowl 25
  Norwalk 54
  Ridgefield xvii, 49, 50, 52, 54, 55, 56, 87, 110, 111, 244, 355, 402
    Ridgefield Chapel 49
    Ridgefield Press 52
    West Mountain 52
      Ridgefield Novitiate 49, 52, 55, 56, 59
  Route 95 (Interstate) 75
  Southington Mountain 9
  Stamford 1, 41
    Stamford Catholic High School (later Trinity High School) (Stamford Catholic; Stamford) 42, 43, 44, 45, 46, 50, 55
  Waterbury xvi, 5, 6, 7, 8, 12, 15, 16, 19, 20, 22, 23, 24, 25, 41, 44, 54, 61, 69, 70, 74, 75, 81, 83, 92, 95
    Crosby (high school) 20
    Immaculate Conception Church 74
    Saint Cecilia's Church xvi, 22
    Saint Francis Xavier Church 12, 13, 19, 20, 22, 402
    Scovill Manufacturing Company 16
    Sylvan Avenue 12, 13
    Washington Park 12

Waterbury Catholic High School (Waterbury Catholic; Catholic High) 20, 21, 22, 31, 32, 33, 35, 41, 402
    Waterbury YWCA 7
    WBRY 23, 32
    Wolcott 5
        Hitchcock Lake 5, 6, 7, 9, 13, 69, 115, 116, 127
        Figgy's Point 6
Connolly, Bridget (Delia). *See Senier, Bridget (Delia) Connolly*
Copley Square. *See Massachusetts: Boston*
Cotswolds. *See England*
Craigan. *See Scotland*
"Creator Spirit, Come" (Brown Senier, 1964, 2005) 331, 341-347
Credo 37
"Creed" (Brown Senier, 1964-1965, 2005) xii, 331, 366, 374-385
Crichton, Elizabeth (formerly Sister Elizabeth Crichton) 61, 69
Crosby (high school). *See Connecticut: Waterbury*
Cunningham, Martin 402
Cuny, Father Peter 22, 23, 402
Curran, Father Thomas 355, 356
Curtis, Bridgeport Bishop Walter 52, 55, 61

D

Daly, Ellen "Nell" Finley. *See Downey, Ellen "Nell" Finley Daly*
de los Angeles, Victoria 123
"De Profundis" (Brown Senier, 2004, 2005) xi, 123, 126, 127, 140-162, 408
Debussy, Claude 23, 118
Deignan, Sister Kathleen, CND vi, xi, xix, 119, 402
Denniston, Donald E. 403
DePaul University. *See Illinois: Chicago*
DeVita Palmieri, Mary-Ann. *See Palmieri, Mary-Ann DeVita*
DiDeo, Ugo 402
Diocese of Bridgeport, Connecticut. *See Connecticut: Bridgeport*
Disney 101
Dixieland band 109
Dodge, Martha 121
Dogs, A Musical (DOGS) 121, 126
Donegal. *See Ireland*
Dorchester. *See Massachusetts*
D'Orio, Rocco 10, 15
Douay-Rhiems (bible) 139
"Down Here, Lord" 402
Downey, Ellen "Nell" Finley Daly (Aunt Nell; Aunt Nellie) 6, 8, 16, 31
Dublin. *See Ireland*
Dudley, Lynn 128, 132, 133
Duncan. *See Scotland*
Durgin Park. *See Massachusetts: Boston: Faneuil Hall Marketplace: North Market*
Dylan, Bob 57

E

"Early One Morning" 402
East Boston. *See Massachusetts: Boston*
East Eighty-sixth Street. *See New York: New York City: Manhattan*
East Seventy-sixth Street. *See New York: New York City: Manhattan*
East Sixty-eighth Street. *See New York: New York City: Manhattan*
Easter 49
Eastertide xvi
Eastham. *See Massachusetts*
Ehrlich, Miryam. *See Williamson, Miryam Ehrlich*
Eleanor Roosevelt. *See Roosevelt, Eleanor*
Eldridge, Dr. Olive 63, 402
Elizabeth (Mother of John the Baptist) 33, 34
Elvis 117, 402
Emil, Dr. Anders 402
Emmanuel College. *See Massachusetts: Boston*
England 14, 44, 45, 51, 81, 97. *See also British Isles; Great Britain*
    Cotswolds 45
        Chipping Campden 45
English 100, 126, 139
Epiphany xvi
Esquire 17
Essex House Hotel. *See New York: New York City*
Eternal One 218
Etude, Opus 10, Number 3 39
Etude, Opus 25, Number 1 39
Europe 45, 65, 99, 111, 118
European 34, 82
European Restaurant. *See Massachusetts: Boston: North End*

F

Faneuil Hall. *See Massachusetts: Boston: Faneuil Hall Marketplace*
Faneuil Hall Marketplace. *See Massachusetts: Boston. See also Massachusetts: Boston: Quincy Market*
Farley 84, 85, 86, 89, 100, 105, 106, 119
Father Fox. *See Fox, Monsignor Robert J.*
Father John Sullivan. *See Sullivan, Father John*
Father Peter Cuny. *See Cuny, Father Peter*
Father Philip Hussey. *See Hussey, Father Philip*
Father Thomas Curran. *See Curran, Father Thomas*
Fauré, Gabriel-Urbain 54
Feast of the Assumption of Mary 275
Fiddler on the Roof 25, 63, 64
Figgy's Point. *See Connecticut: Wolcott: Hitchcock Lake*
Finley, Ellen "Nell." *See Downey, Ellen "Nell" Finley Daly*
Firenze. *See Italy*
Fleet National Bank vi
Florida 57, 58, 59, 72, 73, 75, 403
    Fort Pierce 57
        Shamrock Village 57
    Indian River 57
    Miami 72
"Flower Song" 401
Foley, Sister Mary Ann 64, 361
"For He Comes" vi
Ford, Mary 33
Fordham (University). *See New York: New York City*
Fort Pierce. *See Florida*
Four Songs for a Woman of Galilee xii, 137, 273
Fox, Monsignor Robert J. 355
France 36, 48, 97, 402
    Solesmes 48, 402
        Benedictine monastery 48
Franciscan 91, 352
French 25
Friends and Neighbors 121, 123, 298
From Sacred Song to Ritual Music xx
Frye, David (Dave) 116, 125
Flye, Dylan 124, 298
Fyne, Loch. *See Scotland: Loch Fyne*

G

Gabriel (archangel) 37
Gaelic 56
Gagliardi, Marcia Haley vi, xi, xxiii, 403, 405. *See also her publishing house at Massachusetts: Athol: Haley's*
Gagliardi, Peter 405
Gajard, Dom 48, 402
Garrity, Faith 24
German 23, 100, 401
Germany 352
Gershwin, George 63, 64
Gershwin, Ira 63
Giannini guitar 355
Gilbert and Sullivan 406
Giroux, Sister Margaret (Sister Saint Patricia) 46
Gitanjali (Rabindranath Tagore) ix, 1, 28, 66, 112, 134, 406, 412
"Gloria" 37
"Glory to God" (Brown Senier 1964-1965, 2005) 51, 331, 366, 369-373
God xvii, xviii, 35, 39, 65, 111, 139, 219, 291, 355
Gothic 48
Grady, Robert (Bob) vi, xi, 25
Graham, Aine vi, xi, 82, 84, 93, 101
Grand Central Station. *See New York: New York City*
"grand silence" xvii
Grannett, Kathy 107, 108
Great Britain. *See also British Isles, England, Scotland*
    Wales 97
Great Hotel, The. *See Scotland: Inverary: The Great Hotel*
Greek 367
Greenock. *See Scotland*
Gregorian chant xvii, 48, 50, 53, 54
Grimes, Anna 94
Guinness Stout 57
Gump, Andy 9
"Gypsy Love Song" 24

H

Haight, Dorothy 57, 59
Haight, Paul 26, 59
haiku 355, 356
"Hail, Mary (Supplication in Time of War or Sorrow)" (Brown Senier, 1964, 2005) xii, 274, 291-293
Haitian 103
Haley's. *See Massachusetts: Athol. See also owner Gagliardi: Marcia Haley*
Halloween 17, 108
Hammerstein. *See Rodgers and Hammerstein*
Hanukkah 108
Hartford. *See Connecticut*
Harlem. *See Spanish Harlem*
Harvard University. *See Massachusetts: Cambridge*
Haven, Edna vi, 405, 405
Haven, Rand vi, 403, 405
Hawaii
    Honolulu
        Pearl Harbor 11
Hayden, Dorothy E. 405
Haydn, Franz Joseph 401
Hebert, Peter 405
Hebert, Shirley 405
Hebrew 106, 126, 139, 218, 219, 403, 404
Helmuth, Dr. Paul J. 132, 133

Hepburn, Katharine 91
Herman's Hermits 43
Hfd. *See Connecticut: Hartford*
Highland Press. *See Massachusetts: Athol*
Hindu *Vedas* xviii
Hitchcock Lake. *See Connecticut: Wolcott*
HMS *Mauritania* 45
Hoffman, Josef 10
Holmes, Sherlock 63
Holy Cross. *See Brothers of the Holy Cross*
"Holy, Holy, Holy" (Brown Senior, 1964-1965, 2005) xii, 331, 367, 386
Holy Spirit xix
Holy Week Triduum xv
Home Movies 121, 123, 126, 298, 403
Hopkins, Gerard Manley xviii
Horman, Ted vi, 403
Horowitz, Vladimir 43, 44, 401
"How Much Is That Doggie in the Window?" 25
Howe, John 122
Howe, Lee vi, xi, 120, 122, 405
Hub. *See Massachusetts: Boston*
Hudson, Geoffrey (Geoff) vi, xi, 126, 127, 128, 130, 131, 132, 404
Hunter College. *See New York: New York City: Manhattan: East Sixty-eighth Street: City College of New York*
Hunter, Ralph 402
Hussey, Father Philip 22
Hypodorian mode 218

I

"I'd Give You the Moon" (Brown Senior, 1999, 2005: lyrics by Dorothy Johnson) xii, 121, 126, 298, 300-303, 403, 411
"I Want to Hold Your Hand" (Beatles, 1964) 351
Illinois 32, 34, 35, 49, 273, 275, 402
    Bourbonnais 34, 37, 273, 275, 402
        Nazarene College 273
    Chicago 32, 34, 35, 402
        DePaul University 35
    Kankakee 33, 34, 275
Immaculate Conception Church. *See Connecticut: Waterbury*
"In Praise of Names" (Brown Senior, 2005) xi, xvii, 127, 163-217, 407
Indian. *See Pocumtuck; Sioux indians*
Indian River. *See Florida*
Industrial Development Board of Northern Ireland. *See Northern Ireland*
Inner Sanctum 17
International Music and Art Foundation. *See Liechtenstein: Vaduz*
Interstate 95. *See Connecticut: Route 95*
Inverary. *See Scotland*
Iraq war 140
Ireland 10, 70, 71, 81, 84, 96, 97, 99, 100, 103, 118. *See also Northern Ireland*
    Connemara 84
    County Galway 70, 96
        Ballyconneely 70, 96
    Donegal 94
    Dublin 88, 94, 97
    Wexford 10
Irish xxi, 5, 8, 45, 69, 70, 71, 75, 76, 80, 81, 82, 84, 86, 87, 88, 90, 95, 96, 97, 100, 101, 111, 118, 218, 338, 352
Irish-American 8
Irish Boston 88
Irish Export Board 80
Irish goods 96
Isaac 355
Italian 76, 91, 100, 123. *See also Italian American*

Italian American 81
Italy 50, 73, 74, 81, 96, 97, 98, 99, 115, 118, 122, 352
    Firenze 99
    Lake Como 98, 115
    Milan 31, 98
        LaScala 99
    Rome 31, 50, 73, 74, 91, 97, 99, 118, 351
    Sicily 75, 94, 108
        Mount Etna 75, 94
    Siena 98, 99
    Venezia 99

J

JFK. *See Kennedy, United States President John F.*
James, Jesse 38
Jane Eyre 118
Jesu, Joy of Man's Desiring 41
Jesuit 355
Jesus 17, 33, 37, 119, 273, 361
Jewish xvi
Jiffy. *See Jiffy Pie Crust Mix*
Jiffy Mix. *See Jiffy Pie Crust Mix*
Jiffy Pie Crust Mix (Jiffy Mix; Jiffy) 83, 84
Jiggs. *See Maggie and Jiggs*
Jimmy ("dear Jimmy") 8
John the Baptist. *See Elizabeth*
Johnson, Dorothy vi, xi, 120, 121, 122, 126, 298, 300, 304, 403, 405
Joncas, Jan Michael xx
Judah 361

K

Kanawa, Kiri Te 123
Kankakee. *See Illinois*
Kelley, Shana 103
Kelly, Bonnie 102, 120
Kennedy, United States President John F. (JFK) 46, 47, 351
Kennedy Gym. *See New York: Purchase: Manhattanville College: Pius X School of Liturgical Music*
ketchup (catsup) 72, 85
Kiley, Sister Ann (Sister Saint Ann of Jesus) 23, 31
Kiley, John 13
Knights of Columbus 25
koans. *See Zen koans*
"Kyrie" 37, 367

L

L. A. *See California: Los Angeles*
La Cucina Italiana 123
Labrecque, Sister Cecilia (Sister Saint Mary Achille) 37, 403
Lady in Black 62
LaFontaine, Sister Reine (Sister Saint Reine Marie) 22, 23, 31, 35, 41, 54, 402
Lake Como. *See Italy*
Lake Hitchcock. *See Connecticut: Wolcott*
Lake Mattawa. *See Massachusetts: Orange*
Lake Mattawa Association 122
Lake Mattawa Singers, The 127, 128, 131, 132, 133, 404
    Albritton, William "Britt" 132, 133
    Behnke, Matthew 128, 132, 133
    Bergeron, Adam 132, 133
    Boudreau, Lynn 132, 133, 140
    Chilton, Elizabeth 132, 133
    Clay, Sarah 132, 133
    Dudley, Lynn 128, 132, 133
    Helmuth, Paul J. 132, 133

    Metcalf, Sarah 132, 133
    Stoessel, Brian 132, 133
    Wardlaw, Judy 132, 133
Lamontagne, Amy 109
"Lamb of God" (Brown Senior, 1964, 2005) xii, 331, 334-337
"Lamb of God" (in the Mass) (Brown Senior, 1964-1965, 2005) xii, 367, 331, 388-389
Lamontagne, Claire vi, xi, 109, 110, 111, 116, 403
Lamontagne, Eileen 109
Lamontagne, Jeannette. *See Brown, Jeannette Lamontagne*
Lamontagne, Paul 109, 110
Larrivee, Beverly 24
La Salle, Jules 33
LaScala. *See Italy: Milan*
Latin xix, xx, 21, 23, 33, 37, 50, 51, 54, 65, 139, 140, 273, 274, 275, 332, 367
Latin America 47
Latin Mass 50
Latta, Paul 102
Lawlor, Bill 17, 37, 273, 401
Lemons, Dr. Jack 60, 64, 402
Lent xv, xvi
Leonard, Elizabeth 52
Leonard, Sister Anne C. (Sister Saint Anne Christine) vi, xi, 40
"Let the Heav'ns Be Glad" (Brown Senior, 1964, 2005) xii, 331, 361, 362
Lewis, Sinclair 17
Lexington Avenue. *See New York: New York City: Manhattan*
Lichtenberg, Andrew (Andy) 121, 122, 123, 126, 298
Liechtenstein vi, 404, 405
    Vaduz vi, 404, 405
        International Music and Art Foundation vi, 404, 405
Life 17
Lincoln, Diane vi
"Listen to Your Heart" (Brown Senior 2001, 2005: lyrics by Dorothy Johnson) xii, 298, 304-311
Liszt, Franz 54, 95, 111, 118
Little Miss Sunbeam 7. *See also Sunbeam Bread Company*
Loch Fyne. *See Scotland*
Löfblad's 6
"Long Before I Knew You" 403
Long Island Sound. *See New York*
Longy School of Music *See Massachusetts: Cambridge*
"Lord Have Mercy" (Brown Senior 1964-1965, 2005) 331, 366, 368
"Lorica" of Saint Patrick 338
Los Angeles. *See California*
Louisiana
    New Orleans 71, 73
"Lowly Shepherds" (Brown Senior, 1956, 2005) xii, 331, 361, 363
"Lullabye to a Black Man Child" 402

M

MacDonald, Sister Anna (Sister Saint Anna) 35
Maceoin, Gary 47, 90, 107, 119
Machu Pichu. *See Peru*
Macqueen, Ann Burns vi, xi, 64
Maggie and Jiggs 38
"Magnificat" xv, xvi, xvii, 31, 33, 163
Mahler, Gustav 45, 118
Malin, Cantor Bruce 403
Mallinckrodt, Pauline von. *See von Mallinckrodt, Pauline*
Malone, Molly 81

Maloney, Don 15
Manhattan. *See New York: New York City*
Manhattanville College. *See New York: Purchase*
Margolis, Leon 88
Marian feast day 274
Marian year 37
Marier, Theodore 49, 402
Mark Morris Dance Company 127, 404
Mark, Katherine Brown (Kaye) vi, xi, 6, 7, 13, 14, 23, 27, 31, 38 (as "Kay"), 57, 60, 78, 95, 109, 115, 163, 198, 401, 406
Mark, Emil 6, 7, 18, 26, 109, 406
Mark, Emil, Sr. 23
Martha's Vineyard. *See Massachusetts*
Mary (Mother of Jesus) 33, 34, 37, 273
Maryland 76
   Baltimore 76
   Columbia 76
Mass in Honor of Marguerite Bourgeoys, Founder of the Congregation of Notre Dame (Brown Senier 1964-1965, 2005) xii, 139, 366
Massachusetts vi, 5, 6, 25, 49, 63, 64, 80, 123, 126, 128, 298, 402, 403, 405
   Athol v, vi, 405
      Haley's v, vi, 403
      Highland Press vi, 405
      Stan's Liquor Mart 405
   Boston (Hub) vi, xvi, xviii, xx, xxii, 20, 31, 40, 43, 44, 47, 60, 61, 62, 63, 69, 73, 75, 76, 77, 78, 80, 81, 83, 87, 88, 89, 90, 95, 96, 101, 103, 105, 115, 116, 120, 122, 123, 125, 126, 403, 416
      700 Commonwealth Avenue (Boston University dorm) 61
      Arnold Arboretum (Arboretum) 100, 104, 105, 106, 117, 125
      Boston Bay Shoreline cruise 62
      Boston Esplanade 111
      Boston Harbor 111
      Boston Pops 111
      Boston Public Gardens 69
      Boston Symphony 98
      Boston University 40, 60, 62, 64, 398, 402, 403, 408
         Boston University Magazine 61
         Boston University School of Fine and Applied Arts 61
      Bostonian Hotel 91
      Copley Square 73, 111
         Trinity Church 73
      Charles River Publishers vi
      Dorchester 71, 81, 90
         Mather School 98
         Upham's Corner 81
      East Boston 81
      Emmanuel College 31, 120
      Faneuil Hall Marketplace (Faneuil Hall) xviii, 20, 56, 69, 75, 76, 77, 78, 79, 81, 84, 85, 87, 91, 92, 95, 100, 102
         Quincy Market 75, 76, 80, 83, 88, 92
            Alexander Parris room 89
            North Market 95, 103
               Celtic Weavers xviii, xxii, 56, 77, 78, 79 (photo), 81-89, 91-93, 95-97, 99-104, 118, 120, 127, 403
               Durgin Park 95, 103
         South Market 81, 82, 102, 103
      Massachusetts Eye and Ear Infirmary 73

      North End 76, 77
         European Restaurant 90
      Paulist Center (Catholic Church) 90
      Roslindale 89, 90, 104, 105
         Mendum Street 94, 104, 106, 107, 108, 109, 110, 111, 125
   Brookline 73, 74, 90, 111, 117
      Novak's 69
   Cambridge 49, 56, 352, 403
      Harvard University 104
      Saint Paul's Church 49
      Longy School of Music 111, 352, 403
   Cape Cod 16, 75, 80, 103, 126
      Cape Cod Synagogue 403
      Centerville 405
      Eastham 16
   Erving 115
   Martha's Vineyard 94
      Oak Bluffs 94
   Millers River 116
   New Salem (Town of New Salem) 116, 120, 122, 123, 125, 128, 298, 404, 405
      1794 Meetinghouse 121, 122, 124, 125, 126, 127, 128, 298, 403, 404
      New Salem Common 122
      Common Reader Bookshop (Common Reader) 121, 122
   Newton xxii, 25, 63, 64, 73, 81, 103, 402
      Boston College 14
      Memorial School 63
      Oak Hill Elementary School (Oak Hill) 63, 64, 65, 75
   North Pond 116
   North Pond Brook 116
   Orange 5, 6, 80, 115, 116, 117, 405
      Holtshire Road 122
      Lake Mattawa (Mattawa) xxii, 1, 5, 13, 25, 36, 60, 80, 81, 96, 98, 100, 109, 105, 110, 111, 114, 115, 116, 117, 118, 122, 123, 124, 125, 126, 135, 401, 403
      Orange Municipal Airport 126
   Pelham 39, 122
   Petersham
      Petersham Common 126
      Unitarian Church 126
   Provincetown 11, 16
      Race Point 16
      Race Point Beach 11
      Sandra Lodge 16
   Route 2 115
   Swift River 116
   Quabbin Reservoir 116
   Waltham 56, 61
   Wellesley 17
Massachusetts Eye and Ear Infirmary *See Massachusetts: Boston*
Massachusetts Teachers Association 65
MasterCard 91
Mastroiani, Sister Lena (Sister Saint Paul) 39
Mather School. *See Massachusetts: Boston: Dorchester*
Mattawa (Lake Mattawa). *See Massachusetts: Orange*
Mattawa Song Cycle, The. See The Mattawa Song Cycle
Mauritania. *See HMS Mauritania*
Maxwell, Gavin 97
McElligott, Claire. *See Lamontagne, Claire McElligott*
McElligott, Edward (Ed) 14, 38, 55, 401, 406

McElligott family 18
McElligott, Joan Brown xxi, 6, 7, 13, 14, 18, 20, 27, 37, 38, 55, 110, 163, 199, 273, 401, 406
McElligott, Mark (Carolyn's nephew) 98
McGrail, Lola vi, xi, 98, 99
McGrath, Caroline 109
McGrath, Erin 109
McGrath, Joan vi, xi, 86, 87, 90, 109
McGrath, Lauren 109
McGrath, Mrs. Helen 18
McGrath, Richard 109
McGrath, Sean 109
McLaughlin & Reilly Co. vi, xvi, xxi, 47
McManus, Sister Frances (Sister Saint John Joseph) 35, 36, 402
McNally, Harry 352
"Meditation Doxology" (Brown Senier, 1966, 2005) 390-399
Mellotones 24, 25, 50
Memorial School. *See Massachusetts: Newton*
Mendelssohn, Felix 402
Mendum Street. *See Massachusetts: Boston: Roslindale*
Merchant marines 12
Meriden. *See Connecticut*
Merritt Parkway. *See Connecticut*
Metcalf, Sarah 132, 133
Metropolitan Opera (Met) 17, 19, 75, 123
Mexico 118
Michigan 56. *See also Chiara, Margaret Mary (United States Attorney for the Western District of Michigan)*
Middle Ages 61
Middletown. *See Connecticut*
Mignon 17
Milford. *See Connecticut*
Monagan, John 25
Monagan, Rosemary 25
Monagans 32
Monsignor Austin Vaughan. *See Vaughan, Monsignor Austin*
Monsignor Robert J. Fox. *See Fox, Monsignor Robert J.*
Montealegre, Felicia 45
Mood, John J. L. xv
"Moon Over Miami" 119
"Moonlight Becomes You" 119
"Moonlight Serenade" 119
"Moonlight Sonata" 401
Morgan, Mother Josephine 55, 402
Moriarty, Eddie 401
Moriarty, Mac 38
Moriartys 18
Morris, Cara vi, xi, 90, 99, 100
Morris, Jim 90, 91, 107
Morris, Michael 90, 106
Morris, Patricia (Pat) vi, xi, 90, 91, 94, 97, 105
Morrises 91, 107
Mother's Day 11
Mother Catherine Carroll. *See Carroll, Mother Catherine*
Mother General Eisenhauer 352
Mother Goose Lost 121
Mother Josephine Morgan. *See Morgan, Mother Josephine*
Mother Marguerite Bourgeoys. *See Bourgeoys, Mother Marguerite*
"Mother of Quebec." *See Bourgeoys, Mother Marguerite*
Mount Etna. *See Italy: Sicily*
Mouvements Perpétuels, Number 1 39
Moylan, Joseph (Joe) vi, xi, 103, 104, 108
Moylan, Pat 94, 108

Moylans 104, 107
Mozart, Wolfgang Amadeus 100, 401
Mrazik, Gloria (Carolyn's niece) 109
Mrs. Brown. *See Brown, Rosalene Carolan*
"Mrs. Brown, you've got a lovely daughter . . . " 43, 46
Mrs. Senier. *See Brown Senier, Carolyn*
Mrs. Smith's Homemade Pie 83
Mullen, Sister Helen (Sister Saint Helen) 40, 41
Music as an integral part of contemporary liturgical celebrations (master's thesis) 416-429
Muzio, Claudio 401

N

Nabucco 19, 403
Namur. *See Sisters of Notre Dame de Namur*
Native American xviii
Nazarene College. *See Illinois: Bourbonnais*
Nestel, Hattie 404, 405
Newton. *See Massachusetts*
New England Confraternity of Christian Doctrine. *See Confraternity of Christian Doctrine*
New England Congress 51
New Haven. *See Connecticut*
New Haven Pops Concerts 25
New Jersey 27, 351, 405
    Mendham 351
    Pennsauken 405
New Orleans. *See Louisiana*
New Salem. *See Massachusetts*
New Year's Eve 90
New York, Archdiocese of. *See Archdiocese of New York*
New York vi, xxi, 10, 17, 26, 38, 39, 40, 41, 42, 43, 44, 45, 50, 54, 58, 80, 97, 98, 111, 123, 127, 274, 355, 404, 405
    Bronxville 80
    Long Island Sound 94
    New York City vi, 10, 26, 41, 45, 97, 111, 404, 405
        America House 355
        American Music Center vi, 404, 405
            Composer Assistance Program vi, 404, 405
        Bronx 37, 39
            Villa Maria Academy (Villa Maria) 37, 39, 40
        Carnegie Hall 26, 43
        Central Park South 97
        Columbia (University) 39
        Essex House Hotel 97, 98
        Fordham (University) 41
        Grand Central Station 41
        Manhattan 39, 41
            East Eighty-sixth Street 39
            East Seventy-sixth Street 40
            Saint Jean Baptist (convent) (Saint Jean's) 40, 41
        East Sixty-eighth Street 40
        City College of New York 40
        Hunter College 40, 41, 402
        Lexington Avenue 40
        New York College of Music 39, 402
        New York Harbor 45
        New York University 39
        Philharmonic Hall 45
        Staten Island 40, 45, 46, 47, 55, 56, 274, 351, 361
            Notre Dame Academy (NDA) 40, 45, 56
        Steinway Piano Company 26
    Purchase xxi, 44, 48
        Manhattanville College (of the Sacred Heart) 48, 50, 402
            Pius X School of Liturgical Music (Pius X School; Pius X) xxi, 44, 48, 49, 55, 402
                Kennedy Gym 48
    Schenectady 54
    Woodstock 60
New York City. *See New York*
New York College of Music. *See New York: New York City*
New York Harbor. *See New York: New York City*
New York Metropolitan Opera. *See Metropolitan Opera*
New York University. *See New York: New York City*
New Zealand 99, 118
Newton. *See Massachusetts*
Nicholas Mosse Pottery 101
Northern Ireland 100. *See also Ireland*
    Industrial Development Board of Northern Ireland 99
North American Buyers Association 95
North End. *See Massachusetts: Boston*
North Market. *See Massachusetts: Boston: Faneuil Hall Marketplace*
North Pond. *See Massachusetts*
North Pond Brook. *See Massachusetts*
North Quabbin Women in Black 126, 140, 141
Northeast 54, 89
Norwalk. *See Connecticut*
Notre Dame, Congregation of. *See Congregation of Notre Dame*
Notre Dame. *See Sisters of Notre Dame de Namur*
Notre Dame Academy. *See New York: Staten Island*
Novak's. *See Massachusetts: Brookline*
Nuclear War 274

O

"O, Praise the Lord, All Ye Nations" (Brown Senier, 1964, 2005) xii, 331, 348-350
"O, Praise Ye the Lord" (Brown Senier, 1961-2005) vi, xvi, xii 47, 91, 110, 331, 351, 353, 354
Oak Bluffs. *See Massachusetts: Martha's Vineyard*
Oak Hill. *See Massachusetts: Newton: Oak Hill Elementary School*
Oak Hill Elementary School. *See Massachusetts: Newton*
"Oh, What a Beautiful Morning" 49
O'Brien, Barbara. *See Brown, Barbara O'Brien*
O'Brien, Fergus, Lord Mayor of Dublin 88, 89
O'Farrell, Fergus xi, 96, 97
O'Farrell, Maire 96, 97, 111
O'Seanora Products 81
Oklahoma 49
Oliver 64
Olmstead, Frederick Law 105
"Opus 21, #2" 299
Orange. *See Massachusetts*
Orange Municipal Airport. *See Massachusetts: Orange*
Orkney Islands. *See Scotland*
Our Lady of Bon Secours Chapel. *See Canada: Montreal*

P

Padua, Vladimir 402
Page, Joan, R.N. vi, xi, 71, 72, 73
Page, Larry 71, 73
"Pageant Song" ("The Pageant Song"; "Annunciation"; "Ave Maria") (Brown Senier, 1953, 2005) ii, iii, xi, 37, 273, 276-280, 403, 405
Palmieri, Mary-Ann DeVita v, vi, xi, 1, 125, 403, 405
Palmieri, Tony 122, 123, 125, 403, 405
Parris, Alexander 88. *See also Massachusetts: Boston: Quincy Market: Quincy Market Alexander Parris room*
Partlow, Mary Rita 35, 402
Passover Seders. *See Seder(s)*
Paul, Les 33
Pavarotti, Luciano 17
Paulist Center (Catholic Church). *See Massachusetts: Boston*
peace activist. *See Maceoin, Gary*
Pearl Harbor. *See Hawaii: Honolulu*
Pelham. *See Massachusetts*
Pennsauken. *See New Jersey*
Pennsylvania
    Philadelphia 88
        Bourse Building 88
Pentecost xvi
Pepe 59, 61
Peru
    Machu Pichu 99
Peruvian 99
Peter, Paul, and Mary 57
Petersham. *See Massachusetts*
Petersham Common. *See Massachusetts: Petersham*
Philadelphia. *See Pennsylvania*
Philharmonic Hall. *See New York: New York City*
Philippines 14
Phillips, Michael D. vi
Phrygian mode 218
Pirates of Penzance 69, 406
Pius X. *See New York: Purchase: Manhattanville College: Pius X School of Liturgical Music. See also Pope Pius X*
Pius X School of Liturgical Music. *See New York: Purchase: Manhattanville College*
Pleasant Sound 132
Plymouth Fury 61
Pocumtuck (An Indian language) 116
Pope, the 111, 352
Pope John XXIII 30, 47, 52
Pope Pius X (Pius X) 48, 50. *See also New York: Purchase: Pius X School of Liturgical Music*
Pope Pius XII 37
Portree. *See Scotland*
Poulenc 39
Protestant 51, 139
Providence. *See Rhode Island*
Provincetown. *See Massachusetts*
"Psalm 99 / 100" (depending on which version of the Bible one consults) 358, 359
"Psalm 103 /104" 37, 244, 245, 251
"Psalm 116 / 117" 348, 349
"Psalm 129 / 130" 140, 141
"Psalm 138 /139" xxi, 126, 258, 259
"Psalm 150" 47, 351, 353
Puccini, Giacomo 403
Pugliese, Terri 22, 23
Purchase. *See New York*

Q

Quabbin Reservoir. *See Massachusetts*
Quabbin Valley Pro Musica 124, 126, 127, 404
Quebec City. *See Canada*
Quincy Market. *See Massachusetts: Boston. See also Massachusetts: Boston: Faneuil Hall Marketplace*
Quincy Market Alexander Parris room. *See Massachusetts: Boston: Quincy Market See also Parris, Alexander*

R

Race Point. *See Massachusetts: Provincetown*
Race Point Beach. *See Massachusetts: Provincetown*
Raitt, John 59
Ravel, Maurice Joseph 118
Reilly, Mr. Arthur 47
Requiem 401
"Respice Stellam" (Brown Senier, 1962, 2005) xi, 273, 274, 281-290
Reston. *See Virginia*
"Resurrection" 403
Rheumatoid arthritis 88, 111
Rhode Island 40, 41
    Providence 88, 91
        Arcade 91
Ridgefield. *See Connecticut*
Ridgefield Chapel. *See Connecticut: Ridgefield*
Ridgefield Press. See Connecticut: Ridgefield
Riley, James Whitcomb 5
Rilke, Rainer Maria xv
Ring of Bright Water 97
Rittman, Trude 49
Ritucci, Louis 109
Robb, Arthur 106, 107
Roberts, Sister Mary 58
Rodgers, Richard 48, 49, 401. *See also Rodgers and Hammerstein*
Rodgers and Hammerstein 23. *See also Rodgers, Richard*
Roman Catholic(s) xix, xx, 30, 31, 33, 37, 47, 48, 50, 51, 54, 65, 91, 103, 106, 366
Roman Catholic Church (Catholic Church) xix, 33, 47, 48, 50, 51, 52, 57, 65, 90, 139
Roman Catholic Diocese of Bridgeport, Connecticut. *See Connecticut, Bridgeport: Diocese of Bridgeport*
Romans 8:14 65
Roosevelt, Eleanor 14, 15, 42
Roslindale. *See Massachusetts: Boston*
Rouse, James 76, 77, 101
Route 2. *See Massachusetts*
Route 95. *See Connecticut*

S

SBA. *See Small Business Association*
SCORE. *See Service Corps of Retired Executives*
Saathoff, Gretchen 132, 403
Sacred Heart University. *See Connecticut: Bridgeport*
Sacrosanctum Concilium xix
"Saint Bernard's Prayer" 273, 281
Saint Cecilia's Church. *See Connecticut: Waterbury*
Saint Francis Xavier Church. *See Connecticut: Waterbury*
Saint Jean Baptiste (convent) (Saint Jean's). *See New York: New York City: Manhattan: East Seventy-sixth Street*
Saint Matthew, gospel of 17
Saint Patrick. *See "Lorica" of Saint Patrick*
Saint Patrick's Day 102
Saint Peter (statue). *See Vatican City: Vatican Square*
Saint Peter's Basilica. *See Vatican City*
Saint-Saëns 27
Saldarini, Signora 98
Sammy 105, 106
"Sanctus" 37, 367
Sandra Lodge. *See Massachusetts: Provincetown*
Saturday Evening Post 17
Schenectady. *See New York*
Schoenberg, Steven 122
School of Fine and Applied Arts. *See Massachusetts: Boston: Boston University*
Schubert 54
Scotland 95, 96, 99. *See also British Isles; Great Britain*
    Armandale Pier 97
    Craigan 96
    Duncan 96
    Greenock 96
    Inverary 96
        The Great Hotel 96
    Loch Fyne 96
    Orkney Islands 95
    Portree 97
    Skye 97
Scottish 82, 95
Scott, Sister Mary Eileeen (Sister Saint Miriam of the Temple), CND 273, 281
Scottish fashion 95
Scovill Manufacturing Company. *See Connecticut: Waterbury*
Scully, Marty 27
Second Vatican Council. *See Vatican Council II*
Seder(s) 80, 126
Selma. *See Alabama*
Senier, William (Bill) 77, 90
Senier, Bobby 77
Senier, Bridget (Delia) Connolly 70
Senier, James 77
Senier, Leo 77, 96
Senier, Mr. *See Senier, Thomas*
Senier, Mrs. *See Brown Senier, Carolyn*
Senier, Richard (grandfather of Richard Senier, Carolyn's husband) 77
Senier, Richard (Dick; Carolyn's husband) vi, vii, xviii, xxii, 1, 16, 36, 44, 45, 47,56, 68, 69, 70, 71, 72, 73, 74, 75, 76, 80-91, 93-111, 115-127, 218, 298, 299, 317, 352, 402, 403, 404, 406
Senier, Thomas (Tom) 71, 77, 78, 81
Senier(s) 64, 80, 81, 82, 83, 87, 88, 91, 96, 97, 99, 101, 102, 103, 104, 105, 107, 108, 110, 111, 122
Service Corps of Retired Executives (SCORE) 88
700 Commonwealth Avenue. *See Massachusetts: Boston: 700 Commonwealth Avenue (Boston University dorm)*
1794 Meetinghouse. *See Massachusetts: New Salem*
Seville. *See Spain*
Shamrock 57, 105
Shamrock Village. *See Florida: Fort Pierce*
Shea, Navy Lieutenant Joseph D. (Joe) 14, 15, 42, 406
Shea, Roselyn Brown 7, 10, 13, 14, 15, 26, 27, 32, 36, 41, 42, 44, 45, 57, 163, 198, 351, 401, 406
Shine on Harvest Moon 119
Shoo Fly, Fly 54
Shove, Helen 17
Sicily. *See Italy*
Siena. *See Italy*
"Silent Night" 401
"Sing Joy to the Lord" (Brown Senier, 1961, 2005) xii, 331, 358-360
Sioux indians 73
Sisters of Notre Dame de Namur 31
Sisters of the Congregation of Notre Dame. *See Congregation of Notre Dame*
Sisters of Saint Joseph 31
Sister Anne C. Leonard. *See Leonard, Sister Anne C.*
Sister Barbara Arnesen. *See Arnesen, Barbara*
Sister Carolyn Brown. *See Brown Senier, Carolyn*
Sister Gail Charron. *See Charron, Sister*
Sister Elizabeth Crichton. *See Crichton, Elizabeth*
Sister Florence Bertrand. *See Bertrand, Sister Florence*
Sister Kathleen Deignan. *See Deignan, Sister Kathleen*
Sister Mary Ann Foley. *See Foley, Sister Mary Ann*
Sister Mary Roberts. *See Roberts, Sister Mary*
Sister Saint Andre Marie. *See Chevrette, Sister Claudette*
Sister Saint Anna. *See MacDonald, Sister Anna*
Sister Saint Ann of Jesus. *See Kiley, Sister Ann*
Sister Saint Edward. *See Young, Sister Margaret*
Sister Saint Helen. *See Mullen, Sister Helen*
Sister Saint John Joseph. *See McManus, Sister Frances*
Sister Saint Martin of Lima. *See Bowes, Sister Martha Bowes*
Sister Saint Mary Achille. *See Labrecque, Sister Cecilia*
Sister Saint Miriam of the Temple. *See Scott, Sister Mary Eileen*
Sister Saint Patricia. *See Giroux, Sister Margaret*
Sister Saint Paul. *See Mastroiani, Sister Lena*
Sister Saint Reine Marie. *See LaFontaine, Sister Reine*
Sister Saint Roselyn of Jesus (Sister Saint Roselyn). *See Brown Senier, Carolyn*
Sisters of Christian Charity. *See Congregation of Sisters of Christian Charity*
Sisters of Notre Dame de Namur 31
Sisters of the Congregation of Notre Dame. *See Congregation of Notre Dame*
Sixth Symphony 45
Skye. *See Scotland*
Small Business Association (SBA) 86
Small Town Life 122
Snow, Edgar Rowe
Solesmes. *See France*
Solomon Islands 14
Sonata, Opus 10, Number 1 39
Sonata, Opus 14, Number 2 39
Sonata in C Major 100
"Song of Abraham" (Brown Senier, 2004, 2005) xi, 126, 127, 218-243, 403
Sound of Music 48
South America 99, 118
South Atlantic 32
South Market. *See Massachusetts: Boston:*

Mary-Ann DeVita Palmieri, right, above, with Carolyn, taught for more than sixteen years at a variety of levels from second grade to first year in college. Her longest stint was as a language arts teacher of seventh and eighth grade students at Great Falls Middle School in Turners Falls. She enjoys her retirement and continues to work part-time with the Western Massachusetts Writing Project located at UMass where she helps publish student writing as well as develop writing and the teaching-of-writing workshops for teachers. She lives in New Salem with her husband Tony. She has three grown children, Gioia, Cristina, and David. Mary-Ann wrote the biographical profile at the beginning of this book, entitled "Luminous Spirit."

Kathleen Deignan, above, is an educator, theologian, composer, and performer. A sister of the Congregation of Notre Dame, she is a professor of religious studies at Iona College in New Rochelle, New York, where she founded and continues to lead the Iona Spirituality Institute. As a CND novice, she sang in Carolyn's choirs and closely assisted Carolyn in her work with the Bridgeport Liturgical Commission. Kathleen has written hundreds of songs. She is the author of many books, including the recent When the Trees Say Nothing, *about the faith and life of Thomas Merton. She and Carolyn have remained close friends. She wrote the foreword to this book, "One Ordained to Praise."*

about the typefaces used in this book

Antique Olive was designed by Roger Excoffon for the French typefoundry, Olive, which it issued in different weights and widths from 1962 to 1966. In France, "antique" is the generic term for sans serif designs. Antique Olive was initially designed to rival the popular sans serifs Helvetica and Univers, but is almost humanistic in its design approach, with no indication of a mechanical look. Although the x-height is large and the ascenders and descenders are short, the design maintains an elegant, statuesque quality. Antique Olive is a distinctive typeface that can be used in a variety of ways, from text work to display. It is the main title typeface.

ITC Leawood was begun by Leslie Usherwood, founder and president of Typsettra in Toronto, and completed by staff designers after Usherwood's untimely death. His original drawings were models for the finished type, which was produced using interpolated instances on a computer. ITC Leawood was released in 1985; it is a text design with angular serifs, slightly flared stems, and a large x-height. It is the main text typeface.

Designer: Leslie Usherwood

ITC Leawood is a trademark of International Typeface Corporation.

Optima is elegant and highly readable, qualities remarkable in a sans serif design. Created in 1958 by Hermann Zapf for the Stempel foundry, Optima combines features of both serif and sans serif types into one humanistic design. The tapered strokes are reminiscent of the calligraphic pen, and the character shapes are soothing to the eye. This sophisticated typeface is excellent for a variety of uses ranging from corporate identities to packaging to medium-length text. It is the secondary text typeface.

Designer: Hermann Zapf

Optima is a Trademark of Heidelberger Druckmaschinen AG exclusively licensed through Linotype Library GmbH, and may be registered in certain jurisdictions.

Faneuil Hall Marketplace
Southeast Asia (war) 60
Southington Mountain. *See Connecticut*
Spain 352
    Canary Islands
        Tenerife 99
    Seville 65
Spanish 98, 361
Spanish Harlem 355
Spartan 5
Spellman, Francis Cardinal. *See Cardinal Spellman scholarship*
SS *Bahama Star* 59
Stamford. *See Connecticut*
Stamford Catholic. *See Connecticut: Stamford*
Stan's Liquor Mart. *See Massachusetts: Athol*
Staten Island. *See New York*
states. *See United States*
Steinway Piano Company. *See New York: New York City*
"Stille Nacht" 23
Stoessel, Brian 132, 133
Streisand, Barbra 118
Studebaker 32
Sullivan, Father John 15, 22
Sullivan, Patrick (Pat) 102, 103
Sullivan, Tarin (Patrick Sullivan's daughter) 103
"Summer Days" (Brown Senier, 2003, 2005) xii, 127, 299, 312-316, 331
Summer in the City 355
Sunbeam Bread Company 7, 20. *See also Little Miss Sunbeam*
Swanson, Lorraine. *See Brown, Lorraine Swanson*
Sweet, Diane vi, xi, 101
Swift River. *See Massachusetts*
Sylvan Avenue. *See Connecticut: Waterbury*

T

Tabasco 72
Tagore, Rabindranath ix, 1, 28, 66, 112, 134, 406
Tchaikovsky, Pyotr Ilich 7
Tenerife. *See Spain: Canary Islands*
Texan 35
Thanksgiving 22, 69, 78
Thaw, Nicholas vi, 404
The Company of Mary. *See Company of Mary*
"The Battle Hymn of the Republic" 47
"The Brook" 401
The Great Hotel. *See Scotland: Inverary*
The Harp 39
The King and I 23
The Lake Mattawa Singers. *See Lake Mattawa Singers, The*
The Last Smile 20
The Lion in Winter 91
The Mattawa Song Cycle (2005) cover, i, v, xviii, xxi, 127, 132, 163, 274, 401, 403, 405
"The Pageant Song." *See Pageant Song*
"The Passing of the Backhouse" 5
"The Ram" (Brown Senier, 1965, 2005) xii, 331, 355-357

The Swan 27
The Telephone Hour 401
"Thou Makest the Winds Thy Messengers" (Brown Senier, 1954, 2005) vi, xi, 47, 244-257
Tomas 17
Transcendent Being 273
Trinity xvii
Trinity Church. *See Massachusetts: Boston: Copley Square*
Trinity High School. *See Connecticut: Stamford: Stamford Catholic*
Tumarkin, Professor Leon 61, 402
Turandot 403
Turner, Flo 111, 402
Turner, Principal Samuel (Sam) A. vi, xi, 63, 64, 111, 402
Turner family

U

U. S. *See United States*
USA. *See United States*
"Uncle Louis". *See Boisvert, Louis ("Uncle Louis")*
Unitarian Church. *See Massachusetts: Petersham: Petersham Common*
United States (USA; U.S.) 8, 11, 34, 46, 47, 70, 71, 75, 97, 99, 118, 275
United States Attorney for the Western District of Michigan. *See Chiara, Margaret Mary*
University of Bridgeport, Connecticut. *See Connecticut: Bridgeport*
Upham's Corner. *See Massachusetts: Boston: Dorchester*

V

Valley Charitable Fund vi
van Buskirk, Jeremy vi, 403
Vatican City (Vatican) 92
    Saint Peter's Basilica 91, 352
    Vatican Square 74
    Saint Peter (statue) 74
Vatican Council II (Second Vatican Council; Vatican Council) xvi, xix, xx, 30, 50, 52, 56, 57, 65, 73, 139
Vatican Square. *See Vatican City*
Vaughan, Monsignor Austin 58, 61
Vedas. *See Hindu Vedas*
Venezia. *See Italy*
"Veni Creator Spiritus" 341
Venus 40
Verdi, Giuseppe Fortunio Frencesco 401, 402
Vermont 95, 115
    West Halifax 115
Vespa 97
Victorian 118
Victory garden 12
Vietnam 108
Villa Maria Academy. *See New York: Bronx*
Virginia 76
    Reston 76
Vivaldi, Antonio Lucio 99
von Mallinckrodt, Mother Pauline 91, 351

W

WBRY. *See Connecticut: Waterbury*
www.susanwilsonphoto.com 405
Wagner, Mel 120, 405
Waldman, Mildred 41, 402
Wales. *See Great Britain*
Wallenhaupt 20
Waltham. *See Massachusetts*
Wardlaw, Judy 132, 133
Warner Bros. Publications U.S. Inc. (Warner Brothers) vi, 101, 403
"Warsaw Concerto" 401
Washington Park. *See Connecticut: Waterbury*
Waterbury. *See Connecticut*
Waterbury Catholic High School (Waterbury Catholic; Catholic High). *See Connecticut: Waterbury*
Waterbury YWCA. *See Connecticut: Waterbury*
Watson, Eddie 69
Waverly Inn. *See Connecticut: Cheshire*
Wellesley. *See Massachusetts*
West Halifax. *See Vermont*
Western Massachusetts Community Foundation 404, 405
Wexford. *See Ireland*
"When I Knew" (Brown Senier 1996, 2005) xii, 127, 299, 317-328
"When I Marry Mr. Snow" 25
"When I Was a Lad" 406
Whipps, Susannah 405
Whitney 105
Wilhousky, Peter 47
Williams, William "Buck" "Bucky" vi, xi, 124, 405
Williams, Jane 124
Williams, Dorothy 124, 405
Williamson, Miryam Ehrlich vi, 403
Wilson, Susan. *See www.susanwilsonphoto.com*
Wizard of Oz 64
Woodstock. *See New York*
Woody 105
Woollen, Russell 56
World War II 5, 11, 14

Y

Yale Bowl. *See Connecticut: New Haven*
Yankee Spirits 120, 122
"You Are Too Beautiful" 403
"You Know Me" (Brown Senier, 1966, 2002, 2005) xi, 137, 258-272
Young, Sister Margaret (Sister Saint Edward) 31
Young Stars On Parade 23, 25, 402
You're A Good Man, Charlie Brown 64

Z

Zen koans xviii